celebrate the Sunday readings

cycle C

david brehm

Scripture Background from the
Seasons of Faith program

Harcourt
Religion Publishers

Dubuque, Iowa

Harcourt Religion Publishers

Our Mission

The primary mission of Harcourt Religion Publishers is to provide the Catholic and Christian educational markets with the highest quality catechetical print and media resources. The content of these resources reflects the best insights of current theology, methodology, and pedagogical research. The resources are practical and easy to use, designed to meet expressed market needs, and written to reflect the teachings of the Catholic Church.

Printed in the United States of America

ISBN 0-15-950608-5

10 9 8 7 6 5 4 3

Contents

Introduction

This resource book invites people of all ages to walk with Jesus in their daily lives. Jesus gave us his word, thus making us a promise: He will be with us always until the end of time. (See Matthew 28:20.) Consequently, after the historical Christ event—the life, death, and resurrection of Jesus—we have the opportunity to experience the risen Lord in the Sacred Scriptures, the Eucharist, and the faith community. Jesus is really present in all three. Jesus has given these to us so that we may encounter his love, forgiveness, goodness, joy, and healing. If we open our hearts and minds to the gift of relationship that Jesus offers us, we cannot help but have a deeper desire to serve others. Our faith becomes "life-giving" and freeing to all we meet.

An Invitation to Dream

All men and women dream, but not equally.
Those who dream by night, in the dust recesses of their minds
Wake in the day to find that it was vanity.

But the dreamers of the day are dangerous people;
for they may act out their dream with open eyes,
to make it possible.

T.E. Lawrence
The Seven Pillars of Wisdom

Before You Begin

Pray the Holy Scriptures

How can we, as ministers for the Lord, touch the lives of others if we don't pray? Spend time with Scripture—read it, reflect on it, let the Lord speak to you through it. The more you are open to God touching your life, the more the students and their families will be open to the experience of God.

Each day of the week, ask Jesus to speak to you. You'll be surprised at the ways Jesus makes himself known each day. Let each experience speak for itself. Our personal encounters with the risen Lord enable us to be authentic teachers, leaders, and ministers. The Lord will use many different ways to share his message with the children and their families. But you need to be willing to use the gifts that God has given you.

I've found it helpful to read the Scriptures before I go to bed at night. There are many examples in the Bible where God speaks to people in their dreams. So I invite Jesus into my sleep and rest. Many mornings, I wake up with God's word in my mind and heart. After my second cup of coffee, I hope to find Jesus in my actions as well.

Mornings are also a good time to read and encounter the Lord in the Scriptures; by doing so, I find images of and links to the Scripture passage throughout the day. The Scripture passage is uniquely revealed as I wait at a red light, attend a staff meeting, and interact with people. This allows me to see God's word in my life. God's word comes to life.

This method works very well for me. If it doesn't work for you, that's okay. God speaks to each of us in different ways. Listen carefully, and ask God to speak to you. God will respond, and you will discover the method that works best for you.

Keep your own journal

The following are questions to reflect on as you encounter God's word. As director, catechist, or volunteer, keep a journal of your own encounters with Jesus in the Sacred Scriptures while you prepare for your presentation. I have found these questions very powerful. However, if other questions move you to a deeper relationship with God's word, use them instead.

1. What is the basic human experience being considered in the Scripture passage?
2. How have I experienced this basic human experience in my own life?
3. What is Jesus saying to me in this passage?
4. What are some practical ways for me to respond to Jesus' message?
5. What message does this Scripture passage have for the People of God, and how could the Church respond to Jesus' message?
6. What questions or difficulties do I have with this Scripture passage?

Be creative and adapt, adapt, adapt

I had fun creating these prayer assemblies. Each lesson went through many refinements—six presentations per week with more than 1,280 elementary students to critique each lesson. By the sixth prayer assembly, we were moving and shaking with the Lord. I learned quickly to adapt, adapt, and adapt.

You know the needs of your students better than anyone. Therefore, be creative! Use these ideas and have some fun, but do not lock yourself into these lessons. The Spirit moves where it will! Follow it. If some of these activities don't fit your needs, use them as a springboard to create better ideas that will touch the hearts of your students. Never limit the Holy Spirit.

This resource book was written for a thirty-minute prayer assembly for elementary religious formation. However, it would also work well in the following settings:

- Weekly, bimonthly, or monthly family nights: With minor adaptation, there's enough material for an hour gathering with children and adults.

- Children's Liturgy of the Word: Trim down to twenty minutes.

- Classroom: Portions of the lesson can be used throughout the week or on Friday.

- Seasonal celebrations: Family nights for Advent, Christmas, Ordinary Time, Lent, and Easter.

- Children's Bible study: Children meet once a week to explore each Sunday's readings.

- Other: Who knows the possibilities?

Dress the part

Some prayer assemblies require the assembly leader to dress up. Costumes help you get into the part and have fun. There are certain themes for which your attire will set the stage and create the needed environment. If the students see you having a good time, they will also. If you feel uncomfortable about dressing the part, please find someone who will enjoy it. Remember, if you aren't open, the students won't be open. The students will mirror your enthusiasm and grace.

Recognize your gifts and find the right support
You do not have to do it all.

This is not the pope's Church, the bishops' and priests' Church, my Church, nor your Church; this is Jesus' Church. Therefore, let Jesus work through you. Use your gifts and talents, and encourage others in your parish to share their gifts. In other words, invite others to get involved in these prayer assemblies. Jesus' Church grows when people come together to share their God-given gifts.

No one has all the gifts; therefore, find singers, storytellers, hospitality ministers, good readers, a set-up crew, and actors. Get your priest(s) and pastoral ministers, deacon(s), older parishioners, parents, and college-age students involved. High school students make great small-group leaders. By involving the whole parish community, you will increase the environment of fun and excitement.

Role-play the Scriptures

Children and adults of all ages really enjoy watching the Scriptures come alive by acting out particular passages or by having one of the Biblical characters come and share. From twenty-two years of working with children and adults, I guarantee that the Scripture passage will come alive and be remembered and experienced in a new way if you invite to your class Jesus, John the Baptist, Mary, Elizabeth, Mary, Peter, Paul, some of the disciples, Pilate, lepers, Lazarus, Pharisees and scribes, or any biblical person.

The students love listening to the Bible characters and asking them questions. The key is to find "spiritually balanced" and creative parishioners who love to act. Pray for guidance; then go out and start asking parishioners or call other local parishes. Believe it or not, you may even be surprised if you call the catechetical office of your diocese. They may know DREs or coordinators, volunteers, and priests who can assist you or direct you to other resources. Don't forget about your own youth ministry resources or local colleges.

Don't underestimate what the power of God can do with a lively discussion of biblical persons who were healed by Jesus, a woman at the well, or the bride and groom who witnessed Jesus turning water into wine.

God's word is alive; it lives and moves.

Time

There's enough material in each lesson to easily fill an hour. I would suggest thirty minutes, but it really depends on the format you choose to use. For example, if you are using these assemblies for family catechesis or seasonal catechesis during Advent and Lent, an hour to an hour and a half would work well. There are many settings and uses for this resource book. Again, be creative! There's lots of material—pick and choose to create the ideal setting for you.

Location

Set the mood and environment.

I feel that the church building is the perfect place for a prayer assembly. For some students, this will be the only time they are inside the church—sad, but true. Furthermore, it's holy and healthy to let the students experience ownership of the church building. All the people of the parish should feel welcome in the church; this is their home also. It's a sacred place to experience God in many different ways and with many expressions. However, please check with the pastor first.

If you are open to the Spirit and use some of these ideas, I guarantee a prayer experience that is communal, loud, fun, creative, and enjoyable. But one should never forget that we are in God's presence, and the church building needs to be respected. Remind the students that being a child of God in God's house is a privilege as well as a right and should be treated as such.

No matter where you gather—in the church building, parish hall, outside in the courtyard—if you gather in Jesus' name, he will be there also. So gather the students in the best location you have; they deserve it. In choosing a location, consider the points on the next page.

- Visibility: Everyone needs to see. A location with a raised platform or stage is ideal.

- Sound system: A good sound system ensures that everyone will be able to hear. The assembly depends a great deal on the children's responses. Make sure that they are heard by everyone.

- Room to spread out: The students will need room. You don't want them on top of each other, and you don't want them too spread out. Choose a location that is conducive to singing, sharing, laughing, and teaching.

- Sacred space: If you aren't meeting in the church building, don't forget the importance of creating sacred space. Set up a table with candles, a Bible, a crucifix, a picture of Jesus, and some flowers. This will reinforce the presence of Jesus and the lessons that he will be teaching. You might cover the table in the liturgical season's color.

Format

Opening page

This page lists the Sunday, readings, theme, and background for each lesson. Prepare for the session by reading the Scripture Background carefully.

Part I: Gathering for God's Word

Introduction

Sometimes you will be reminded of any preparations that need to be made before the lesson. You will be given all the preliminary information you need to map out your prayer assembly. (For space consideration, this information is sometimes on the opening page.)

There is an introduction each week. Use it as a guide to welcome the students and prepare them for the Opening Prayer. Always begin by calling them the "Church." For example: "Will the Church please stand?" This will remind them that **they** are the **Church**. If they are baptized, they are the Church. Understanding this gives them ownership.

Opening Prayer

The Opening Prayer can be led by one of the students or by you. You can use a prayer of your choice or the one provided. Structure the prayer for the assembly to fit your needs.

If you choose to have the students lead the Opening Prayer, give them at least a week to prepare. They may need some guidance. Let them know that prayer doesn't have to be memorized. Prayer can take the form of poetry, a song, reflection, or a spontaneous dialogue. You may want to send a handout about prayer home with the children to use it as a guide when preparing for Opening Prayer.

The prayers that are provided attempt to bridge the themes from the previous week's readings with the upcoming week's readings.

Song

There are recommended songs for each assembly, and these are meant to reinforce the themes of the readings. However, feel free to choose other songs that fit your plan and the repertoire of the children. Children love to sing. Pick fun and lively songs, and, where possible, create hand gestures to use with the songs.

Some great sources for song available from Harcourt Religion Publishers: *Glory Day*, by David Haas; *Walking by Faith*, by David Haas and Robert Piercy; *Celebrating Our Faith*; *When Children Gather*, compiled by Robert Piercy and Vivian Williams.

Announcements

Communicate with the students important upcoming events. This is also a time to acknowledge birthdays.

Part II: Remembering God's Word

"Remembering God's Word" connects last week's readings with the upcoming readings. It contains questions that reinforce and review the gospel message of the previous week.

In early childhood, repetition of concepts is important. The children will be exposed to God's word four times: at the prayer assembly, in class, at Sunday liturgy, and again at the prayer assembly when they recall the previous Sunday. Furthermore, "Remembering God's Word" encourages the children to attend Sunday liturgy. The children know the questions that will be asked are based on the Sunday readings; consequently, they listen more intently to the readings. And some children who normally don't attend Sunday liturgy on a regular basis will come more regularly. I've witnessed this for five years now.

Here's a true story: I received a call one Sunday morning at my office from a mother who was somewhat upset. She demanded to know what we were teaching during our faith formation classes. Her daughter was upset and was pestering her father because she didn't want to miss church that morning. The little girl wanted to know the answers for "Remembering God's Word." After I explained to the mother our format for our weekly faith formation classes and that her daughter only wanted to be prepared for our prayer assembly, the mother understood. But the father was still upset. I asked her why this was so, and the mother responded that the father wanted to stay home to watch Sunday football. His daughter's demands to go to church were interfering with his plans. The child didn't win; the family stayed home that Sunday morning, and the little girl was disappointed at the next faith formation assembly. I let her pick from the grab bag anyway.

Don't worry about wrong answers. Make sure the children understand that it's their trying that is important to Jesus. God prefers that we try to live our faith every day. When we try to live our faith, God uses us to touch the lives of others. This draws us into a deeper relationship with God. It works for adults and children.

Grab bag

Have a grab bag available. You can use any bag, even a pillow case. Fill the bag with simple prizes: prayer cards, inexpensive rosaries, crosses, stickers, and so on. Ask parish members to donate gifts for the grab bag. Avoid food, candy, and gum in the grab bag. These are all big, "messy" mistakes.

Each child who answers a reflection question get to choose from the grab bag. The answer doesn't have to be correct. Trying is what is important to Jesus. Remind the children that it's in giving that we receive; by responding they help each grow in faith.

What happens when you run out of goodies? Ask the parish community to help. Some people will buy religious items for the children. Others will go through their closets and drawers. You'll be amazed at the beautiful crosses, holy cards, and rosaries that people will freely give to the children. The children will love it, and so will the adults who know they are contributing something very special to the children. This is definitely a win-win situation.

Part III: Understanding God's Word

Materials Needed

In this section, the necessary materials are listed. Sometimes there are some helpful hints or notes about preparation. Some of the materials are used only for the younger students and some are used only with the older students. In these cases, you will find them specifically marked (Younger Students and Older Students).

Scripture

This is the heart of the assembly. It lists the readings that you will be proclaiming. Before you proclaim God's word, have the children sit in a circle. Then join the circle and proclaim the gospel or reading.

Sometimes questions or activities will precede the Scripture. This is especially true of the parables. This allows the children to get in the right mind-set before the word is proclaimed. It helps children focus on the meaning of difficult readings before they're read, while they're read, and after they're read. Repetition is the key.

Reflection

Reflection questions are divided into two sections, for younger students and for older students. This is helpful because, as children mature, they process the readings on different levels. As their lives change with maturity, the readings are applied on deeper levels.

You will need to decide where to draw the line between younger students and older students. This line will depend on your students and their needs.

Reflection is designed to let the students process the readings and apply them to their daily lives. This section will vary with each assembly. Sometimes it will be discussion only, and other times will include drawing, journaling, or a hands-on craft. Sometimes it will include all of these. If you are limited by time, the reflection questions or activity can also be sent home with the students to share with their parents. Again, this is your assembly. Structure it to meet your needs.

Activity

Each assembly has a fun activity that gets the children excited about the readings. These activities are intended to make God's word come to life as the children interact with that word. The message of the gospel takes on new meaning when the students and teachers take ownership by entering into the movement of the Holy Spirit in the Scriptures.

Closing Prayer

The Closing Prayer allows the students to think and pray about what they learned in the assembly. Various prayer forms are used to show the children that there are many different ways to pray. Begin each prayer by gathering in a circle and holding hands. This emphasizes the unity of the Church—struggling and growing together.

Making God's Word Our Own

Making God's Word Our Own challenges the students to apply the gospel messages to their daily lives. It is also helps the students build a personal relationship with Jesus. At the end of each session, invite the students to spend time reflecting on the gospel message with Jesus. You can read the challenge to the children as it appears in the book or adjust it to fit the needs of your students.

Ideas to Incorporate

Following is a list of ideas that can be incorporated into prayer assemblies.

- A tour of the rectory and the church building: altar, sanctuary, prayer corners, confessionals, reconciliation room, baptismal font, and so on. This is a wonderful way to educate the children and adults on Church symbols, traditions, and worship.

- Learn one prayer a week as a large group. This especially helps the students who don't pray at home. Learn the simple yet basic prayers of our faith: the Lord's Prayer, the Hail Mary, the Rosary, Glory to the Father, the Sign of the Cross, and so on.

- Focus on one part of the Liturgy of the Word. Explain what happens and what the assembly's responses are. Take the role of the priest (or ask the pastor to participate) and ask the children to respond as they do on Sunday. Afterward, explain (or have the pastor explain) the meaning behind the actions and responses. This is a wonderful way for the students to better understand the liturgy.

Good luck and have fun!

First Sunday *of* Advent

Readings

Jeremiah 33:14–16
1 Thessalonians 3:12–4:2
Luke 21:25–28, 34–36

Theme

Fear is not of God. As Jesus' friends, we wait with joyful hope!

Scripture *Background*

The readings for the First Sunday of Advent offer three perspectives of our waiting for the day of the Lord. The reading from Jeremiah offers the perspective of the prophet. The prophets believed that the fullness of the kingdom could be experienced within history. Jeremiah was writing for an audience that was facing exile. Jerusalem had been destroyed, and many of its citizens taken captive to Babylon. Those left behind were forced to live in caves. Jeremiah assured the people that even in this disaster God would remain faithful. A righteous king would again sit on the throne of David as God had promised. This king would bring justice and security to the land. Their current king, Zedekiah, whose name meant "The LORD is our righteousness," failed. However, in the restoration God promised, the whole people would be called "the Lord our justice."

The Gospel of Luke presents the perspective of *apocalypticism*. Developed two centuries before Christ, this approach held that history itself was too corrupt to be redeemed. Evil was greater than human strength. There would ensue a great battle between good and evil involving cosmic powers, spirits, and all creation. Humankind would be destroyed. In the end, good would triumph over evil. God would emerge victorious. God would bring the righteous into a new life in the kingdom. Today's gospel uses apocalyptic imagery to describe the return of Christ. When the great cataclysm begins, Christians should rejoice because Christ is coming, and their redemption is at hand. Christians must always be ready because no one knows when the great day will come. God will keep the promise at the appointed time. Christians must watch and pray.

Luke's audience recognized that the wait for Christ's return could be long. The Christians at Thessalonica, however, believed that the day would come in their lifetime. Paul's letter encourages them to live wisely in anticipation of Christ's coming. They should persevere in the way of life they had learned from Paul, to emerge blameless and holy when Christ arrived. Then the day of the Lord would truly be a day of rejoicing.

Irene Nowell OSB

PART I: Gathering *for God's Word*

Opening Prayer

Alternative: *Ask one of the students to lead the opening prayer.*

Open the session by saying: **Welcome. May God's peace be with you, the Church of God. Please stand. "Stand up and raise your heads, because your redemption is drawing near"** (Luke 21:28).

> *Lord Jesus, bless these students. Fill them with hope, love, and the need to prepare their hearts for your arrival. Be our guide as we begin this new Church year. Keep us warm in your blanket of love, and never let us forget that we belong to you. We are your children of the light, children of hope, and children of love. We ask all this in your name.*

The students respond loudly: **Amen!**

Song

"City of God" by Dan Schutte from *Glory & Praise* (OCP [NALR]), *Gather (Comprehensive)* (GIA), *Today's Missal* (OCP).

"Future Full of Hope" by Paul Hillebrand from *Promise* (OCP).

"Soon and Very Soon" by Andre Crouch from *Glory and Praise 2* (OCP [NALR]).

Announcements

Affirming and acknowledging the students is very important. Use this time to recognize birthdays and individual or group accomplishments. Celebrate a student or saint of the week. Be honest and creative in your affirmation.

When there is a birthday, invite all those with birthdays to stand. Sing "Happy Birthday." Then, as a class, extend your hands over the standing students and pray the following:

> *Creator God, through your Son Jesus, all things came into being and were made wonderfully good. We thank you for the gift(s) of* (name students)*, and we ask you to continue to bless them and fill them with your Holy Spirit. You have given them the gift of life. May they live their lives to the fullest, and may their actions always be pleasing to you. Amen.*

- news of the week or liturgical season
- birthdays
- special events or Advent projects
- other

PART II: Remembering *God's Word*

Review last week's session. Have an Advent wreath in a visible location. (If possible, borrow the one used in the parish's liturgical celebrations.)

1. What feast did we celebrate last Sunday?

- Christ the King

2. What did you learn about Jesus? About yourself?

- Jesus is Lord and King of our lives. We are children of the light—kingdom kids. The closer we stand to the light of Christ, the more we reflect God's kingdom.

3. What are the symbols of the Advent wreath? What do they represent?

- The **circle** represents God's eternal love for us. There is no beginning or end; God's love is always present.

- The **evergreens** symbolize Jesus' presence. Just as an evergreen tree is always green—never changing—Jesus is always near. His spirit is always present for us.

- The **four candles** represent the four Sundays in Advent. This is a time of preparation and celebration as we joyfully wait for Jesus. The candles remind us that Jesus is the *true* light of the world. We are called to be Jesus' light so that others may see Jesus in us. Because of our Baptism, we, the Church, are living Advent wreaths. We bring hope, light, and love into the world.

- The **colors of the candles** are symbolic as well. Purple represents hope and waiting. Pink symbolizes joy and happiness.

PART III: Understanding *God's Word*

Scripture

Encourage the students to listen carefully to Jesus' words. Proclaim Luke 21:25–28, 34–36. Ask the students to respond to each question below. Make two separate lists of their responses.

List one: How do we act when we fear Jesus?

List two: How do we act when we recognize Jesus as our friend and the true King of our lives?

Compare the two lists. Then proclaim the gospel again. Say: **Jesus will come again. As his friends, we have nothing to fear. Jesus tells us to stand up straight and raise our heads. Don't be afraid; trust Jesus. If we love Jesus, we must try as hard as we can to follow him. Open your hearts to him. This is called "waiting in joyful hope." Come, Lord Jesus, come!**

Reflection

Use the following questions to explore the reading further.

Materials Needed

All Students
- poster paper or chalkboard
- markers or chalk
- Bible
- Advent wreath
- evergreens, one per student (optional)

Younger Students
- paper
- crayons

Older Students
- journals
- pens

Younger Students

1. What would you say if Jesus visited you today?

2. Distribute to the students paper and crayons. Instruct them to draw a picture of Jesus coming in his power and glory. Allow time for the students to share their pictures with the class.

3. What can you do to prepare your heart for Jesus' coming?

Older Students

Allow time for the students to respond in their journals to the last question.

1. How would you feel if Jesus came back today in his full power and glory to establish the fullness of his kingdom here on earth?

2. Have you ever been surprised or caught off-guard by someone or something? What happened? How did you feel?

3. Jesus tells us to be prepared for his coming. This Advent, how are you going to prepare your heart and mind for Jesus?

Closing Prayer

Have the students gather around the Advent wreath. Turn out the lights, and light the first candle. Review what the symbols of the Advent wreath mean (see page 4). Ask the students to think about one thing that frightens them. Invite them to silently ask Jesus to take away that fear and replace it with courage and trust in him. After a few moments of silence, join hands and conclude with the Lord's Prayer.

Optional: Give each student a piece of an evergreen branch to take home as a reminder that we are called to be living Advent wreaths to the world.

Making God's Word Our Own

If you are choosing a student for next Sunday's opening prayer, do so now.

Choose one thing you are afraid of. Ask Jesus to help you face that fear. Alone it may be difficult, but with Jesus you can overcome any fear. Try it for one week; you may be surprised at what Jesus will do.

For the next session, you will need to find someone to role-play John the Baptist. Your pastor, associate priest, or a priest from another parish are always good choices. Or ask your DRE for suggestions; this would be a great opportunity to involve a parishioner or a parent. If possible, give the volunteer the script on pages 9–10 to study prior to the session.

Second Sunday *of* Advent

Readings

Baruch 5:1–9
Philippians 1:4–6, 8–11
Luke 3:1–6

Theme

We, the Church, are called to be signs of God's kingdom.

Scripture *Background*

Today's readings anticipate the great joy of God's coming. The prophetic passage from Baruch, which borrows the vocabulary of Second Isaiah, presents a glorious vision of the vindication of God's people. Jerusalem, clothed in the glory and justice of God, would climb to the heights like a sentinel and watch her children gather from the whole earth to share in God's glory. God would lead them home, with mercy and justice as companions. All creation would share in the delight and make a smooth, shady path for the people of God.

Paul's Letter to the Philippians expresses the great hope he had for the people to whom he preached the good news. They had enthusiastically accepted the gospel of Christ. They had supported Paul financially and shown kindness to him during his imprisonment. He prayed that they would continue their faithfulness. Paul reminded them that God would bring that good work to its fullness. He prayed that they might be like plentiful fruit for the harvest of God. If they love one another and value what matters, they will be ready for that great harvest.

In the gospel reading, Luke sets the story of Jesus in historic context for his Gentile audience by listing the important figures of the time. At the end of the list, he introduces John the Baptizer with the passage, "the word of God came to John, son of Zechariah, in the desert." John's purpose was to preach the arrival of God's salvation in Jesus. He did this in two ways. He reminded his listeners of God's promise of salvation and also preached a baptism of repentance. Baptism, or ritual washing, was a practice common to some Jews at the time. It was viewed as a way of cleansing sin and as a way of initiating members into the community. John's baptism indicated that his followers had repented and were being cleansed of their sins. John also reminded his listeners of Second Isaiah's words about the return from exile. God will lead the people home to Jerusalem. Creation would prepare the way. All flesh would see the wonder of God's salvation.

Irene Nowell OSB

PART I: Gathering *for God's Word*

Opening Prayer

Alternative: *Ask one of the students to lead the opening prayer.*

Open the session by saying: **Welcome. It is good seeing you here again. I invite you, the Church, to please stand. We begin in the name of the Father, and of the Son, and of the Holy Spirit** (make the sign of the cross).

Lord Jesus, we thank you and praise you for all the wonderful gifts you have given us. As we prepare for your coming and work to be signs of your kingdom, send us your Spirit of courage and strength. Make us heralds of your love and forgiveness. Open our hearts and minds to know you better so we may prepare for your coming. We ask these prayers and those in our hearts in your name.

The students respond loudly: **Amen!**

Song

"Advent Gathering: Make Ready the Way/Come, O Lord" by David Haas from *Walking by Faith* (Harcourt Religion Publishers, GIA).

"Prepare Ye" by Stephen Schwartz from *Godspell*.

Announcements

- news of the week or liturgical season
- birthdays
- Advent project or special events
- other

PART II: Remembering *God's Word*

Review last week's session.

1. Last week, we lit the Advent wreath. What are the symbols of the Advent wreath? What do they mean?

   - The **circle** represents God's eternal love for us. There is no beginning or end; God's love is always present.

   - The **evergreens** symbolize Jesus' presence. Just as an evergreen tree is always green, Jesus is always near. His spirit is always present for us.

   - The **four candles** represent the four Sundays in Advent. This is a time of preparation and celebration as we joyfully wait for Jesus. The candles remind us that Jesus is the *true* light of the world. We are called to be Jesus' light so that others may see Jesus in us. Because of our Baptism, we, the Church, are living Advent wreaths. We bring hope, light, and love into the world.

   - The **colors of the candles** are symbolic as well. Purple represents hope and waiting. Pink symbolizes joy and happiness.

2. In last Sunday's gospel reading, Jesus told us to that he would return in power and glory. He told his followers to do three things when he returns. What are these three things?

   - Stand up straight; raise your heads; trust Jesus.

3. How did Jesus help you overcome your fears last week?

　　• Let the students respond openly.

PART III: Understanding God's Word

Scripture

Invite the students to sit on the floor around you for the gospel reading. Proclaim Luke 3:1–4. Stop after the phrase "The voice of one crying out in the wilderness." At this time, a volunteer role-playing John the Baptist enters the room, finishes the reading, and takes over the lesson (utilizing the script on pages 9–10).

Reflection

Use the following questions and activities to help students process the gospel reading further. Have the older students respond to the last question in their journals.

Materials Needed

All Students
- a volunteer to role-play John the Baptist
- John the Baptist's script (pages 9–10)
- white robe
- piece of old rope for a belt
- Bible
- bowl of water
- reflective music
- CD or tape player
- gummy worms in a small bag (optional)

Younger Students
- paper
- crayons

Older Students
- journals
- pens

Younger Students

1. Distribute to the students paper and crayons. Instruct them to write a letter to their parents or guardians telling them that they love them and will pray for them this Advent Season. Or give students the option of drawing an Advent picture that shows their love for their parents or guardians.

2. Allow time for the students to make a card for John the Baptist thanking him for sharing his love and wisdom. Have available paper and crayons.

3. How can you help your family prepare for Jesus' coming?

Older Students

1. If you were John the Baptist living in today's world, how would you share with others the message of conversion, the need for forgiveness, and the coming of Jesus?

2. John the Baptist was a sign of hope and good news to most who heard his message of conversion. Who has been a sign of good news and Jesus for you?

3. How would you feel and what would you do if you were told that because of your own Baptism, you are also called to be a herald's voice in the world, to share Jesus with everyone you meet?

Closing Prayer

Place a bowl of water in a central location. As reflective music plays softly in the background, individually invite the students to come to the water. Have them bless themselves. As they do this, remind them that they are called to be God's messengers and examples of God's love in the world. Conclude with the Lord's Prayer.

Making God's Word Our Own

This week share the good news of Jesus with three people. You can do this through word (tell three people about Jesus) or through your actions (being kind, caring, forgiving, loving, respectful).

If you are choosing a student for next Sunday's opening prayer, do so now.

Role-Play Script—
John the Baptist

John the Baptist enters and loudly proclaims as he walks to the front so all the students can see:

"Prepare the way of the Lord, make his paths straight. Every valley shall be filled, and every mountain and hill shall be made low, and the crooked shall be made straight, and the rough ways made smooth; and all flesh shall see the salvation of God."

That is exactly what I preached. I would say it so much and so loud that my throat got sore sometimes. Do you know what I have noticed over the years? People have heard this reading so many times that they forget to listen and don't understand what it really means. Let me explain it to you. It will only take a minute.

"Prepare the way of the Lord . . ."

It means just that! Get ready, because the Lord is coming. I'll tell you how I got ready for the Lord in my life; maybe it will help you get ready, too. I prayed. I found a place to be alone with no distractions, and I *listened* to God. It was God who told me how to prepare. I also fasted; that means I didn't eat much. I did this to help me better listen to God. And it worked! Try not eating your favorite food or candy. Try fasting from fighting with your brothers and sisters or arguing with your parents.

> *Optional: Have John the Baptist eat gummy worms and tell the students about his diet of honey, locusts, and other bugs.*

> *If time allows, ask students how they will make ready the way of the Lord this Advent.*

"Make his paths straight."

This is really easy to understand; it means clean up! Do God's will; follow God's commandments; love God above everything else with your whole being, heart, soul, and strength; and love others as you love yourself. It's doing what Jesus has asked us to do: love, forgive, care for the poor, be kind to all, and love everyone. If you do this, you will be clearing a straight path to your heart for God.

> *If time allows, ask the students how they can clear a straight path to their hearts.*

"Every valley shall be filled, and every mountain and hill shall be made low."

This may seem a little more difficult to understand, but it's really simple. Let God be God. What seems impossible for us is possible for God. Preparing the way of the Lord and clearing him a straight path is hard work. It may even seem impossible, but we can do it *only* if we try. As we try, we need to ask God to help us. And God will!

> *If time allows, ask the students into which areas of their lives they need to invite God.*

"The crooked shall be made straight, and the rough ways made smooth."

There's that word *straight* again! Let me tell you a little secret. *(Whisper.)* Whenever your hear the phrase *make straight* in the Bible, it usually means "conversion." *(Normal voice.)* *Conversion* means turning away from something and turning toward something else. God wants us to turn away from sin and things that are not of God and turn our hearts toward him. It's that simple! Turn to God. Look to God for "everything" you need or want. If you don't know how to do this, ask Jesus to show you how, and he will! Try it this Advent Season. This may seem difficult, but with God, you can do it!

> *If time allows, ask students what they will turn away from this Advent Season. What can they do to turn their hearts and minds toward God?*

"And all flesh shall see the salvation of God."

This is exciting. If you do the things I just described, others will be able to see Jesus in you, and God's love will touch the lives of others.

- Make his paths straight.
- Every valley shall be filled, and every mountain and hill shall be made low.
- The crooked shall be made straight, and the rough ways made smooth.

You can make a real difference! You bring God's love and salvation to others when you turn your life over to God. This is another way of saying that we, the Church, are called by our Baptism to reflect Jesus in the world.

> *If time allows, ask the students what they can do this Advent Season to best show that God loves everyone.*

Thank you for letting me visit with you. I will pray that this Advent Season will be special and holy for you and your families. Good-bye.

Third Sunday
of Advent

Readings

Zephaniah 3:14–18a
Philippians 4:4–7
Luke 3:10–18

Theme

We need to learn to recognize the Lord working in our lives.

Scripture *Background*

The prophet Zephaniah preached during one of the most difficult times in Israel's history, a generation before the destruction of Jerusalem by the Babylonians. Zephaniah told his listeners that the day of the Lord would be a joyless day because they had not been faithful. It would be a day of destruction. Only a few of them, a "remnant," would be saved. Those who did not hope in themselves, who knew their only hope was in God, would be saved. Today's reading was a joyful promise to this faithful remnant. This remnant, the new Jerusalem, should sing and dance with wild abandon because the God in whom they trusted had saved them. God had turned away the enemies outside, and, through his forgiveness, had also turned away the enemies inside. Now the Lord, the true king of Israel, lives in their midst. The Lord rejoices in their salvation and sings and dances with wild abandon.

The sense of excitement at the arrival of the Lord continues in the second reading. Paul called the Philippians to joy and peace because the Lord was coming. Nothing should disturb them because God would take care of all their needs. Their gratitude should be limitless because God's own peace would stand guard over them. They should live in accord with who they were, people saved by the mercy and love of God.

At the time the Gospel of Luke was written, Christians had begun to realize that Christ's return might not be immediate. They needed to learn how to live in readiness, to be aware that their own deaths might precede the day of the Lord. The Gospel of Luke stressed the value of daily living. John's words in today's passage instructed people in some of the ordinary professions. Rather than abandon their professions, they should live justly within their work. When the Messiah came, he would separate the just from the wicked, just as the thresher separated the wheat from the chaff. Luke's audience knew that the return of Christ might not be imminent. They did know, with certainty, that Christ would indeed arrive.

Irene Nowell OSB

PART I: Gathering *for God's Word*

Opening Prayer   **Alternative:** *Ask one of the students to lead the opening prayer.*

Open the session by saying: **The Lord's peace to all of you. Thank you for joining us. Today we are celebrating the Third Sunday of Advent. Advent goes by quickly; so does life. So get ready for a wonderful and exciting ride. I invite the Church of God to stand.**

> *We ask God to bless us in the name of the Father, and of the Son, and of the Holy Spirit* (make the sign of the cross). *Lord Jesus, bless these students. Give them the strength to question and seek you out. Give them the grace to hear your answers to their questions. We ask this and all the prayers in our hearts in your name.*

The students respond loudly: **Amen!**

Song   "If God Is for Us" by John Foley from *Glory & Praise* (OCP [NALR]).

"Jesus, Come to Us" by David Haas from *Glory & Praise 2* (OCP [NALR]).

"O Come, O Come, Emmanuel" from *Today's Missal* (OCP), *Lead Me, Guide Me* (GIA).

Announcements
- parish news
- birthdays
- Advent project update
- other

PART II: Remembering *God's Word*

Use the following questions to review last week's session.

1. Who was the ruler of Judea when John the Baptist was preaching about the coming of Jesus?
   - Pontius Pilate

2. What did you learn from last week's gospel reading?
   - Let the students respond openly and honestly.

3. What does John the Baptist encourage us to do to prepare our hearts for Jesus?
   - Get ready for God's awesome power.
   - Clean up, and do God's will.
   - Let God be God in your life.
   - Turn your heart to God (conversion of heart).
   - Be alone with God.

4. How did you share Jesus with others last week? What did you learn about God and yourself?
   - Let the students respond openly and honestly.

PART III: Understanding *God's Word*

Scripture

Proclaim Luke 3:10–18. After the reading, play the "Who Am I?" game.

Who Am I?

Say: **In this week's gospel (Luke 3:10–18), there are three groups of people who ask John the Baptist questions: the crowd, the soldiers, and the tax collectors. I am going to read the answers John gave to these groups. You need to guess which group John the Baptist was answering: the crowd, the soldiers, or the tax collectors.**

1. "Do not bully anyone. Denounce no one falsely. Be content with your pay."
   - Answer: the soldiers

2. "Let the person with two coats give to the one who has none. The person with food should do the same."
   - Answer: the crowd

3. "Exact nothing over and above your fixed amount."
   - Answer: the tax collectors

Ask the students to think of some questions to ask John the Baptist (knowing his message). Invite older students to answer the questions as John the Baptist would have answered.

> **Materials Needed**
>
> **All Students**
> - Bible
> - bowl of water
> - candle
> - matches
>
> **Older Students**
> - journals
> - pens

Reflection

Use the following questions and activities to help students get to the heart of the gospel.

Younger Students

1. Jesus promises to baptize us in the Holy Spirit and in fire. Have the students draw pictures of what that would look like. (You may choose to explain that the dove is a symbol of the Holy Spirit.) Invite volunteers to share their drawings with the class.

2. Do you like to wait? What is the hardest part about waiting for something special?

3. What are you doing while you are waiting for Jesus to return? Give an example.

Older Students

Allow time for the students to respond in their journals to the following questions. Invite volunteers to share their responses to the first question with the class.

1. Sometimes in our lives we miss what we are looking for. And most of the time, what we are looking for is right in front of us—very close to us. Yet we miss it. Has this ever happened to you? Describe the experience.

2. Though Jesus promises to come again in his glory and in the fullness of love, he is still here with us in a very special and intimate way. What may prevent you from seeing and experiencing Jesus?

3. All of John the Baptist's responses pointed to action. Carefully reread the gospel reading. How can you prepare for Jesus in your life?

Closing Prayer

Place in the middle of the room a bowl of water and a candle (the Easter candle, if possible). Invite the students to stand in a circle around the water and candle. Proclaim Philippians 4:4–7. After a moment of silence, invite all the students to bless themselves with the water and make the sign of the cross as a symbol of how they are preparing for the Lord. Join hands, and conclude with the Lord's Prayer.

Making God's Word Our Own

This week reflect on how near Jesus truly is to you and your family. Ask the following question of seven family members: "How have you experienced Jesus' closeness in your life?" Listen to their answers, and be ready to share their responses next week.

> *If you are choosing a student for next Sunday's opening prayer, do so now.*

Fourth Sunday *of* Advent

Readings

Micah 5:1–4a
Hebrews 10:5–10
Luke 1:39–45

Theme

We are called to share the good news of Jesus with others.

Scripture *Background*

The prophet Micah was a contemporary of the great prophet Isaiah. He preached in and around Jerusalem in the eighth century B.C. Micah proclaims that hope would arise from another "city of David," Bethlehem, and not Jerusalem. Jerusalem was David's capital, but Bethlehem was his birthplace. The new king, the new anointed one (messiah) who would bring salvation, would come like David from Bethlehem. Now even Bethlehem participated in the glory. The new king would be a shepherd like David. He would guide his flock through God's strength. His kingdom would reach to the ends of the earth. There would be peace in his kingdom, not because he would defeat all the surrounding countries as David did, but because he himself would be peace.

The gospel centers on another little town in the hill country of Judah—Ein Karim, home of Zechariah and Elizabeth. In today's gospel, Mary came to visit Elizabeth. The younger came to greet the elder. When they met, Elizabeth proclaimed the greatness of Mary's child. John the Baptizer, still in the womb, recognized the one for whom he prepared the way and leapt for joy. This vision was made possible by the Spirit of the Lord who filled both mothers and both children. In her delight, Elizabeth proclaimed three beatitudes: Blessed are you among women; blessed is the fruit of your womb; blessed is she who trusted the Lord's word.

The reading from the Letter to the Hebrews presents the incarnation of Jesus from a different perspective. The author was very interested in presenting Christianity as descended from, and yet different from, Judaism. In today's reading, the author discusses the difference between Jewish sacrifice and the one Christian sacrifice, the death of Jesus. Jesus' sacrifice of himself, a sacrifice offered only once, was made possible by his assuming a human body and human existence. Jewish sacrifice was the offering of animals. The single Christian sacrifice was Jesus' offering of himself. This sacrifice was the purpose of the birth awaited in the gospel. It was this sacrifice that fulfilled the prophecy of Micah.

Irene Nowell OSB

PART I: Gathering *for God's Word*

Opening Prayer

Alternative: *Ask one of the students to lead the opening prayer.*

Open the session by saying: **May God's Spirit fill us all with hope and love. I invite the Church to stand.**

> *Jesus, our friend, brother, and Messiah, we welcome you into our hearts and to this gathering. Grant all of us, especially these students, the courage and strength to put our trust in you as Mary did. Fill our hearts with your joy and love as we wait for your return. We ask these prayers and the ones we hold in our hearts in your name.*

The students respond loudly: **Amen!**

Song

"An Angel Came from Heaven" by Christopher Walker and Paul Freeburg from *Stories and Songs of Jesus* (OCP).

"Find Us Ready" by Tom Booth from *Find Us Ready* (OCP).

"Jesus, Come to Us" by David Haas from *Glory & Praise 2* (OCP [NALR]).

Announcements

- parish news
- birthdays
- Advent project update
- other

PART II: Remembering *God's Word*

Use the following questions to review last week's gospel reading.

1. What three groups of people questioned John the Baptist? How did John respond to their questions?
   - The crowd: "Let the man with two coats give to him who has none. The man who has food should do the same."
   - The tax collectors: "Exact nothing over and above your fixed amount."
   - The soldiers: "Do not bully anyone. Denounce no one falsely. Be content with your pay."

2. John the Baptist said he baptized with water only. What did he say Jesus would baptize us with?
   - the Holy Spirit and fire

3. What were some of the responses you gathered from family members to the following question: "How have you experienced Jesus' closeness in your life?" How have your family members experienced Jesus' closeness?
   - Allow the students to respond openly and freely.

PART III: Understanding *God's Word*

Proclaim Luke 1:39–45. After a few moments of silence, choose seven volunteers to play the "What If?" game.

Materials Needed
All Students
• Bible
• index cards
• seven volunteers
• three small prizes
Younger Students
• paper
• crayons
Older Students
• journals
• pens

What If?

Preparation: Write seven "What if?" questions on index cards. Write a question for each of the following characters: Mary, Joseph, John the Baptist, the innkeeper, a wise man, a shepherd, and King Herod. Use the questions below or write your own. Choose seven volunteers, and have each person randomly pick a card. Encourage the volunteers to become the character of the person they choose; this is their chance to be that person.

Give the students time to prepare their answers. Allow ample time for the volunteers to share their questions and responses with the remainder of the class. Have the students vote for the best "What If?" responses in the following categories: most creative, most honest, and most spiritual. Give small prizes for each category.

- What if you were Mary and God asked you to be the mother of the Son of God? What would you do? Would you say yes or no? Why?

- What if you were Joseph and God asked you to be the foster father of the Son of God? What would you do? Would you say yes or no? Why?

- What if you were John the Baptist? How would you prepare the way of the Lord?

- What if you were the innkeeper who sent Mary and Joseph away from the inn? What would you do and why?

- What if you were one of the wise men who followed the star? How long and how far would you follow the star?

- What if you were a shepherd in the fields and angels told you about the birth of Jesus, the king? What would you do?

- What if you were King Herod? What would you do about this new king? What would you do with him?

Use the following questions and activities to help students process the readings further.

Younger Students

1. Describe a time when someone shared happy news with you. How did it make you feel? Do you remember what the news was?

2. How have you shared the good news of Jesus with others this Advent? Who has shared the good news of Jesus with you? How?

3. Distribute to the students paper and crayons. Allow time for them to draw a picture of Mary and Elizabeth greeting each other.

Older Students

Allow time for the students to respond in their journals to the last question.

1. Reread Luke 1:39–45. What is the role of the Holy Spirit in this passage? How does the Holy Spirit help you recognize Jesus in the world around you?

2. In addition to listening to the Holy Spirit, how can we prepare ourselves to see and experience Jesus in the world around us? What prevents us from seeing and experiencing Jesus?

3. How have you shared the good news of Jesus with others this Advent? Who has shared the good news of Jesus with you? How?

Closing Prayer

Gather the students together, and remind them that the first part of the Hail Mary was taken directly from Scripture. Praying it helps us focus on Jesus. Pray the second joyful mystery of the Rosary (Mary visits Elizabeth) slowly and reflectively.

Making God's Word Our Own

This week make room for Jesus. Clean your closets and drawers. Donate the clothes you no longer use to people in need. Make it a prayer. Picture yourself cleaning out your heart to make room in your life for Jesus' love and Holy Spirit.

If you are choosing a student for next Sunday's opening prayer, do so now.

Holy Family

Readings

Sirach 3:2–7, 12–14
Colossians 3:12–21
Luke 2:41–52

Theme

Jesus' family shows our family how to be holy.

Scripture *Background*

In today's gospel, the Holy Family is on a pilgrimage from their hometown of Nazareth in Galilee (northern Israel) to Jerusalem in Judea (the southern part of the country). It is the feast of Passover, one of the high feast days on which devout Jews came to the temple to celebrate. Later in Luke's Gospel, Jesus would speak his first words in the temple on this feast commemorating the exodus from Egypt. It would be during the feast of Passover that Jesus' own exodus or passage to the Father would take place. Luke is giving us a preview of what is to come.

The gospel presents the youth Jesus, in obedience and reverence to those his Father had placed over him, echoing the spirit of today's reading from Sirach. As he lived faithfully as a youth with his parents, Jesus grew in wisdom, maturity, and grace.

The Book of Sirach is among the group of writings known as *wisdom books*. These are practical instructions on leading a good and successful life. Today's reading from chapter 3 of the Book of Sirach focuses on the duties of children toward their parents. A father and a mother are placed in authority over their children by the Lord. Children are to honor their parents as God had ordained through Moses at Mount Sinai. The command to honor one's parents is not just for young children, however. Adult children must also honor their parents. In their old age, parents will have special needs. The kindness or mercy bestowed on parents is a gift of self and resources given because it is the right thing to do.

The reading from Colossians reminds Christians of their duties toward one another, both in their immediate family and in the wider community. Paul's instructions echo the social ethics that non-Christian writers in a patriarchal society of his day would have given. Paul exhorted family members to remain faithful to the demands of their life-situation, as any respectable member of the society ought to do. In all relationships, forgiveness, love, and a positive attitude should predominate.

Anne Marie Sweet OSB

PART I: Gathering *for God's Word*

Opening Prayer

Alternative: *Ask one of the students to lead the opening prayer.*

Open the session by saying: **Merry Christmas! Don't forget that Christmas is more than one day; Christmas is a way of life. That is why we celebrate the Christmas Season for several weeks.**

I invite the Church to stand. We begin our celebration recalling Jesus' great love for us as we sign ourselves in the name of the Father, and of the Son, and of the Holy Spirit.

> *Jesus, thank you for coming in human form and walking among us. You came to show us how much you love us and that you want to be part of our lives. Walk with us, Jesus; teach us the way to God. Bless all of our families; bring joy, laughter, healing, and love. Grant that all the families of the world reflect your love for us. Remind us that no family is perfect, and help our families strive to be holy. We ask all this and the prayers we hold in our hearts in your name.*

The students respond loudly: **Amen!**

Song

"Hark! The Herald Angels Sing," traditional.

"I Want to Walk as a Child of the Light" by Kathleen Thomerson from *Gather (Comprehensive)* (GIA), *Celebrating Our Faith* (Harcourt Religion Publishers, GIA).

"Joy the World," traditional.

Announcements

- parish news
- birthdays
- other

PART II: Remembering *God's Word*

Use the following questions to review last week's session.

1. What happened in last Sunday's gospel reading?
   - Mary visited Elizabeth. Elizabeth recognized the greatness of Mary's child.

2. What did you learn from last Sunday's gospel?
   - Let the students respond openly and honestly.

3. What did you experience last week when you cleaned out your closets and your hearts?
   - Let the students respond openly and honestly.

PART III: Understanding *God's Word*

Note: *Remember every family structure is different. Be sensitive to the children who come from separated and divorced families. There is no perfect family structure. God works in and loves all families.*

Scripture

Proclaim Luke 2:41–52. Ask: **What is a holy family?** Write the students' responses on a chalkboard or dry-erase board. Discuss different family structures, and stress that God works in all families regardless of structure. Stress that there is no perfect family, but every family is called to be a holy family. Say: **When Jesus is at the center of any family, he helps transform and change that family. Jesus lived in a family just as we do. Through his family, he learned obedience and grew in wisdom and grace. Every family is called to be a holy family. No matter what your family structure is like, Jesus invites all families to be holy.**

Have the students sit in a circle. Pass the bowl of M&M's™ around the circle. Invite the students to take as many as they want. After the bowl has been passed around the circle, say: **For every M&M™ you took, share one example of how a family could be more holy.** (Explain that their examples need not be something about their own families, but they can be.) Write the students' responses on the board. Have fun with this activity. If the students get stuck because they took quite a few M&M's™, limit their responses to five. You will be amazed at the students' ideas. You may want to make a copy of their responses to send home with the students the following week.

Materials Needed

All Students
- Bible
- large bowl of M&M's ™ (red and green would be festive)
- chalkboard or dry-erase board
- chalk or dry-erase markers

Younger Students
- paper
- crayons

Reflection

Use the following questions and activities to help students process the idea of what it means to be a holy family.

Younger Students

1. Distribute to the students paper and crayons. Instruct them to make a card for their parents or guardians, thanking them for who they are and letting them know that they love them.

2. Jesus was obedient to his parents. Are you obedient to your parents? How could you be more obedient?

3. Jesus was once a young person just like you. But as he grew, he learned many things. As you grow as Jesus did, what do you think God wants you to learn?

Older Students

1. If you were missing for three days like Jesus was, what do you think your parents would do? How would they feel?

2. What kind of child do you think Jesus was when he was your age? Do you think he experienced the same struggles you and your friends do? Why or why not?

3. Jesus learned obedience and listened to his parents; in doing so, his Father in heaven helped him grow in wisdom and grace. What could you learn from God if you were more obedient and listened to your parents?

Closing Prayer

Say: **Our closing prayer today is different and special. Our gathering is not over until you give your parents or guardians a big hug and tell them that you love them. For some of you this may be difficult to do, but perhaps Jesus is asking you to share his love through you. A holy family can begin with you and an "I love you!" Go and be holy!**

Making God's Word Our Own

This week make an extra effort to do nice things for your family members. Ask Jesus to show you special ways that you can help your family be more holy. Every day ask Jesus to show you one way you can help achieve this goal.

If you are choosing a student for next Sunday's opening prayer, do so now.

Solemnity *of* Mary, Mother of God

Readings

Numbers 6:22–27
Galatians 4:4–7
Luke 2:16–21

Theme

Mary discovered and treasured what is important.

Scripture *Background*

Today the Church celebrates Mary, the Mother of God. A blessing is a gift that leads to the happiness of another. Mary's gift of herself made possible the greatest gift of all—the gift of Jesus.

As Paul tells the Galatians in today's second reading, Jesus is God's gift to all people. He is born in the fullness of God's plan for the salvation of all people. Because Mary gave Jesus birth, Jesus could be God's gift to us.

Paul tells us that a problem arose in the Galatian church regarding the practice of the Jewish law. Some people wanted the Gentile Christians to adopt some of the practices of the Jewish law (such as circumcision) in their Christian way of life. Paul disagreed. Although Jesus was born under the Law, he brought us beyond the Law to a new way of life, a new covenant. God shared the gift of his own life through the Spirit of Jesus, making the people sons and daughters of God. As sons and daughters of God, the Gentile Christians of Galatia were entitled to the same promises that God had made to Israel.

Today's gospel tells the story of the first people, apart from Jesus' family, who believed in him. When the shepherds heard the words of God's angelic message, they believed. They found the child with Mary and Joseph, then went and told other people of the great gift that had been given.

Luke tells us that Mary "treasured all these things and pondered them in her heart." Throughout her life, Mary would come to know more deeply the significance of the gift she treasured.

Like Mary, we ponder the things God has done for us and treasure them in our hearts. We, too, are called to consider the gift of Mary. Because she is the mother of Jesus, she is our mother as well. Through Jesus, we know the full realization of the blessing prayer of the reading from Numbers: "God's face shines on us." All generations call her "blessed" or "favored by God." Because Mary is blessed, we have been blessed.

Anne Marie Sweet OSB

PART I: Gathering for God's Word

Opening Prayer

Alternative: *Ask one of the students to lead the opening prayer.*

Open the session by saying: **Welcome, and Merry Christmas! We are still celebrating the great and wonderful mystery of God entering into creation as Jesus. So, in Jesus' name, I welcome you and invite the Church to stand. We begin our prayer by remembering that we are baptized in the name of the Father, and of the Son, and of the Holy Spirit** (make the sign of the cross).

Jesus, we thank you for the gift of Mary, who shows us how to say yes to you. Grant us the same openness and courage to trust God as Mary did. Bless these students and their families; keep them safe and cover them in your blanket of love. We offer to you these prayers and those that are in our hearts in your name.

The students respond loudly: **Amen!**

Song

"All the Ends of the Earth" by Bob Dufford from *Gather (Comprehensive)* (GIA), *Lead Me, Guide Me* (GIA), *Journeysongs* (OCP), *Glory & Praise* (OCP [NALR]).

"Hail Mary, Gentle Woman" by Carey Landry from *Glory & Praise* (OCP [NALR]), *Gather (Comprehensive)* (GIA), *Journeysongs* (OCP).

"Sing of Mary" by Pleading Savior from *Today's Missal* (OCP).

Announcements

- parish news
- birthdays
- other

PART II: Remembering God's Word

Review last week's session.

God wants every family to be holy. What can you do to help God make your family more holy?

- Allow time for volunteers to share openly and honestly. Be aware and sensitive of the many family situations students experience today. Their responses may include the following: be more obedient; pray for parents, brothers, and sisters; don't fight; help with the chores.

PART III: Understanding God's Word

Scripture

Encourage the students to listen closely to the gospel reading from Luke. Proclaim Luke 2:16–21. Then ask the students: **What did Mary do?** *(Mary treasured all these things and reflected on them in her heart.)*

All Students
• Bible

Younger Students
• paper
• crayons

Older Students
• journals
• pens

Discuss the joy of discovery in this gospel. Mary, Joseph, and the shepherds all discover God's wonderful actions. Point out that Christmas is a time of finding something special—Jesus. At Christmas, we celebrate God entering creation in love and forgiveness as Jesus.

Discuss the importance of taking the time to discover Jesus in the world around us today. We need to take the time to treasure our special moments and place them in our hearts, just like Mary and Joseph did. Ask: **How did Mary, Joseph, and the shepherds respond to God's actions in their world?** *(Mary and Joseph treasured and reflected God's actions in their hearts; the shepherds glorified and praised God.)*

Ask the students: **If you were there, what would you have done?** *(Let the students respond openly and honestly. Listen to and discuss their responses.)*

Reflection

Use the following activity and questions to discuss the gospel further.

Younger Students

1. Distribute to the students paper and crayons. Instruct them to draw a picture of Jesus in the manger. When they have drawn Jesus, have them draw Mary, Joseph, and the shepherds in the same picture. Finally, direct them to include themselves in the picture. When everyone is finished, have volunteers share their drawings and discuss their role in the pictures.

2. What special events do you treasure in your heart?

3. What do Mary, Joseph, and the shepherds teach us about discovering Jesus in the world today?

Older Students

Allow time for the students to respond in their journals to the first two questions.

1. Mary and Joseph are great examples of trusting God. They said yes to God and allowed that yes to unfold in their lives. How can you say yes to God in your life?

2. Do you trust that God will take care of you? Why? Why not?

3. Which person in the gospel passage do you feel closest to—Mary, Joseph, or one of the shepherds? Why? What can they teach us about discovering Jesus in the world today?

Closing Prayer

Gather the students and sing "Silent Night." Using the song as a meditation, allow quiet time for them to reflect on the words of the song. End with the Lord's Prayer and the Hail Mary.

Making God's Word Our Own

Each day this week take a fifteen-minute walk with Jesus. Just ask Jesus to join you. Feel his presence as you walk. Allow Jesus to show you the workings of the Holy Spirit in the world around you. Open your eyes and really look at what Jesus shows you. You will be surprised at what you discover.

If you are choosing a student for next Sunday's opening prayer, do so now.

Solemnity *of* *the* Epiphany

Readings

Isaiah 60:1–6
Ephesians 3:2–3a, 5–6
Matthew 2:1–12

Theme

Jesus is out there. Go find him!

Scripture *Background*

Today's gospel suggests the manifestation of God's promise. God's covenant promises were first made to Israel. In the descendants of Abraham, all nations find blessing. The royal title given to Jesus by the Magi in today's gospel also points to Jesus' role as Messiah. The Jewish people hoped for a messiah who would be descended from the line of King David. Jesus is born in Bethlehem, David's hometown.

The association of a star with the messiah came from a Jewish interpretation of Numbers 24:17. In ancient times, the birth of a great person was frequently associated with some astrological phenomenon. The Magi, from Eastern countries, were associated with astrology and dream interpretation.

The reading from Isaiah occurs after the exile. It was a time of great hope. Jerusalem, the capital of Israel, would soon be rebuilt. The city that had been destroyed by foreign nations would now be honored by those nations. Riches and wealth would be brought to Jerusalem rather than carried out of it, as happened when the city was destroyed by the Babylonians in the sixth century B.C. Jerusalem would "rise up" in a new beginning as the people return from exile and the whole world joins in rebuilding the city.

In the Old Testament, God's presence and guidance was frequently associated with light. This reading is filled with such words as *shine* and *radiance* that evoke this connotation.

Today's second reading is from Paul's Letter to the Ephesians. The Jewish Paul of Tarsus was overwhelmed by the brilliant light of Christ. He came to see himself as the Lord's "chosen instrument" who was sent to proclaim the gospel to the Gentiles.

Paul stressed that it is always God who takes the first step. It was God who confronted him with the gospel and gave him his apostolic commission. He "revealed" or made it known to Paul. God's ways are "mysterious" and can be known only through his revelation. God's promises to the chosen people were fulfilled in Jesus. All peoples, Gentiles as well as Jews, share in salvation in Christ.

Anne Marie Sweet OSB

PART I: Gathering *for God's Word*

Opening Prayer

Alternative: *Ask one of the students to lead the opening prayer.*

Open the session by saying: **Welcome. Thank you for joining us today as we prepare to celebrate the Epiphany.** *Epiphany* **is a Greek word that means "to manifest or to be revealed." We will examine how God reveals his plan to all who seek God in their hearts. I invite the Church to stand as we begin our prayer by remembering who we are—daughters and sons of God. In the name of the Father, and of the Son, and of the Holy Spirit.**

> *Jesus, accept the gift of our hearts, which we know you value more than gold, frankincense, or myrrh. We ask that you give us the strength, wisdom, and courage to seek you out and find you. It is through your grace and love that you freely reveal yourself to us; give us the faith to see you. We ask all these prayers and those in our hearts in your name.*

The students respond loudly: **Amen!**

Song

"Oh, How I Love Jesus" by Carey Landry from *Hi God!* (OCP [NALR]).

"We Three Kings," traditional.

"What Child Is This?" traditional.

Announcements

- parish news
- birthdays
- other

PART II: Remembering *God's Word*

Use the following questions to review the Feast of the Holy Family.

1. What did Jesus do in last Sunday's gospel reading?

- Twelve-year-old Jesus was separated from his parents. He was found speaking with the religious leaders in the temple in Jerusalem. After Jesus returned home with his parents, he was obedient to them, and he grew in wisdom and grace.

2. What is a holy family?

- Let the students respond openly. Make sure they understand that Jesus is at the center of all holy families. Also remind the students that all families are special and called to be holy—regardless of a family's shape and size.

3. God wants every family to be holy. What can you do to help God make your family more holy?

- Let the students respond openly and honestly.

Use the following questions to review the Solemnity of Mary, Mother of God.

1. What did Mary do in last Sunday's gospel reading?

- She treasured the recent events and everything that was said and reflected on them in her heart.

2. How did the shepherds respond to God's actions in their world?

- They glorified and praised God.

3. What did you discover last week as you spent time and walked with Jesus?

- Let the students respond openly and honestly.

PART III: Understanding *God's Word*

Scripture

Choose from two options.

Option One

Proclaim Matthew 2:1–12. Then show approximately seven minutes of the video *Jesus of Nazareth* (tape 1, 0:52:00 to 0:59:00). Discuss as a class the significance and meaning of the gifts of gold, frankincense, and myrrh.

- gold—gift for kings and royalty
- myrrh—ointment used when burying the wealthy and royalty (sign of prophecy indicating Jesus' death)
- frankincense—incense used by priests in temple worship

These gifts symbolize the threefold character of Jesus as priest, prophet, and king.

Option Two

Proclaim the gospel. Divide the students into four groups, and assign each group one of the following questions.

- What led the wise men to Jesus?
- What do you think the wise men expected to find?
- Why didn't King Herod and all the other wise men and women of Judea see and follow the star?
- How do you think Mary and Joseph felt when the wise men came and offered Baby Jesus gifts of gold, frankincense, and myrrh?

Allow five or ten minutes for the groups to discuss their question and to decide on one answer they will share with the class. After all the answers have been shared, say: **Just like the wise men, we are sometimes led toward Jesus by circumstances that we don't understand. Have you ever felt called to do something that you believed to be the right thing even though you didn't know why?** (Give time for the students to respond.) **We must learn to trust the Holy Spirit. If we *try* to live a good life and follow what Jesus taught, we will be guided in our actions toward God—just as the wise men were.**

Reflection

Use the following questions to help explore the reading further.

Younger Students

1. What gift could you give to Jesus that would make him really happy?

2. The wise men had to travel a long way to find Jesus. How can you find him right here or at home?

3. How can you help others find Jesus?

Older Students

1. What did the wise men know about Jesus before they found him? What do you think they learned during their travels and when they finally found Jesus?

2. When we truly seek out Jesus, what helps us along the way? What stops us from finding him?

3. Herod and his important men of the kingdom were very near to the place where Jesus was born, yet very few people were aware of Jesus' existence. How can we be very near Jesus and not be aware of him?

Closing Prayer

Gather the students together, and have them sit in a comfortable position. Invite them to close their eyes while they talk to Jesus. Remind them that he is always present with us. Jesus listens to our prayers, and he wants us to be aware of his presence now. Have the students repeat the following prayer after you.

> *Lord, Jesus,*
> *like the wise men,*
> *draw me to you.*
> *May your love discover me*
> *as I look for you.*
> *Open my heart, Jesus,*
> *and fill it with your Holy Spirit.*
> *I will follow the Holy Spirit.*
> *I will trust the Holy Spirit*
> *to lead me and guide me to you.*
> *You are everywhere;*
> *open my eyes to see you everywhere.*
> *Thank you, Jesus.*
> *I love you.*
> *Amen.*

Making God's Word Our Own

If you are choosing a student for next Sunday's opening prayer, do so now.

This week, ask God for an epiphany. (Give each student an index card with the following prayer written on it: "Jesus, open my eyes to see you; open my heart to love you; open my mind to know you.") Place this card next to your bed. Say this prayer before you go to sleep at night and when you awake. Say the prayer twice a day until we gather again.

Baptism of the Lord

Readings

Isaiah 42:1–4, 6–7
Acts 10:34–38
Luke 3:15–16, 21–22

Theme

Our Baptism makes us children of the light—a new creation in God.

Scripture *Background*

Today's gospel selection begins with John's affirmation of his unworthiness in the face of "one who is mightier than I." The phrase may refer to John's role as "one who prepares the way," or it may point to the powerful presence of God's Spirit in Jesus. The presence of the Spirit is strongly emphasized throughout the Gospel of Luke. Jesus is "filled with the Holy Spirit," and his actions are done through the power of the Spirit. Jesus will baptize his followers in the Holy Spirit and in fire.

In the Gospel of Luke, the words "You are my beloved son" are addressed to Jesus. The baptism of Jesus was a revelation of his unique relationship to the Father. It also affirms who he was and his ministry of proclaiming the good news and bringing healing and liberation to the people.

Luke's words evoke the image of the servant of God, the subject of today's first reading from Isaiah. Isaiah spoke of the "servant" in four passages: Isaiah 42:1–9; 49:1–7; 50:4–11; 52:12–53:12. It is not clear whether the servant was believed to be an individual, such as the prophet himself, or merely an image for the Israelite people. Perhaps the servant is both. Early Christians believed these passages referred to Christ.

In today's passage, we hear how the Lord empowers the one he has chosen with the gift of his Spirit. The servant is a gentle person who willingly meets people where they are, inviting them to fuller life. His words bring healing, enlightenment, and freedom.

The mission of the servant is to bring justice to the nations, not just to the people of Israel. Yet even the apostles were sometimes surprised by the idea of the Gentile nations sharing in God's salvation. Today's reading is an excerpt from Peter's address to the household of Cornelius. Cornelius was a Gentile "godfearer," someone supportive of Jewish beliefs and practices but not a circumcised Jew. Following the instructions of a vision, Peter went to preach at the house of Cornelius. Cornelius had a shared vision from God. Peter then understood that it was God's will that both the Gentiles and the Jews were to share in his salvation. Cornelius and his household believed Peter's testimony. They received the gift of the Spirit and were baptized.

Anne Marie Sweet OSB

PART I: Gathering *for God's Word*

Opening Prayer

Alternative: *Ask one of the students to lead the opening prayer.*

Prior to class, place the Easter candle in a central location of the room. Open the session by saying: **May the Spirit you received at your Baptism fill you with love, laughter, and joy! Today we are reminded of our own Baptism as we celebrate Jesus' baptism. It is because we share the same Baptism in Jesus that I now invite the Church to stand. We begin our prayer in the same way we were baptized—in the name of the Father, and of the Son, and of the Holy Spirit** (make the sign of the cross).

> *Jesus, on the day of your baptism the Holy Spirit came upon you. Help us realize that at our Baptism we were given the same Holy Spirit and the power to live as members of your family. We are God's children—children of the light because you placed your light deep in our hearts. Thank you for your wonderful gifts of light and life.*

The students respond loudly: **Amen!**

Song

"By Name I Have Called You" by Carey Landry from *Glory & Praise* (OCP [NALR]).

"Christ Be Our Light" by Bernadette Farrell from *Glory & Praise 2* (OCP [NALR]), *Journeysongs* (OCP).

"This Little Light of Mine," traditional.

"We Are the Light of the World" by Jean Anthony Greif from *Glory & Praise 2* (OCP [NALR]), *Journeysongs* (OCP).

Announcements

- parish news
- birthdays
- other

PART II: Remembering *God's Word*

Use the following questions to review last week's gospel reading.

1. What does the word *epiphany* mean?

- Epiphany means to be revealed, to manifest.

2. What did you learn from last Sunday's gospel?

- Let the students respond openly.

3. What three gifts did the wise men give to Jesus? What do the gifts symbolize?

- The wise men brought Jesus gifts of gold (gift for kings and royalty), myrrh (ointment used for burying the wealthy and royalty that was a sign of prophecy), and frankincense (incense used by priests in temple worship). These gifts symbolize the threefold character of Jesus' ministry: priest, prophet, and king.

4. Last week you were invited to pray a special prayer each day: "Jesus, open my eyes to see you; open my heart to love you; open my mind to know you." What special epiphany did God grant you this week?

- Allow time for the students to share openly and honestly.

PART III: Understanding *God's Word*

Scripture

Write one of the following verses on each of the seven poster boards:

- I am baptizing you in water,
- but there is one who is
- mightier than I.
- I am not fit
- to loosen his sandal strap.
- He will baptize you
- in the Holy Spirit and in fire.

Materials Needed
All Students
• Bible
• seven sheets of poster board
• seven volunteers
• reflective music
• CD or tape player
• holy water
• large bowl
Younger Students
• paper
• crayons
Older Students
• journals
• pens

Mix up the seven poster boards. Give each volunteer a poster board to hold in random order. Ask the class to put the poster boards in order so that the verses make sense. (The students really enjoy trying to figure it out!) Once the poster boards are in order, ask the students what the verses mean. Say: **At our Baptism, we received the Holy Spirit. Through the Holy Spirit, we received the gifts of wisdom, understanding, right judgment, courage, knowledge, reverence, and wonder and awe. Through the waters of Baptism, we were cleansed of sin. God's light was lit inside of us to shine for everyone to see. We are God's children—children of the light. Now let's listen to what happened at Jesus' baptism.**

Proclaim Luke 3:15–16, 21–22.

Reflection

Use the following questions and activities to review the gospel reading further.

Younger Students

1. Distribute to the students paper and crayons. Direct them to draw a picture of Jesus being baptized. When everyone is finished, invite volunteers to share their pictures with the class. Display the pictures near the baptismal font, in the church lobby, or in the church hall for the parish community to enjoy.

2. Have you ever been to a Baptism? What do you remember about it?

3. When you were baptized, God was saying, "You are my beloved (son or daughter); on you my favor rests." What does that mean? How do you feel when you hear that?

Older Students

Allow time for the students to respond in their journals to the last question.

1. When were you chosen to do something special? What was it? How did you feel about being chosen?

2. When you were baptized, God was saying, "You are my beloved (son or daughter); on you my favor rests." What does that mean? How do you feel when you hear that?

3. At your Baptism, you were anointed with the Holy Spirit. When have you felt the Holy Spirit working in you? What gifts or talents do you have? Which of those are gifts of the Holy Spirit?

Closing Prayer

Place a large bowl of holy water in a central location of the room. As reflective music is playing in the background, invite the students to come forward one at a time to bless themselves with the holy water by making the sign of the cross. As the students bless themselves, have the rest of the students say together, "(Student's name), you are God's child—a child of the light." Do this for each student and catechist. Conclude by joining hands and praying the Lord's Prayer.

Making God's Word Our Own

Pray the Sign of the Cross three times each day this week. Each time you pray the Sign of the Cross, remember that you are a child of the light—a child of God.

If you are choosing a student for next Sunday's opening prayer, do so now.

Second Sunday *in* Ordinary Time

Readings

Isaiah 62:1–5
1 Corinthians 12:4–11
John 2:1–11

Theme

Grace is God's free gift to us.

Scripture *Background*

Today's readings use the symbols of weddings and gifts to discuss God's kingdom.

The Old Testament reading compares the renewed city of Jerusalem to a radiant bride of the Lord. The image of marriage was used often to describe God's covenant relationship with the people. God had promised to be their God forever. In turn, the people had promised to be God's people. As in a marriage, the partners had pledged love and fidelity to each other. This image was designed to give heart to the discouraged Jewish people as they attempted to rebuild their city.

The setting of the gospel reading was also a wedding. This was the first miracle story in the Gospel of John. At the wedding in Cana, the wine was depleted. Jesus' mother conveyed this information to him. He replied to her, "My hour has not yet come." Throughout John's Gospel, Jesus' "hour" referred to the combined moments of his passion, death, resurrection, and ascension. Jesus responded to his mother's request by performing a miracle to symbolize that hour. Throughout Scripture, the messianic age was portrayed as a time of great abundance, especially an abundance of wonderful things to eat and drink. The abundance of wine at the Cana wedding mirrors the wedding feast of God and his covenant people. At this feast, too, the wine will flow unabated.

The second reading is from Paul's First Letter to the Corinthians. The Corinthians were enthusiastic Christians, eager for spiritual gifts. Paul reminds them that they should use these gifts with order and reverence. The gifts are from one Spirit and will build the Christian community into one body. The gifts of the Spirit are poured out like wine on the community for the good of all. The presence and the generous sharing of these gifts are signs of the messianic age, the glorious wedding feast of God's kingdom.

Irene Nowell OSB

PART I: Gathering *for God's Word*

Opening Prayer

Alternative: Ask one of the students to lead the opening prayer.

Open the session by saying: **Welcome. I ask the Church to stand. Hold the hand of the person next to you as we begin our prayer in the name of the Father, and of the Son, and of the Holy Spirit** (make the sign of the cross).

Jesus, you freely offer us your grace, the special life and love that only you can give. Please grant us the courage and wisdom to accept your wonderful gift of grace. Help us remember that our gift of grace is free; all we have to do is open our hearts, and you will generously pour forth your grace. We thank you for your gift of grace.

The students respond loudly: **Amen!**

Song

"All the Ends of the Earth" by Bob Dufford from *Journeysongs* (OCP), *Glory & Praise* (OCP [NALR]), *Gather (Comprehensive)* (GIA), *Lead Me, Guide Me* (GIA).

"Amazing Grace," traditional.

"You Are Near" by Dan Schutte from *Gather (Comprehensive)* (GIA), *Today's Missal* (OCP), *Glory & Praise* (OCP [NALR]).

Announcements

- parish news
- birthdays
- special events
- other

PART II: Remembering *God's Word*

Use the following questions to review last week's session.

1. Last Sunday we celebrated and remembered Jesus' baptism. Who can remember what John the Baptist said about Jesus?
   - "One mightier than I is coming."
   - "I am not fit to loosen his sandal strap."
   - "He will baptize you in the Holy Spirit and fire."

2. What three things happened when Jesus was baptized by John?
   - The skies opened, the Holy Spirit appeared in the form of a dove and descended on Jesus, and a voice was heard saying, "You are my beloved Son; on you my favor rests."

3. What happened last week when you prayed the Sign of the Cross three times during the day, remembering that you are baptized in the name of the Father, and of the Son, and of the Holy Spirit?
   - Let the students respond openly and honestly.

PART III: Understanding *God's Word*

Scripture

Preparation: Print on index cards the words *manna, covenant,* and *grace*. There should be a group of five index cards for each of the three words. Four of the cards in each group should have just the word, and one card in each group should have the word and definition. Do this for each of the words.

Choose five older volunteers. Invite them forward, and give each one an index card. All five students will have the same word, but only one student will have the word and its definition. The other four will receive an index card with only the word on it. Direct these students to create a definition for the word. All five students need to convince the rest of the class that his or her definition is the correct definition. After all five students have shared their word and definition, ask the audience to vote. Keep score by awarding one point per vote for each volunteer. Thank the volunteers, and invite them to sit down. Then choose five new volunteers. Repeat this process for each of the words. (The students and teachers really enjoy this activity. If you have time, add more words. Use the dictionary as a source for fun and unique words.)

> **Manna** *(four cards with just the word; one card with word and definition)*: the special food God gave to the Israelites as they wandered in the desert for forty years.

> **Covenant** *(four cards with just the word; one card with word and definition)*: an agreement or promise; God made an agreement or covenant with Abraham.

> **Grace** *(four cards with just the word; one card with word and definition)*: love; grace is God's gift of loving presence to us.

After the correct definition of the word *grace* is revealed, tell the students: **There are many understandings of the word *grace*.** However, the theological understanding of grace is "life and love." Grace is God's life and love that he freely offers to all who accept it. When we accept God's gift of grace, we are connected to Jesus in an intimate way. Let me give you an example of how God freely gives grace to those who ask.

Invite a student to come to the front of the classroom. Have him or her ask you for a dollar. After they have asked for the dollar, reach into your pocket or purse and take out a bundle of play money, telling him or her that they are $100 bills. Pour the money over the student. Tell the students that God does the same to us when we pray and are open to his grace in our lives. If we ask for even a little, God will give us more love than we could imagine.

Say: **Let's listen to what Jesus did when someone asked him for wine. Imagine what he would give us if we asked for grace.** Proclaim John 2:1–12.

Reflection

Use the following questions and activities to help students process the gospel reading further.

Younger Students

1. Have you ever been to a wedding? What was it like? Did you have fun?

2. At the wedding, Jesus didn't just make a little bit of wine from the water; he made a lot of wine. What does this story tell you about Jesus and his care for us?

3. As a class, list on a chalkboard or dry-erase board miracles that happen in the world around us that show us how much Jesus loves us and wants to share his life and love with us.

Older Students

Allow time for the students to respond in their journals to the first question.

1. Is there any water in your life that Jesus could change into wine (for example, self-esteem, family, work/school, appearance, spirituality, physical fitness, mental attitude)? Explain your answer.

2. Jesus could have made a little bit of wine, but he made a lot of wine. What does this tell us about Jesus?

3. Do you find it easy or difficult to freely accept God's grace (God's life and love) in your life? Explain your answer. What prevents you from receiving God's grace?

Closing Prayer

Invite the students to stand and raise their hands, palms up, to God. Say: **This gesture is an ancient prayer posture. As we stand together before God in the depth and silence of our hearts, repeat after me:**

Lord, Jesus, pour out your grace on me now.

Let it cover all of me from my head to my toes.

Let it sink into my mind and my heart.

Let me receive it with openness.

And give me the spirit of sharing so that

I will freely give your love and grace

to everyone I meet.

Thank you, Jesus, thank you.

(Allow a moment of silence to rest in God's grace.) Amen!

> *If you are choosing a student for next Sunday's opening prayer, do so now.*

Making God's Word our Own

This week, spend some quiet time alone with Jesus. Invite him to change you from water into his wine or ask him for his free gift of grace. Try this for fifteen minutes each day this week. Jesus' grace just might change you, fill you with peace and healing, and give you a sense of joy that you cannot imagine.

Third Sunday *in* Ordinary Time

Readings

Nehemiah 8:2–4a, 5–6, 8–10
1 Corinthians 12:12–30
Luke 1:1–4, 4:14–21

Theme

Jesus is present in the sacraments, the Word, and the community of faith.

Scripture *Background*

The readings for today reflect the gift of the Word of God to the community.

The first reading tells the story of Ezra, a priest whose major contribution was the teaching of the Torah to his people. The Torah (or *Pentateuch* in Christian terminology) consists of the first five books of our Bible. In today's reading, Ezra presents this collection of books to the people as the Word of God. This was the first Sacred Scripture, the first authoritative revelation of God. The people listened, wept, and said "Amen." Then they rejoiced with a great celebration for God's great gift of the Word.

The opening verses of Luke explain the writer's purpose and method. Luke acted as a reporter, collecting and organizing accounts concerning Jesus so that Theophilus, the friend of God, could see how reliable his instruction was.

The story of the beginning of Jesus' ministry follows this introduction to this gospel. After his baptism and sojourn in the desert, Jesus returned to his hometown of Nazareth. He read a passage from the prophet Isaiah concerning the arrival of the messianic age. The messiah would bring liberation to all who were enslaved. When Jesus finished the reading, he announced to the amazed congregation that the promise of the passage had now been fulfilled. Compassion and liberation were to be the theme of Jesus' ministry and concern for the weakest members of society the mark of his identity as Messiah.

The continued reading from 1 Corinthians presents Paul's image of the Christian community as one body alive in one Spirit. Whatever happens to one part of the body affects the whole. In a healthy body all parts serve for the welfare of the whole.

One of the gifts held by the Christian community is the gift of Scripture, the Word of God. It is the community that recognizes the authority and inspiration of Scripture. It is the community that preserves Scripture.

Irene Nowell OSB

PART I: Gathering *for God's Word*

Opening Prayer

Alternative: *Ask one of the students to lead the opening prayer.*

Open the session by saying: **Welcome! Thanks for joining us again. Will the Church please stand for our opening prayer? We begin in the name of the Father, and of the Son, and of the Holy Spirit** (make sign of the cross).

Lord, Jesus, we thank you for calling us together again. You promised to be present when two or more are gathered in your name. We ask that you keep your promise as we gather here today in your name. Jesus, thank you for the gift of the Sacred Scriptures, where you reveal your love, forgiveness, and healing. May our hearts and minds be open to you in your word; grant us the courage to live what we hear. We ask all this in your name.

The students respond loudly: **Amen!**

Song

"All the Ends of the Earth" by Bob Dufford from *Gather (Comprehensive)* (GIA), *Lead Me, Guide Me* (GIA), *Journeysongs* (OCP), *Glory & Praise* (OCP [NALR]).

"Great Things Happen When God Mixes with Us" by Carey Landry from *Glory & Praise* (OCP [NALR]).

"Sing a New Song" by Dan Schutte from *Glory & Praise* (OCP [NALR]), *Journeysongs* (OCP).

"The King of Glory" by Willard Jabusch from *Today's Missal* (OCP), *Gather (Comprehensive)* (GIA).

Announcements

- parish news
- birthdays
- other

PART II: Remembering *God's Word*

Use the following questions to review last week's session.

1. Jesus did something special last Sunday. What did he do?

- Jesus changed water into wine.

2. What does the word *grace* mean?

- Grace is God's free gift of his life and love. Grace is God's loving presence in our lives.

3. How did you experience God's grace last week?

- Let the students respond openly and honestly.

PART III: Understanding *God's Word*

Materials Needed

All Students
- Bible
- gift to be given way (a new Bible would be great)
- "The Hidden Incarnation" from *St. George and the Dragon and the Quest for the Holy Grail* by Edward Hays (Forest of Peace Publishing) (option one)
- four or five meaningful pictures of your family and friends (option two)
- slips of paper with Luke 4:17–19, 21 written on them

Younger Students
- 2" X 6" strips of poster board (one for each student)
- paper
- crayons
- art supplies
- stickers (optional)
- soft music
- tape or CD player

Older Students
- journals
- pens

Show the students the gift you are going to give away. Explain that whoever answers the question correctly will receive the prize. Question: **Where do we believe Jesus is 100 percent present?** (Hint: Think about the Sunday liturgy and recall today's opening prayer.)

Answer: Jesus is 100 percent present in the Sacred Scriptures, Holy Eucharist, and in the gathered community of the people of God—us! When we gather in Jesus' name, he is "really" present.

Option One: God's love for us is present in the word.

Read the story "The Hidden Incarnation" from *St. George and the Dragon and the Quest for the Holy Grail* by Edward Hays. This is a wonderful parable about God's desire to communicate more clearly with God's people through Sacred Scripture. Read the short story with great excitement and animation. Both students and adults love it! Afterward, ask the students to share their thoughts about the meaning of the parable.

Proclaim Luke 1:1–4, 4:14–21.

Option Two: God's word comes alive in the faith community—the Church.

Divide the students into small groups. Take four or five pictures from your personal photo album, and give one picture to each group. Ask them to look closely at the picture and develop a story of what's going on in the picture. They can be as creative as they want, but they must use the details found in the picture. After about five to seven minutes, have each group share their story of the picture with the large group. When everyone is finished, choose one or two pictures, and briefly share with the students the history of the event and the people found in each picture.

The students may come close to the story of what the picture is about. However, you may have been there when the picture was taken, and you know the family story concerning the event in the picture. You can add more depth and share the experienced reality of what the picture represents. The same is true with Sacred Scripture. We can experience God in the Scriptures alone—and it is good to read the Bible—but we need the faith community to help us deepen our understanding of God and his word. We are all part of God's family, and we need each other to help us experience and celebrate God's word. "When two or more are gathered . . . I will be with you."

Proclaim Luke 1:1–4, 4:14–21.

Use the following questions and activities to discuss the gospel reading further.

Younger Students

1. What is the good news that Jesus speaks about?

2. Do you think it is easy or hard to live the good news?

3. Distribute to the students paper and crayons. Play soft music. Direct them to draw a picture of themselves and their families living the good news. When everyone is finished, invite volunteers to share their pictures with the large group.

4. Distribute strips of poster board. Have the students make bookmarks for their Bibles by decorating the poster-board strips. (Stickers work well for decorating.)

Older Students

Have the students respond in their journals to the second question.

1. What five things does Jesus say he is anointed to do?

2. As a follower of Jesus, you are required to do what Jesus did. Have you brought good news to a friend or family member? Have you tried to liberate someone who was oppressed? When a friend is doing something you know is not of God and is not good, how do you help this person see that his or her actions are harmful or wrong? Do you forgive others, or do you keep them prisoners by reminding them of their mistakes? How can you share with others the goodness of God?

3. What do you think Jesus really means when he says, "Today this scripture has been fulfilled in your hearing"?

Closing Prayer

Gather the students into a circle. Read the gospel again, and ask them to reflect quietly on what Jesus is personally inviting them to hear today. Do they need glad tidings, liberty, sight, release, or to experience the favor of the Lord?

> *. . . the scroll of the prophet Isaiah was given to him. He unrolled the scroll and found the place where it was written:*
>
> *"The Spirit of the Lord is upon me,*
>
> *because he has anointed me*
>
> *to bring good news to the poor.*
>
> *He has sent me to proclaim release to the captives,*
>
> *and recovery of sight to the blind,*
>
> *to let the oppressed go free,*
>
> *to proclaim the year of the Lord's favor. . . .*
>
> *Today this scripture has been fulfilled in your hearing."*

Luke 4:17–19, 21

> *If you are choosing a student for next Sunday's opening prayer, do so now.*

Making God's Word Our Own

Distribute to the students slips of paper with Luke 4:17–19, 21 written on them.

Your spiritual challenge for the week is to memorize Luke 4:17–19, 21. Use your own Bible, and invite your parents to help you. If you read this passage and work on it for fifteen minutes each day this week, you'll be able to share it with us at our next gathering. If you have difficulties, ask Jesus to help you memorize it.

Fourth Sunday *in* Ordinary Time

Readings

Jeremiah 1:4–5, 17–19
1 Corinthians
  12:31–13:13
Luke 4:21–30

Theme

Jesus' words and love are for everyone!

Scripture *Background*

Jeremiah was commissioned as a prophet, not only for God's covenant people, but "to the nations." This idea was repeated in the reassurance and in the sign: "To whomever I send you, you shall go. . . . This day I set you over nations and over kingdoms." His message would meet with great opposition. He was given twice as many destructive tasks (destroy, demolish, root up, tear down) as constructive (build, plant). But God promised not to leave him crushed by opposition. Rather, God would make him a brass wall, an iron pillar, a fortified city. Jeremiah's prophetic task would be painful, but God's presence would deliver him in the end.

In the passage from the Gospel of Luke, Jesus met with great opposition from the people of his hometown. The congregation was so angry at his preaching that they led him to the cliff. Jesus escaped their wrath.

The people were angry because Jesus had said that prophets ordinarily minister outside their own home territory. He cited two examples in which prophets left the covenant people and worked miracles for Gentiles. He reminded them of the proverb, "No prophet is accepted in his native place." They could not bear the truth that God's word moves freely anywhere God chooses.

Chapter 13 of Paul's First Letter to the Corinthians is one of the most beautiful and beloved passages of the New Testament. Paul tries to persuade his audience that love is worth more than all other gifts. Love always seeks the good of another. Love is the touchstone of the mature Christian. Love will never end. Love is not jealous when gifts are given to others. Rather, love rejoices, even when the nonbeliever receives the blessings of God.

Irene Nowell OSB

PART I: Gathering *for God's Word*

Opening Prayer

Alternative: *Ask one of the students to lead the opening prayer.*

Open the session by saying: **Again, I welcome you, and I honor your commitment to grow in our Lord. I invite the Church to stand for our opening prayer. Many times people ask "Who is God?" "What does God look like?" or "How do we know how God acts?" In today's prayer, Paul helps us understand God's actions. We begin by recalling our special relationship with God that began at baptism;** (make the sign of the cross) **in the name of the Father, and of the Son, and of the Holy Spirit.**

Read 1 Corinthians 13:4–8. After you read this passage, say: **Our Catholic tradition—written and oral—states that "God is Love." Let's take a closer look at God.** Read 1 Corinthians 13:4–8 one more time, replacing the word *love* with the word *God.*

> *God is patient; God is kind; God is not envious or boastful or arrogant or rude. [God] does not insist on [his] own way; [God] is not irritable or resentful; [God] does not rejoice in wrongdoing, but rejoices in the truth. [God] bears all things, believes all things, hopes all things, endures all things. God never ends.*

The students respond loudly: **Amen!**

Song

"Anthem" by Tom Conry from *Glory & Praise* (OCP [NALR]), *Today's Missal* (OCP), *Gather (Comprehensive)* (GIA).

"Celebrate God" by Carey Landry from *Hi God!* (OCP [NALR]).

"His Banner Over Me Is Love" by Carey Landry from *Hi God!* (OCP [NALR]).

"The King of Glory" by Willard Jabusch from *Today's Missal* (OCP), *Gather (Comprehensive)* (GIA).

Announcements

- parish news
- birthdays
- other

PART II: Remembering *God's Word*

Use the following questions to review last week's session.

1. Last week, you were challenged to memorize Jesus' words from Luke's Gospel. Who would like to recite it for us? (Or, if all the students are prepared, you may wish to recite the passage together as a group.)

The scroll of the prophet Isaiah was given to [Jesus]. He unrolled the scroll and found the place where it was written:

> *"The Spirit of the Lord is upon me,*
>
> *because he has anointed me*
>
> *to bring good news to the poor.*
>
> *He has sent me to proclaim release to the captives*
>
> *and recovery of sight to the blind,*
>
> *to let the oppressed go free,*
>
> *to proclaim the year of the Lord's favor. . . .*

"Today this scripture has been fulfilled in your hearing."

Luke 4:17–19, 21

2. What did you learn about Jesus from last Sunday's gospel?

   • Let the students respond openly and honestly.

PART III: Understanding *God's Word*

Scripture

Review Game

Divide the students into two groups. Appoint an official scorekeeper. Choose one student from each group, and position the two so that they face each other with their hands at their sides. Place between them the table with the desk bell on it. Read one of the questions that follow this paragraph. The first one to ring the bell gets to answer the question for five points. If they don't know the correct answer, they can ask the other students and catechists on their team to help for one point. When a student or team answers incorrectly, the opposing team gets to answer; if they answer correctly, they score five points. Keep going until everyone has had a turn. Feel free to add some questions of your own. After all the students have had a turn, ask the scorekeeper to add up the points and announce the winning team.

Materials Needed

All Students
   • Bible
   • desk bell
   • small table
   • score pad

   • True or false: King Herod wanted to visit the baby Jesus and bring the newborn king a present. **(False. He wanted to kill Jesus.)**

   • What are the three gifts the wise men gave Jesus? **(gold, frankincense, and myrrh)**

   • What does the Greek word *epiphany* mean? **(to be revealed, brought to light, to make known, to manifest or show forth)**

   • Who said these words: "I am baptizing you in water, but there is one to come who is mightier than I. I am not fit to loosen his sandal strap"? **(John the Baptist)**

   • John the Baptist said that someone would come after him who would baptize in the Holy Spirit and fire. Who was that person? **(Jesus)**

   • In what river did John baptize? **(the Jordan River)**

   • What three things happened after Jesus was baptized? **(The sky opened; the Holy Spirit descended on him in the form of a dove; a voice from heaven was heard saying "You are my beloved Son. On you, my favor rests.")**

   • True or false: As Christians, we can earn God's gift of grace. **(False. God's grace is a free gift; it can never be earned—it's free!)**

- What does the word *grace* mean? (**God's free gift of his life and love; grace is God's loving relationship with us.**)
- Where did Jesus' first miracle take place? What happened? (**Jesus' first miracle was at a wedding in Cana. He changed water into wine.**)
- What did Jesus' disciples do after his first miracle? (**They believed in Jesus and followed him.**)
- Name three ways God is really present when we gather in God's house on Sunday? (**in Sacred Scripture, the Eucharist, and the faith community**)
- Fill in the blanks: When Jesus went to the synagogue and read from the Sacred Scriptures, he read:

  "The Spirit of the Lord is __(upon me),__

  because he has __(anointed me)__

  to bring good news to __(the poor).__

  He has sent me to proclaim release to __(the captives)__

  and recovery of sight to __(the blind),__

  to let the oppressed __(go free),__

  to proclaim the year of the __Lord's favor."__

- After Jesus was finished reading, what did he say? (**"Today this scripture has been fulfilled in your hearing."**)

Have the students sit in a circle and quietly prepare to listen to God's Word. Proclaim Luke 4:21–30, which continues the story of Jesus in the synagogue.

Reflection   Use the following questions to help the students process the reading.

Younger Students

1. Think of a time when someone rejected you. What did it feel like?
2. Do you think Jesus felt rejected by his hometown neighbors? Why or why not?
3. What did replacing the word *love* with the word *God* in 1 Corinthians 13:4–8 teach you about God?

Older Students

1. Jesus tells us that God's word of love, healing, and forgiveness is for everyone who believes in Jesus. Do you think this is true? Or is God's word only for "good Catholic Christian people"?
2. Is it easier to see God working in the lives of your family members and relatives or in other people not related to you? Why?
3. What did replacing the word *love* with the word *God* in 1 Corinthians 13:4–8 teach you about God?

Closing Prayer   Gather the students together and repeat the opening prayer by reading 1 Corinthians 13:4–8. Once again, change the word *love* to the word *God*. Proclaim it reflectively. Then hold hands, and conclude with the Lord's Prayer.

Making God's Word Our Own   This week look for God working in your family. Do this in two ways: First, spend fifteen minutes each day praying for your family; second, do something extra for each family member (without being asked)—help around the house, spend time with your brother or sister, help clean up after a meal, work in the yard with your mom or dad. Each day do whatever is most needed.

> *If you are choosing a student for next Sunday's opening prayer, do so now.*

Presentation *of* the Lord

Readings

Malachi 3:1–4
Hebrews 2:14–18
Luke 2:22–40

Theme

Finding and recognizing the light— Jesus!

Scripture *Background*

As prescribed by the Jewish tradition in Exodus (13:2), Jesus is brought to the temple forty days after his birth and presented to God. Jesus' parents brought with them "a pair of turtledoves and two young pigeons." This is in accord with the dictates of the laws of the Lord. According to Jewish law, the firstborn son belonged to God, and the parents had to redeem the child by offering a sacrifice.

In the temple, Jesus meets Simeon and Anna. Through Simeon, the chosen people welcome Jesus as the one who would fulfill the promise of God and deliver Israel from its oppression. Here is the one who would be the "glory of Israel and revealing light to the Gentiles" (Luke 2:30–32). Simeon also foreshadows the cross as he warns Mary and Joseph of the grief to come. Anna, who is not a "son of the covenant," represents the disadvantaged and excluded people who also find their hope in this child.

In the first reading, the prophet Malachi confronts the temple priests with their infidelity. Malachi was a prophet who tried to regenerate the faith of the people by reminding them of their hope for a messiah. He predicts a time of reckoning. Someday God's messenger will purify the temple and its priesthood. Then there will be true worship in God's temple.

Luke's story of the presentation of the child Jesus in the temple echoes this prophecy. The followers of Jesus retold the story from Malachi after Jesus' death and resurrection. They hoped to regenerate the people's faith in Jesus, the fulfillment of God's promise. Jesus is presented as the trustworthy priest who continues to act on their behalf. He is seen as the anointed one, God's Son, who created a new kingdom in their midst. As the high priest, Jesus offered his sacrifice of self. He gave his whole life so that we might be with our God forever.

Jeanita Strathman Lapa

PART I: Gathering for God's Word

Opening Prayer

Alternative: *Ask one of the students to lead the opening prayer.*

Open the session by saying: **Welcome! I honor your steadfastness in our journey of seeking a deeper understanding of our faith in Jesus. I invite the Church to stand for our opening prayer. We begin** (make the sign of the cross) **in the name of the Father, and of the Son, and of the Holy Spirit.**

> *Lord Jesus, may the same Spirit that enabled Simeon and Anna to recognize you be with us. Help us see you active in the world around us. Fill our hearts. Bless these students, Lord, and protect them from all harm. Keep them warm and safe in your love. We also pray for all those we hold in our hearts. We ask all this in your name.*

The students respond with enthusiasm: **Amen!**

Song

"Be Light for Our Eyes" by David Haas from *Gather (Comprehensive)* (GIA).

"City of God" by Dan Schutte from *Glory & Praise* (OCP [NALR]), *Gather (Comprehensive)* (GIA), *Today's Missal* (OCP), *Journeysongs* (OCP).

"The Spirit Is A-Movin'" by Carey Landry from *Glory & Praise* (OCP [NALR]), *Hi God!* (OCP [NALR]).

"This Little Light of Mine," traditional.

Announcements

- parish news or liturgical season
- birthdays
- other

PART II: Remembering God's Word

Use the following questions to review last week's session.

1. What did you learn about God last week?

- God is kind and patient, never jealous, boastful, proud, or rude. God isn't selfish or quick-tempered. God doesn't keep a record of wrongs that others do. God rejoices in the truth but not in evil. God is always supportive, loyal, hopeful, and trusting. God never fails!

2. True or false: The gift of God's Word, the Bible, is for everyone.

- True

3. Last week you were invited to find Jesus in your own family members—to pray and do something special for them. Where did you find Jesus? What did you experience when you helped your family members?

- Let the students share honestly and openly.

PART III: Understanding *God's Word*

Scripture

Choose from two options.

Option One

In Franco Zeffirilli's film *Jesus of Nazareth,* there is a wonderful five-minute scene of the presentation of Jesus in the Temple. Play the scene for the students, and discuss it with them. Encourage and answer questions. Then proclaim Luke 2:22–40.

Option Two

Proclaim Luke 2:22–40. Then use the script on page 49 of this manual to recreate the presentation of the Lord. Choose students to read the following parts: narrator, Simeon, Anna, Mary, Joseph, group 1, group 2.

Reflection

Use the following questions and activities to help explore the reading further.

Materials Needed

All Students—Option 1
- Bible
- VCR and TV
- *Jesus of Nazareth* video, directed by Franco Zeffireli (Ventura, CA: Gospel Light Publications)
- bowl of holy water

All Students—Option 2
- Bible
- script for presentation skit (page 49)
- bowl of holy water

Younger Students
- crayons
- paper

Older Students
- journals
- pens

Younger Students

1. Distribute to the students paper and crayons. Have them draw a picture of the baby Jesus being presented to God.
2. How were Simeon and Anna able to recognize Jesus as being special?
3. How can you become more aware of Jesus' presence in the world and in your life?

Older Students

Allow adequate time for the students to respond to the last question in their journals.

1. Do you think God had a special plan for Jesus, Mary, and Joseph?
2. Do you think God has a plan and purpose for your life—like God did for Mary and Joseph? How can you become more aware of that plan?
3. Simeon and Anna prepared themselves and patiently waited to see the Messiah. What can you do to prepare your hearts to better recognize Jesus as he touches the world around you?

Place a bowl of holy water in a central location. Invite the students to come forward one at a time and bless themselves with the holy water. As they bless themselves, ask them to silently present themselves to God. When everyone is finished, hold hands and pray the Lord's Prayer.

Closing Prayer

Making God's Word Our Own

This week spend fifteen minutes each day outside with Jesus. Ask Jesus to join you and show you God's activity in the world.

If you are choosing a student for next Sunday's opening prayer, do so now.

Role-Play *Script—*
Presentation *of the* **Lord**

Narrator: When Jesus was forty days old, Mary and Joseph took him to the Temple in Jerusalem to present him to God.

Group 1: This is what is written in the Law of the Lord: "Every firstborn male shall be dedicated to the Lord." They also went to offer a sacrifice as required by the Law—a pair of doves or two young pigeons.

Group 2: Now there was a man living in Jerusalem named Simeon. He was a good and God-fearing man, waiting for Israel to be saved. He had been assured by the Holy Sprit that he would not die before he had seen the promised Messiah.

Narrator: When the parents brought the child, Jesus, into the temple, Simeon took him into his arms and gave thanks to God saying:

Simeon: Now Lord, you have kept your promise; let your servant go in peace. For with my own eyes, I have seen your salvation, which you have prepared in the sight of all people—a light to reveal your way to the Gentiles and to give glory to your people Israel.

Mary: Joseph, I am amazed at the things Simeon has said about our son, Jesus! We must thank God as he gives us the blessing.

Joseph: Yes, you are right. This child is special. Mary, I think this man is going to speak to you.

(Simeon turns to Mary.)

Simeon: This child is chosen by God for the destruction and salvation of many in Israel; he will be a sign from God that many people will speak against. And sorrow, like a sharp sword, will pierce your own heart.

Narrator: There was an old prophetess named Anna. Day and night, she worshiped God with fasting and prayer. That very hour she arrived at the Temple. Upon seeing Jesus, she spoke about the child saying:

Anna: Listen, all you who look for salvation and who wait for God to redeem Jerusalem. Praise the Lord, for this child will save us! Give thanks to God!

Narrator: The Word of the Lord.

All: Amen.

Fifth Sunday *in* Ordinary Time

Readings

Isaiah 6:1–2a, 3–8
1 Corinthians 15:1–11
Luke 5:1–11

Theme

Jesus performs miracles all around us. We are continually invited to follow him.

Scripture *Background*

Today's readings center on the experience of being called by God.

In the first reading, the prophet Isaiah has a vision in which God is attended by seraphim (burning, perhaps burning serpents). The seraphim cried out the holiness of God, and smoke filled the house (from the incense?). The prophet protests his unworthiness: "I am a man of unclean lips being among a people of unclean lips." A seraph touches Isaiah's lips with a hot coal from the incense burner. This is a sign: his lips are cleansed to preach God's word.

The gospel story presents Luke's account of the call of the first disciples. In contrast to the story told by Matthew and Mark, here the disciples had a more resounding reason to respond to the call from Jesus. They had witnessed a miracle and heard Jesus teaching. They knew both his message and his power.

Simon Peter's response to the call reminds us of the response of Isaiah: "Leave me, Lord. I am a sinful man." The disciples are reassured by Jesus' words: "Do not be afraid. From now on, you will be catching people." With Jesus' help, they would catch a great number of "fish."

The reading from 1 Corinthians precedes the Gospel of Mark by fifteen years and is the oldest formal statement of resurrection faith that we have. Paul presents this statement of Christianity's central faith in the formal pattern of rabbinical tradition: "I handed on to you what I myself received. . . ." He lists the essential tenets in simple terms:

1. *Christ died for our sins in accordance with the Scriptures.*

2. *He was buried and, in accordance with the Scriptures, rose on the third day.*

3. *He was seen by . . .*

4. *Christ died, rose, appeared.*

This is what we preach; this is what you believe.

The truth of the resurrection was confirmed by appearances of the Risen Christ. These people were witnesses that he was alive: Cephas (Peter), the Twelve, the five hundred, James, all the apostles, and, finally, Paul. Paul declared his unworthiness. But the vision of the Risen Christ was a call. Therefore, Paul spent his life preaching the good news of the resurrection.

Irene Nowell OSB

PART I: Gathering *for God's Word*

Alternative: *Ask one of the students to lead the opening prayer.*

Open the session by saying: **Greetings and God's peace to each and every one of you. Thank you for being here. Will the Church please stand for our opening prayer? We begin by first remembering who we are—children of God—children of the light.** (Make the sign of the cross.)

> *Jesus, continue to bless us and make us strong. Give us the courage to do what is right and the wisdom to understand and use the gifts and talents that you have given us. Open our eyes to see the miracles that you do all around us; let us experience a deep need for you in our lives. We ask all this and the prayers we hold in our hearts in your name.*

The students respond enthusiastically: **Amen!**

Song

"Great Things Happen When God Mixes with Us" by Carey Landry from *Hi God!* (OCP [NALR]), *Glory & Praise* (OCP [NALR]).

"Michael Row Your Boat Ashore," traditional.

Announcements

- parish news
- birthdays
- other

PART II: Remembering *God's Word*

Use the following questions to review the Fourth Sunday in Ordinary Time.

1. What did you learn about God last week?

- God is kind and patient, never jealous, boastful, proud, or rude. God isn't selfish or quick-tempered. God doesn't keep a record of wrongs that others do. God rejoices in the truth, but not in evil. God is always supportive, loyal, hopeful, and trusting. God never fails!

2. True or false: The gift of God's Word, the Bible, is for everyone.

- True

3. Last week you were invited to find Jesus in your own family members—to pray and do something special for them. Where did you find Jesus? What did you experience when you helped your family members?

- Let the students share honestly and openly.

Use the following questions to review the session on the Presentation of the Lord.

1. Summarize the gospel story for the Presentation of the Lord.

- Joseph and Mary take Jesus to the Temple in Jerusalem to present him to God. There, they meet Simeon and Anna, who welcome Jesus as the one who will fulfill the promise of God and deliver Israel from its oppression.

2. Last week you were invited to spend time each day outside with Jesus. Where did you see God's active role in the world?

- Let the students respond openly and honestly.

PART III: Understanding *God's Word*

Scripture

Materials Needed

All Students
- Bible
- fishing gear
- six poster boards
- six volunteers
- bowl
- fish cut from colored paper (one per student)
- bowl

Younger Students
- paper
- crayons

Prior to this session, write on six pieces of poster board six different professions—one profession per poster board (computer programmer, real estate agent, doctor, mechanic, author, priest).

Gather together some fishing gear (waterproof fishing pants, hat, rod and reel, tackle box, net, and so forth). Share with the students some real or fictional fishing stories. Stress that fishing for a living is hard work, and, as a profession, is unpredictable. The income depends on the amount of fish that is caught.

Proclaim Luke 5:1–11, or use the following paraphrase of the gospel. Feel free to use your own paraphrase.

Jesus invites Simon Peter to go fishing again after he has been fishing all day long. Simon has just returned from fishing and, although he didn't catch many fish, is tired. Trusting in Jesus, Simon goes out again and catches more fish than he could have ever imagined; there was so much fish that the nets were breaking and the boat was about to sink. Simon witnessed the greatness of God in Jesus and experienced his own need for God in his life. Jesus then invites Simon to follow him. And Simon does! He leaves behind everything that he knows, values, and loves and follows Jesus.

Choose six volunteers to hold up the signs with the different vocations written on them. Have the students stand up front so that everyone can see. Say: **Jesus performed a fishing miracle to reveal his love and power for Simon, who was a fisherman. What type of miracle would Jesus do for the following groups of people to show his love and power?**

Listen to the students' responses. Ask: **In what ways could these people use their special gifts and talents to *catch* people for Jesus? Or, how could they share the message of Jesus with others?**

Reflection

Use the following activity and questions to discuss the gospel reading further.

Younger Students

1. Distribute to the students crayons and paper. Direct them to draw a picture of Jesus, Simon Peter, and all the fish.

2. Who is the best fisher in your family? What kind of fisher are you?

3. What are you willing to leave behind to follow Jesus?

Older Students

1. Why did Simon Peter fall on his knees and exclaim that he was a sinful man after seeing all the fish Jesus helped him catch? What would you do if the same thing happened to you?

2. What are you willing to leave behind to follow Jesus?

3. What prevents you from following Jesus? What would you **not** be willing to leave behind? Why?

Closing Prayer

Pass out fish cut from colored paper. List the seven gifts of the Holy Spirit (wisdom, understanding, right judgment, courage, knowledge, reverence, wonder and awe of God) on the chalkboard. Direct the students to write on the fish one of the seven gifts. Ask the students to place the fish in a bowl in the middle of the room.

Gather the students around the bowl. Say: **Jesus, send your Holy Spirit to open our eyes, minds, and hearts to the miracles that happen all around us. Give us the courage and wisdom to leave behind our old ways so we can follow you—our true source of life. Teach all of us the way of Jesus; teach us your way.**

Hold hands, and conclude class with the Lord's Prayer. Invite the students to take a fish from the bowl and listen to the call of the Holy Spirit.

Making God's Word Our Own

If you are choosing a student for next Sunday's opening prayer, do so now.

This week, focus on using the gift written on your fish. Use your gift to serve others. Be open to God's opportunities for you to use this gift at home, at school, while playing with friends, during sporting events—anywhere the opportunity presents itself. It's like riding a bike—to use it you have to practice and practice before you get really good. The same is true with becoming fishermen and fisherwomen; it takes practice and help from the Holy Spirit.

Sixth Sunday *in* **Ordinary Time**

Readings

Jeremiah 17:5–8
1 Corinthians 15:12,
  16–20
Luke 6:17, 20–26

Theme

Trust in Jesus. Jesus shows us the way to true happiness.

Scripture *Background*

The reading from Jeremiah draws a clear distinction between the person who is blessed and the one who is cursed. The one who trusts God is blessed; the one who does not trust God is cursed. Blessing is always a share in life; curse always implies death. Water is a significant aspect of the image. The one who is cursed is like a parched desert bush. The one who is blessed is like a watered, fruitful tree. It can survive a dry season. No third option is given, no possibility for trust in God **and** in created things. The passage presents a straightforward choice. Trust God and live; trust flesh and die.

The gospel reading presents a similar scenario. Jesus pronounces four blessings (beatitudes) and four curses (woes). The four blessings portray life; the four woes signify death. (The word *woe* in early use was a funeral lament.)

The blessings and woes, however, reverse our expectations. People who seem to be cursed and on the verge of death are pronounced blessed. Those who are poor, hungry, weeping, and rejected are declared the living. These people know that trust in people or things is futile. They know their only hope is in God. Conversely, the rich, the satisfied, the merry, and the honored are declared the living dead. Their funeral lament is already proclaimed. They have succumbed to what is easily attained. It will not last.

Paul presents the greatest paradox of Christianity and the greatest challenge to faith: the resurrection. The way to life is through death. Paul's argument is clear: "If the dead are not raised, then Christ was not raised. If Christ was not raised, your faith is worthless." Belief in the resurrection of Christ demands belief that we will join him in risen life. If we fail to take this second step, Paul said, "We are the most pitiable people." This challenge calls us to the most radical trust of all. We are called to abandon trust even in life itself and to enter death without despair. All our trust is anchored in the God who raised Jesus from the dead, who promises to raise us to new life along with him.

Irene Nowell OSB

PART I: Gathering *for God's Word*

Opening Prayer

Alternative: *Have one of the students lead the opening prayer.*

Open the session by saying: **Welcome, and peace to you all. Will the Church please stand for our opening prayer? How do we begin our opening prayer?** Let the students respond.

> *We begin in the name of the Father, and of the Son, and of the Holy Spirit* (make the sign of the cross). *Jesus, you gave us the map that leads to true blessing and peace. We thank you and praise you for that gift. Your way is different from the ways of the world. So I ask that you bless these students and give them the wisdom and courage to follow your path to happiness. Your way leads to life. We lift all of our prayers to you—those spoken and those still in our hearts.*

The students respond loudly: **Amen!**

Song

"Be Not Afraid" by Bob Dufford from *Glory & Praise* (OCP [NALR]), *Today's Missal* (OCP), *Gather (Comprehensive)* (GIA), *Lead Me, Guide Me* (GIA).

"Beatitudes" by Darryl Ducote from *Glory & Praise* (OCP [NALR]), *Today's Missal* (OCP).

"His Banner Over Me Is Love" by Carey Landry from *Hi God!* (OCP [NALR]).

"Walking by Faith" by David Haas from *Walking by Faith* (Harcourt Religion Publishers, GIA).

Announcements

• parish news
• birthdays
• other

PART II: Remembering *God's Word*

Review last week's session.

1. Why did Simon Peter fall at Jesus' feet and say, " I am a sinful man"?

• He had just witnessed a powerful miracle of Jesus.

2. What did Jesus say to Simon, James, and John?

• "Do not be afraid. From now on you will be catching people."

3. What was their response to Jesus?

• They left everything and became his followers.

4. How did you use your gift of the Holy Spirit last week to help others? What happened when you used your gift for the first time? How did you catch others for Jesus?

• Let the students respond openly and honestly.

PART III: Understanding *God's Word*

Materials Needed

All Students
- Bible
- eight volunteers
- old clothes
- empty bowl
- spoon
- box of tissues
- red cloth
- fake jewelry
- large gift box
- funny hat
- sunglasses
- eight signs, one for each volunteer

woe—a condition of deep suffering from misfortune, affliction, or grief

Prior to class create signs for each volunteer to hold. The signs should read:

- I am poor.
- I am hungry.
- I am sad.
- I am an outcast.
- I am rich.
- I am satisfied.
- I am funny.
- I am famous.

Choose eight students to dress in costume and/or hold props for the Scripture activity. Suggestions for costumes:

- I am poor.—old clothes
- I am hungry.—empty bowl, spoon
- I am sad.—box of tissues
- I am an outcast.—red cloth draped over shoulder
- I am rich.—fake, expensive-looking jewelry
- I am satisfied.—large gift box
- I am funny.—funny hat
- I am famous.—sunglasses

Group together the first four students ("I am poor"; "I am hungry"; "I am sad"; "I am an outcast"), and have the group introduce themselves (in character) to the class. Invite the remaining four students (the second group) to introduce themselves. Place the groups on opposite sides of the room.

Ask the students to listen carefully while you proclaim the gospel. Say: **Listen closely to what the gospel says. When I'm finished reading, we will examine it more closely. Look for anything that seems odd.**

Proclaim Luke 6:17, 20–26, and then discuss the following questions.

1. What point was Jesus making?
2. What meaning does Jesus' words have for us today?
3. How should we, as baptized followers of Jesus, respond to this reading?

Ask if anyone in the two groups would like to switch groups. (Let them switch if they wish.) Ask them why they would want to change or not want to change after hearing what Jesus says in the gospel.

Reflection

Use the following questions to discuss the lesson further.

Younger Students

1. What encouragement does Jesus give those who have experienced poverty, hunger, sadness, or who have been made fun of?

2. Would you rather be rich in this world or rich in the Spirit of God?

3. Together as a class write a prayer asking for the strength and courage to follow God's way rather than the world's way. Point out the differences between God's way and the world's way.

Older Students

1. What encouragement does Jesus give those who have experienced poverty, hunger, sadness, or who have been made fun of?

2. Jesus is very clear. Yet many of us have a difficult time with what he says. Why is it so hard for us to hear this passage and believe it?

3. How do we need to act if we really believe what Jesus says in this passage?

Closing Prayer

Gather the students, and reflectively and slowly read the gospel again. Let Jesus' words sink in with a moment of silence. Hold hands and end with the Lord's Prayer.

Making God's Word Our Own

This week read the gospel passage (Luke 6:17, 20–26) every day. After you read it, spend fifteen minutes praying for those who are rich and full, those who don't take life and others seriously, and those who are famous for their own sake.

If you are choosing a student for next Sunday's opening prayer, do so now.

Seventh Sunday
in Ordinary Time

Readings

1 Samuel 26:2, 7–9,
  12–13, 22–23
1 Corinthians 15:45–49
Luke 6:27–38

Theme

We are called to love as Jesus loves.

Scripture *Background*

The reading from 1 Samuel discusses a time when David was being pursued by Saul. The prophet Samuel had anointed as king both Saul and David. However, Samuel told Saul that God had rejected him. Saul was on the decline; David was on the rise. In this scene, David had an opportunity to kill Saul. David, however, spared Saul's life because Saul was the Lord's anointed (messiah). At the end of the passage, David suggested that his own life should be protected because he, too, was the Lord's anointed. He had treated Saul as he wished to be treated.

The gospel states the ideal that the passage from 1 Samuel illustrated: Love your enemies, and do good to those who hate you; bless those who curse you, and pray for those who maltreat you.

The section of the gospel from verse 27 to verse 35 is held together by three key directives: "love," "do good," "lend." The directives were repeated three times in the same order. The verbs, however, are not as difficult as the object of the action. We are to love, do good, and lend to the most undesirable recipients: enemies, violent and greedy people, incessant borrowers. Only then will we be children of God, who is good to all people.

In the second section (verses 36–38), the fundamental basis of the Law is introduced. This is the command to be like God. Here we are told to be compassionate like God. Then we will love and give, regardless of cost (a reference to verses 27–35). We will forgive rather than judge (a reference to verses 37–38).

The Golden Rule was stated in two forms here: Do to others what you would have them do to you (verse 31) and with whatever measure you measure will be measured back to you (verse 38).

Being like God is possible since we are made in the image of God. Jesus, the human who is the Son of God, the one who is God, is our model for being like God. This was Paul's argument in 1 Corinthians as he moved to the conclusion of his treatment of resurrection.

Irene Nowell OSB

PART I: Gathering *for* God's Word

Opening Prayer

Alternative: *Have one of the students lead the opening prayer.*

Open the session by saying: **Welcome, and God's peace to all of you. I invite the Church to stand. We remember that we were baptized and that through our Baptism God has given us the power to love. With this in mind, we begin in the name of the Father, and of the Son, and of the Holy Spirit** (make the sign of the cross).

> *Lord Jesus, give your children the courage and strength to follow you. Let us live by your examples of love and forgiveness. Help us not judge but share your compassion freely with everyone we meet. It is hard for us at times to live like you want us to. But with your help and the help of the Holy Spirit, we can do anything. Thank you for hearing our prayer. In your name, we pray.*

The students respond: **Amen!**

Song

"Give a Little Love" by Ziggy Marley and the Melody Makers from *For Our Children* (Walt Disney Records).

"I Like God's Love" by Carey Landry from *Hi God!* (OCP [NALR]).

"Love Can Move Mountains" by Celine Dion from *Love Celine* (Sony Music Entertainment).

"Love That Is Kept Inside" by Carey Landry from *Hi God!* (OCP [NALR]).

"They'll Know We Are Christians" by Peter Scholtes from *Today's Missal* (OCP), *Gather (Comprehensive)* (GIA).

Announcements

- parish news
- birthdays
- other

PART II: Remembering *God's Word*

Review last week's gospel.

1. Whom did Jesus bless last week? Whom did he despair?

- Jesus blessed those who are poor, those who hunger, those who weep, those who are hated, those who are ostracized and insulted because of him. He despaired the rich, the full, those who laugh and are spoken well of now.

2. What is this special passage called?

- the Beatitudes

3. How did reading the gospel every day last week and praying for those Jesus despaired affect your week? What did you learn about yourself while you were praying for others?

- Let the students respond freely and openly.

PART III: Understanding *God's Word*

Scripture

Materials Needed

All Students
- Bible
- eight volunteers
- sixteen chairs

Younger Students
- paper
- crayons

Older Students
- journals
- pens

Prior to class, arrange sixteen chairs at the front of the room. Put eight chairs on one side of the room and eight chairs on the other side. During the activity the lead catechist should stand between the two groups of chairs.

Invite eight student volunteers to come to the front of the classroom. Request that all eight students sit in the chairs on one side of the room. Stress to all students the value and importance of honesty.

As an introduction to the gospel, tell them that Jesus' message contains powerful statements. Ask the students to listen carefully to Jesus' statements. Tell the eight volunteers that if they agree with the statements and try to live these statements in their lives, then they should remain in their chairs. If they don't agree with or live what the statements teach, they must move to one of the chairs on the other side of the room. Remind them to be honest.

Slowly read Luke 6:27–38. Pause after each powerful statement to allow the students to reflect on the gospel reading and decide whether or not to move. Let them know its okay to move if they don't agree with or if they don't live what the statements suggest.

> *Jesus said to his disciples . . .*
>
> *Love your enemies.*
>
> *Do good to those who hate you.*
>
> *Bless those who curse you.*
>
> *Pray for those who maltreat you.*
>
> *When someone slaps you, turn and offer him the other cheek.*
>
> *When someone takes your coat, let him have your shirt as well.*
>
> *Give to all who beg from you.*
>
> *When a man takes what is yours, don't demand it back.*
>
> *Do to others what you would have them do to you.*
>
> *Love your enemy and do good.*
>
> *Lend without expecting repayment.*
>
> *Be compassionate.*
>
> *Don't judge.*
>
> *Don't condemn.*
>
> *Pardon.*
>
> *Give.*

Ask the class for examples of how everyone can live each of the statements. After the sharing, inform the class that the only way to live out what Jesus says for us to do is by the power of the Spirit or the Risen Christ—the Holy Spirit. It is Jesus who gives us the power to love and the desire to follow him. It is through prayer, practice, and Jesus' power that the Beatitudes are lived.

Conclude by inviting everyone to stand. Ask them to extend their hands over one another and repeat after you: **Jesus fill us with your Holy Spirit. Help us love as completely as you do. Give us the courage to live your commandments of love. Amen.**

Reflection

Use the following questions and activities to help the students process the reading further.

Younger Students

1. Is it easy to live as Jesus tells us to in the gospel? Why?

2. How does it make you feel to know that God will not judge us if we do not judge others, will not condemn us if we do not condemn others, will pardon (forgive) us if we pardon (forgive) others, and will give to us if we give to others?

3. The passage "Do to others what you would have them do to you" is known as the Golden Rule. Ask the students to name some other rules that help us love others and ourselves. As a group, discuss which of these rules should be added to Jesus' rules.

4. Distribute to the students paper and crayons. Direct them to draw a picture of themselves sharing Jesus' love with someone. Share their pictures with the group.

Older Students

Allow ample time for the students to respond in their journals to the last question.

1. Reread the gospel. If you tried to live what Jesus suggests in our world, what would happen to you?

2. Was what Jesus said easier to live when he was here on earth or is it easier to live today? Why?

3. Who are some people who live or truly try to live the Golden Rule? How do they do it?

4. How can you better live the Golden Rule? What changes do you need to make in your life?

Closing Prayer

Gather the students together and reflectively proclaim Luke 6:27–38 again. Invite the students to bless each other with these or similar words: "May you hear Jesus and have the courage and strength to follow his way of life." Hold hands as you conclude the session with the Lord's Prayer.

Making God's Word Our Own

Each day this week read Luke 6:27–38 and choose one of Jesus' rules to live that day. Try a new rule each day, or choose one to live throughout the week. Ask Jesus to help you. Give it a try; it could change your life.

If you are choosing a student for next Sunday's opening prayer, do so now.

Eighth Sunday *in* Ordinary Time

Readings

Sirach 27:4–7
1 Corinthians 15:54–58
Luke 6:39–45

Theme

Christians are known by their actions.

Scripture *Background*

Ben Sira was a sage who lived at the beginning of the second century B.C. He tutored young men in wise living. The book that bears his name is a collection of his teachings, loosely organized by topic. Today's reading is part of a section on honesty and wise speech. The sage teaches the wisdom gained by the experience of living well.

Ben Sira gave his students several vivid images to impress his teaching on their minds. As the sieve and the potter's kiln test quality, so a person's speech is a test of the true self. As the fruit shows the worth of a tree, so speech shows the worth of a person.

Jesus used the same image of the tree in the collection of sayings found in Luke's Gospel. Only the good tree produces good fruit. Only the good person spreads goodness by word and action. One can give only what one has.

This same principle anchors the sayings about teachers and guides. Only those who can see may act as guides, especially for the sightless. A blind guide is a contradiction. Only those who have gained some knowledge or skill may function as teachers. Only those people have some benefit to offer their students. Every Christian teacher, however, must remember that he or she is still a disciple or student of Christ. No disciple is greater than the Master.

Verses 41–42 carry the theme of judgment from verse 37. They deal with the human inclination to see faults in others and only goodness in ourselves. As teachers often do, Jesus exaggerated the example to make the point memorable. A person unaware of a plank in the eye is more than blind.

The reading from 1 Corinthians served as the conclusion of Paul's treatise on the resurrection. He arrives at the heart of the mystery: the corruptible will take on incorruptibility. It is true that, corruptible as we are, we cannot share in the kingdom of God. Through Christ and the power of his resurrection, we share in incorruptibility. Our share in Christ's resurrection is our share in life. Death has met defeat.

Irene Nowell OSB

PART I: Gathering for God's Word

Opening Prayer   **Alternative:** *Ask one of the students to lead the opening prayer.*

Open the session by saying: **Welcome! Thank you for coming to learn about our faith and about how to live as Jesus did. I invite the Church to stand. We begin by remembering our relationship with God;** (make the sign of the cross) **in the name of the Father, and of the Son, and of the Holy Spirit.**

Lord Jesus, we thank you for this beautiful day and for all creation. We ask you to help us produce good fruit. May your Spirit open our eyes so that we will truly see you; fill our hearts with goodness and love. Continue to bless these students; keep them and their families warm and safe in your love. We ask all this in your name.

The students respond: **Amen!**

Song   "Christians, Let Us Love One Another" by Picardy from *Today's Missal* (OCP), *Journeysongs* (OCP), *Glory & Praise* (OCP [NALR]).

"Love One Another" by Bob Dufford from *Today's Missal* (OCP), *Journeysongs* (OCP), *Glory & Praise* (OCP [NALR]).

"Nothing Can Keep Us from God's Love" by David Haas from *Today's Missal* (OCP).

"Prayer of Saint Francis" by Sebastian Temple from *Today's Missal* (OCP), *We Celebrate* (J.S. Paluch Co., Inc.).

"They'll Know We Are Christians" by Peter Scholtes from *Today's Missal* (OCP), *Gather (Comprehensive)* (GIA).

Announcements
• parish news
• birthdays
• other

PART II: Remembering God's Word

Use the following questions to review last week's session.

1. What did you learn about Jesus in last week's gospel?

• Let the students respond openly and honestly.

2. What did you learn about yourself and your desire to follow Jesus?

• Let the students respond openly and honestly.

3. How did Jesus help you live his laws last week? What did you experience?

• Let the students respond openly and honestly.

PART III: Understanding *God's Word*

Scripture

Step 1: Invite two volunteer students to the front of the classroom. Tie a blindfold over one student's eyes. Ask the other student to lead the blindfolded student around the room. After a few minutes, tie the blindfold over the guide's eyes. Ask the guide to continue leading the other student around the room—this time blindfolded. Ask the rest of the students what would happen if a blind person acted as a guide for another blind person. Remove the blindfolds, and ask the volunteers to return to their seats. Proclaim Luke 6:39–40.

Step 2: Invite two different volunteers to the front of the classroom. Blindfold one of the volunteers. Have the two students face each other. Ask the person who is blindfolded to make fun of the eyesight of the person who is not blindfolded. After a few minutes, ask the rest of the students what they think about the blindfolded person making fun of the person who can see. Remove the blindfold, and let the volunteers return to their seats. Proclaim Luke 6:41–42.

Step 3: Place a bowl of mixed fruit on a table in front of the room. (There should be a combination of good and rotten fruit.) Hold up each piece of fruit. For each piece, ask: **From what kind of tree did this piece of fruit come? If this is the way the fruit looked when it was picked, was the tree that produced the fruit healthy or sick?** Proclaim Luke 6:43–45.

Reflection

Help the students process the reading further using the following questions and activities.

Materials Needed

All Students
- Bible
- two blindfolds
- bowl of mixed fruit (some fruit should be good and some rotten)
- four volunteers
- fruit shapes cut from colored paper (one for each student)
- paper punch
- string
- artificial tree or large branch

Younger Students
- paper
- crayons

Older Students
- journals
- pens

Younger Students

1. Distribute to the students crayons and paper. Direct them to draw a picture of one of the stories Jesus told in the gospel reading: the blind guide, the log in the eye, or the tree that produces good fruit.

2. What do you think Jesus is trying to say to us in these stories? What can we learn about others and ourselves?

3. Jesus talks about the good person producing goodness for the good in his or her heart. How can we show to others the goodness that is in our hearts?

Older Students

Allow time for the students to respond in their journals to the last question.

1. How can you recognize a good fruit tree? What do you look for? What are the signs of health?

2. What is Jesus really saying about his followers and their actions?

3. If your life were a fruit tree, what would Jesus need to do to make it more healthy and help it produce better fruit?

Closing Prayer

Cut out fruit shapes from colored paper (one for each student). Have the students write one of the fruits of the Holy Spirit on each piece of fruit: charity, joy, peace, patience, kindness, goodness, generosity, gentleness, faithfulness, modesty, self-control, chastity. Punch a hole in each piece of fruit with a paper punch. Tie string through the holes, and hang the paper fruit on a tree. A dead branch or artificial Christmas tree could be used.

Gather the students together. Say: **Because of Jesus' life, death, and resurrection, we have been given many gifts by the Spirit to help us produce good fruit. We receive the fruits of the Holy Spirit when we use these gifts and freely give them away to others. These fruits are charity, joy, peace, patience, kindness, goodness, generosity, gentleness, faithfulness, modesty, self-control, and chastity.**

Form a circle around the tree, hold hands, and pray the Lord's Prayer. Ask each student to pick a piece of fruit from the tree. Have them share the fruit of the Holy Spirit they received. Let them take the fruit home.

Making God's Word Our Own

If you are choosing a student for next Sunday's opening prayer, do so now.

Each day this week, ask Jesus to walk with you and help you examine your actions. Are they truly a reflection of what Jesus taught? Don't forget last week's gospel message about living the Golden Rule. Ask Jesus every day to help you live in a way that produces good fruit in your life. Rely on the fruits of the Holy Spirit you picked to help you. Ask Jesus to help you, too.

First Sunday of Lent

Theme

Lent is a time to open our hearts more fully to Jesus.

Scripture *Background*

The reading from the Book of Deuteronomy reflects the central beliefs of the Israelites. This creed was recited at the spring festival of first fruits. On this occasion the Israelites offered a portion of the first harvest of the year to acknowledge that the land belonged to God. This creed recalled that the land was a gift from their own history. Jacob and his family had immigrated to Egypt, where they were enslaved. Through the mercy of God, they were delivered by God's power and brought into this good land.

In the gospel passage, the Spirit drove Jesus into the desert, the "home of demons," to be tempted by the devil. After Jesus' forty days of fasting, the devil tempted him to abandon trust in God and to use power to ensure his survival. Jesus countered the devil's temptations by recalling God's care of the people in the desert after the Exodus. Just as God led Israel out of Egypt, nourished them for forty years in the desert, and gave them the promised land, so God would care for Jesus during and after his forty days in the desert. Israel did not always resist temptation. Jesus passed the test because his trust in God, his Father, never wavered.

The devil tempted Jesus in the same way he had tempted the man and woman in the garden. Then he had promised they would "be like God." The devil was tempting Jesus to be like God by rejecting God. It was the same temptation Jesus would face on the cross: "Let him save himself if he is the chosen one, the messiah of God" (Luke 23:35). Jesus' response teaches us that the way to be like God is through obedience and trust, not disobedience and pride.

The passage from the Letter to the Romans encourages us to trust in God. The Israelites trusted in God and were given the promised land. Jesus trusted in God, his Father, and was raised from the dead. What we must do to share in that salvation is simply to believe in Jesus as risen Lord and to call upon him.

Irene Nowell OSB

PART I: Gathering *for* God's Word

Opening Prayer

Alternative: *Ask one of the students to lead the opening prayer.*

Open the session by saying: **Welcome, and happy Lent to you! The Season of Lent is a wonderful time to reflect on and celebrate our need for Jesus in our lives. It is a time to look honestly at ourselves, our actions, and the world around us and to ask, "Are we living as Jesus wants us to?" I invite the Church to stand as we begin, remembering that when we were baptized, we died to ourselves so we could live with Jesus. We remember** (make the sign of the cross) **in the name of the Father, and of the Son, and of the Holy Spirit.**

Jesus, you were tempted in the desert by the evil one; we are also tempted. We can overcome temptation as you did if we keep our focus on you and our hearts open to receive your help. Give us the courage and strength to keep trying and to trust that you will come to our aid when we call for help. I pray that these children and catechists will never be afraid to call on you for help. Help us build a strong relationship with you, knowing how much you love us, no matter what! Thank you for hearing us and answering our prayers. We ask all this and all the prayers we hold in our hearts in your name.

The students respond: **Amen!**

Song

"Abba! Father!" by Carey Landry from *Glory & Praise* (OCP [NALR]), *Today's Missal* (OCP).

"Be Not Afraid" by Bob Dufford from *Glory & Praise* (OCP [NALR]), *Today's Missal* (OCP), *Gather (Comprehensive)* (GIA), *Lead Me, Guide Me* (GIA), *Journeysongs* (OCP).

"Blest Be the Lord" by Dan Schutte from *Glory & Praise* (OCP [NALR]), *Gather (Comprehensive)* (GIA), *Today's Missal* (OCP), *Journeysongs* (OCP).

"Lord, Be with Me (Psalm 91)" by David Haas from *Walking by Faith* (Harcourt Religion Publishers, GIA).

"You Are Near" by Dan Schutte from *Gather (Comprehensive)* (GIA), *Today's Missal* (OCP), *Glory & Praise* (OCP [NALR]), *Journeysongs* (OCP).

Announcements

- parish news
- birthdays
- other

PART II: Remembering *God's Word*

Use the following questions to review the Sixth Sunday in Ordinary Time.

1. Whom did Jesus bless last week? Whom did he despair?

- Jesus blessed those who are poor, those who hunger, those who weep, those who are hated, those who are ostracized and insulted because of him. He despaired the rich, the full, those who laugh and are spoken well of now.

2. What is this special passage called?

- the Beatitudes

3. How did reading the gospel every day last week and praying for those Jesus despaired affect your week? What did you learn about yourself while you were praying for others?

- Let the students respond freely and openly.

Use the following questions to review the Seventh Sunday in Ordinary Time.

1. What did you learn about Jesus in last week's gospel?

- Let the students respond openly and honestly.

2. What did you learn about yourself and your desire to follow Jesus?

- Let the students respond openly and honestly.

3. How did Jesus help you live his laws last week? What did you experience?

- Let the students respond openly and honestly.

Use the following questions to review the Eighth Sunday in Ordinary Time.

1. What did you learn about Jesus from last Sunday's gospel?

- Let the students answer openly and honestly.

2. What did Jesus ask us, his followers, to do in last week's gospel?

- The blind cannot guide the blind.
- A student is not above the teacher.
- Remove the plank from your own eye before you remove the speck for your brother's or sister's eye.
- A good person produces goodness from the good in her or his heart.

3. How did your fruit of the Holy Spirit help you live out Jesus' message last week? What happened when you tried to live it out? How did Jesus help you?

- Let the students respond openly and honestly.

PART III: Understanding *God's Word*

Materials Needed

All Students
- Bible
- dry-erase board or chalkboard
- incense
- incense holder
- charcoal
- matches
- reflective music
- CD or tape player
- recording of "To Make You Feel My Love"

Younger Students
- paper
- crayons

Older Students
- journals
- pens

Understanding the Season of Lent

The Season of Lent is a special time in the Church's liturgical year when we as the Body of Christ, the Church, spend time examining how well we are living. Lent is a time to look honestly inside ourselves and at our actions. Do our thoughts, words, and actions reflect Jesus? Lent invites all of us to open our hearts to Jesus. This is known as "on-going conversion," which means we want to turn from a selfish way of living to another way of living—Jesus' way.

Ash Wednesday

Putting ashes on our foreheads reminds us that one day we will die and return to God. We need God's help if we are to be holy and live as Jesus did.

Lenten Activities

Jesus invites us into a deeper relationship with him. He guides us as we grow in his likeness. Christ walks beside us on our Lenten journey. Some traditional ways of spiritual journeying are prayer, fasting from foods or bad actions, doing good things for others, reading Scripture, and daily Mass.

Scripture Proclaim the gospel. Ask the students to pay close attention to the three temptations Jesus overcame. After proclaiming the gospel, invite student volunteers to share temptations with which they are faced. List these temptations on the dry-erase board or chalkboard. Help the students develop concrete ways of overcoming these temptations. Erase each temptation as you devise a way of overcoming it. Say: **With Jesus' help, we can conquer all temptation. We can ask him to help us.**

Reflection Use the following questions and activities to help the students process the reading further.

Younger Students

1. Distribute to the students crayons and paper. Direct them to draw a picture of Jesus conquering his temptations. Have them draw on the back of the paper a picture of themselves conquering their temptations with Jesus' help.

2. Lent is a time to prepare our hearts to celebrate Jesus' forgiveness and love for us. What can you do to open your heart further to Jesus this Lenten season? Give examples.

3. Everyone is tempted. What is the best way to fight temptations and keep your mind and heart open to Jesus?

Older Students

Allow time for the students to respond in their journals to the last question.

1. What does Jesus' ability to conquer temptation mean to you?

2. List five things you can do to avoid temptation. Explain.

3. What can you do this Lent to open up your hearts more fully to Jesus and strengthen or build your relationship with him?

Closing Prayer

Gather the students in a circle. In the center of the circle, set an incense holder and lit charcoal. Next to the holder, place a bowl of incense. Play some reflective music, and allow the students a moment of silence. Invite the students to examine their lives and actions. Ask them to think about what they are willing to do this Lenten Season to open their hearts more fully to Jesus. After a few moments, invite the students (one at a time) to take one piece of incense as a symbol of their prayer and Lenten desire before God and place it in the incense holder.

Have the students return to their circle and sit in quiet reflection. After a few minutes of silence, play "To Make You Feel My Love" from *Billy Joel's Greatest Hits, Vol. III* or from the *Hope Floats* soundtrack. Introduce the song by saying: **This is a song you may have heard. I want you to think about it in a special way. Imagine Christ singing it to you personally as a testament of his love for you.** (Alternative: Sing or listen to an appropriate hymn.)

After the song, say: **Jesus loves each of us deeply—so much that he died for us. Christ calls us to share that love with each other. That is not always easy. But with Christ, we can love each other unselfishly, courageously, and deeply—no matter what the situation.**

Making God's Word Our Own

If you are choosing a student for next Sunday's opening prayer, do so now.

This week spend fifteen minutes alone with Jesus. You could invite him to go on a walk with you, or you could invite him to sit quietly in your room with you as you fall asleep. Perhaps you could invite Jesus to do homework with you. Spending time with Jesus could change your life like you would not believe!

Second Sunday of Lent

Readings

Genesis 15:5–12, 17–18
Philippians 3:17–4:1
Luke 9:28b–36

Theme

*Lent calls us to
transform our lives.*

Scripture *Background*

An ancient way of sealing an agreement in the Near East was for both parties to walk between the split bodies of sacrificial animals. The ceremony was a symbolic way of saying "If I break this covenant, may I be split like these animals." The reading from Genesis tells of such a ceremony for which God instructed Abram to prepare. God had promised Abram many descendants, the land on which he settled, and a special relationship with God. Abram did as he was instructed and then waited. God sealed the covenant by appearing as a flaming torch between the carcasses of the sacrificial animals. God's time, however, is not human time. Abram must continue to wait. Humans must wait upon God.

The gospel story also symbolically portrays God's promise. Immediately after Jesus told the disciples that he would suffer, die, and rise again, he and they were given a vision of the glory to come. Jesus took his closest friends—Peter, John, and James—to a mountain to pray. While they were on the mountain (a favorite biblical place for revelation), Jesus was transformed. He was filled with light, symbolizing the presence of God that shone through him. Moses, representing the Law, and Elijah, representing the prophets, came to speak with Jesus about his "exodus," his passing through death to life.

Peter and the others were captivated by this vision and wanted to cling to Jesus' glory. Jesus would enter into his glory through his passion and death; his disciples must follow the same path. The cloud (another symbol of God's presence) overshadowed all of them, and God's voice proclaimed Jesus as his Son. The glory of the obedient Son of God, who did not succumb to the devil's temptation, would be fully revealed in the Paschal mystery. The disciples must listen to Jesus and wait.

Paul encouraged the Philippians to trust God and wait. Those who lose faith search for immediate gains. Paul scorned them by saying "Their god is their belly!" Those who wait for God's promises will come into the land of promise and will be citizens in heaven. Those who wait for God's promises to be fulfilled will share in Jesus' glory. The disciples must listen and wait.

Irene Nowell OSB

PART I: Gathering for God's Word

Opening Prayer

Alternative: *Ask one of the students to lead the opening prayer.*

Open the session by saying: **Welcome. May the peace of Jesus be with you this Lent. I invite the Church to stand as we begin our opening prayer. The sign of the cross is a transforming sign. It shows us who we truly are, and it shows the power of God working within us. Therefore, we begin our prayer** (make the sign of the cross) **in the name of the Father, and of the Son, and of the Holy Spirit.**

Jesus, our God and friend, help us look deep into ourselves to recognize and see who we truly are—your sons and daughters who share in your love, mercy, power, and eternal life. Give us the strength to put aside anything that is not of you. This Lent, may we open our hearts more freely to receive your love and forgiveness and offer our lives in service of others. Bless these students and keep them warm and safe in your love. We ask all this in your name.

The students respond enthusiastically: **Amen!**

Song

"By Name I Have Called You" by Carey Landry from *Today's Missal* (OCP), *Glory & Praise* (OCP [NALR]).

"The Lord Is My Light" by Christopher Walker from *Today's Missal* (OCP), *Glory & Praise* (OCP [NALR]).

"You Are Near" by Dan Schutte from *Gather (Comprehensive)* (GIA), *Today's Missal* (OCP), *Glory & Praise* (OCP [NALR]), *Journeysongs* (OCP).

Announcements

- parish news/Lenten schedule
- birthdays
- other

PART II: Remembering God's Word

Review last week's session using the following questions.

1. What happened to Jesus in last week's gospel?

- He was led into the desert by the Holy Spirit and was tempted there.

2. What did you learn about your own temptations from Jesus' temptations?

- We can overcome our temptations just as Jesus did. Jesus will help us.

3. How did your relationship with Jesus grow last week? Was it difficult to spend time with Jesus?

- Let the students respond openly and honestly.

PART III: Understanding *God's Word*

Materials Needed

All Students
- Bible
- transformer toy
- index card for each student with one of Jesus' commands written on it

Younger Students
- paper
- crayons

Older Students
- journal
- pen

Jesus' Commands

Jesus said to his disciples . . .

- Love your enemies.
- Do good to those who hate you.
- Bless those who curse you.
- Pray for those who maltreat you.
- When someone slaps you, turn and offer him the other cheek.
- When someone takes your coat, let him have your shirt as well.
- Give to all who beg from you.
- When a man takes what is yours, don't demand it back.
- Do to others what you would have them do to you.
- Love your enemy and do good.
- Lend without expecting repayment.
- Be compassionate.
- Don't judge.
- Don't condemn.
- Pardon.
- Give.

Scripture

Proclaim Luke 9:28b–36.

Use the transformer toy to illustrate how things change. What we see is not all we get. We are limited (the toy), but with Christ we can choose to be transformed into so much more.

Explain that in and through God's grace, we are transformed into what God calls us to be. But because of free will, there is only one obstacle to overcome—ourselves. We must freely allow Jesus to touch us and transform us into what God wants us to be.

Say: **In the gospel, God says, "This is my Son, my Chosen; listen to him" (Luke 9:35). God wants us to listen to Jesus. What do we need to do to listen to Jesus? Think about the gospel readings for the past four Sundays. What were some of the things Jesus asked us to do?**

Give each of the students an index card with one of Jesus' commands written on it. Say: **This card has one of Jesus' commands written on it. Focus on doing what the card directs throughout the week.**

Reflection

Discuss the gospel reading further using the following questions and activities.

Younger Students

1. Distribute to the students crayons and paper. Direct them to draw a picture of Jesus being transfigured. Instruct them to include themselves in the picture. Allow ample time for the students to draw their own transfigurations on the back of the paper.
   Say: **Jesus is calling you to be what is already deep within you. Let it out!**

2. What would you have done if you saw Jesus in his glory with Moses and Elijah?

3. What are you going to change in your life this Lent so that the Jesus within you can shine more clearly in the world?

Older Students

Allow time for the students to respond in their journals to the second question.

1. Where in your life have you experienced God in an unusual way? What happened?

2. God said "This is my Son, my Chosen; listen to him" (Luke 9:35). What are you willing to do so that you are able to listen and hear Jesus more clearly this Lent?

3. Do you believe that Jesus is the Messiah who has come to heal us and save us through his life, death, and resurrection? If so, how does this change the way we see and live in the world around us?

Closing Prayer

Gather the students in a circle. Ask for a moment of silence. Invite the students to listen to the silence. After a few minutes, read Luke 9:35: "This is my Son, my Chosen; listen to him." Go to each student, and sign a cross on his or her ears. Look at the student, and say "Jesus is God's Son, God's chosen one. Listen to him." Hold hands as you conclude the session with the Lord's Prayer.

Making God's Word Our Own

If you are choosing a student for next Sunday's opening prayer, do so now.

This week's prayer challenge is going to be difficult. What will make this so hard is that you are going to say nothing. Every day this week, spend fifteen minutes with Jesus saying nothing—just listen to what Jesus says to you. Let Jesus do all the talking for once! He just might have some wonderful and exciting things to say to you.

Third Sunday *of* Lent

Readings

Exodus 3:1–8a, 13–15
1 Corinthians 10:1–6,
   10–12
Luke 13:1–9

Theme

*Lent calls us to
conversion.*

Scripture *Background*

Today's first reading finds Moses objecting to God's call. He says to God: "If they ask me, 'What is the name of the God who sent you,' what shall I tell them?" God's answer, "I AM sent me to you," has led believers to contemplate the meaning of "I AM," or *YWHW*. Two explanations seem plausible: "I will be who I will be" or "I will be present for you." God will be with the people to save them from oppression and suffering. The God of Israel is a God who will help when needed.

The reading from 1 Corinthians is Paul's meditation on the fate of the people who were delivered in the Exodus. Not all of the people who were freed remained faithful to God. Those who turned away from God met their death. Paul wants his readers to learn from their example. Being delivered from sin through Baptism is not enough. We must continue to remain faithful to God and continue to turn back when we have turned away.

The gospel story was Jesus' answer to those who judged others through the theory of retribution (the good will be blessed, the wicked punished). He pointed to examples that seem to contradict the theory. Jesus described people who had suffered terribly, yet who were not wicked. Then he described a barren fig tree, the favorite symbol for an unfaithful people. The fig tree was allowed a second chance to bear fruit. Jesus' message was that God is free. Humans cannot see enough to judge God's purpose in events. One thing we know: God is present. The parable illustrated God's patience. However, God would not wait forever. Now is the acceptable time to return, to accept God's deliverance, and to live as people freed from the slavery of sin.

Irene Nowell OSB

PART I: Gathering *for God's Word*

Opening Prayer **Alternative:** *Ask one of the students to lead the opening prayer.*

Open the session by saying: **Welcome. May your steadfastness in faith lead you to a deeper relationship with Jesus. Thank you for joining us as we prepare to celebrate the Third Sunday of Lent. I invite the Church to stand as we begin our prayer. We begin by remembering the conversion of life and faith that was celebrated at our Baptism. May that conversion be ongoing as we pray** (make the sign of the cross) **in the name of the Father, and of the Son, and of the Holy Spirit.**

> *God our Father, the Creator of all good things, you have revealed yourself in many ways throughout history. You have spoken through nature—in fire and floods—in whispers, and in a burning bush. But it was through your Son, Jesus, that you spoke the clearest and revealed the fullness of who you are and shared with us your love. Bless these students gathered here today, and continue to embrace them in your loving arms. Thank you, God, for hearing our prayer. We ask these prayers in Jesus' name.*

The students respond loudly: **Amen!**

Song "Standin' in the Need of Prayer," spiritual from *Gather (Comprehensive)* (GIA), *Lead Me, Guide Me* (GIA).

"You Are Near" by Dan Schutte from *Gather (Comprehensive)* (GIA), *Today's Missal* (OCP), *Glory & Praise* (OCP [NALR]).

"City of God" by Dan Schutte from *Glory & Praise* (OCP [NALR]), *Gather (Comprehensive)* (GIA), *Today's Missal* (OCP).

Announcements
- parish news
- birthdays
- other

PART II: Remembering *God's Word*

Review last week's readings.

1. Who did Jesus take with him when he went up the mountain to pray?

- Peter, John, and James

2. Jesus changed while he was praying. Who appeared and talked to him?

- Moses and Elijah

3. A voice from the cloud said "This is my Son, my Chosen; listen to him." What does this means for us today?

- Let the students respond openly and honestly.

4. Was it hard to sit quietly and listen to Jesus last week? What did Jesus say to you? What happened?

- Let the students respond openly and honestly.

PART III: Understanding *God's Word*

Scripture

Choose two students to role-play Moses and the burning bush. Have them get into costume. Have the two students act out Exodus 3:1–8a, 13–15 as it is being read. Direct them to echo their speaking parts after you read them. This makes it easier and more fun. When you are finished role-playing, discuss the reading with the students.

1. Share your own need for conversion that is ongoing; God is calling you and all of us just like God called Moses.

2. Point out that by God revealing to us the name " I am who am," God is inviting us into a personal relationship. God wants a relationship with us just like God had with Moses.

3. Look for the burning bush in your own lives. Jesus is all around us. What forms of burning bushes do you have in your lives? How does God appear to you?

Reflection

Use the following questions and activities to help the students process the reading further.

Younger Students

1. Distribute to the students paper and crayons. Direct them to draw a picture of Moses and the burning bush. Remind them to include themselves in their pictures.

2. What would you do if you met God in a burning bush? What questions would you ask God?

3. Jesus loves us. He wants us to accept his love. What can you do this Lent to allow Jesus' love into your heart?

Older Students

Allow time for the students to respond in their journals to the last question.

1. Would it be easier to see God's actions in a burning bush or to see God actions in the life, death, and resurrection of Jesus? Why?

2. Moses changed after his encounter with God in the burning bush. How do we change when we encounter Jesus in the Eucharist?

3. Lent provides us with an opportunity to change our hearts, to experience a conversion. How have you opened your heart to Jesus' love and healing this Lent?

Materials Needed

All Students
- Bible
- two students to role-play Moses and the burning bush
- brown robe
- a staff
- sandals
- tree branch with red paper flames

Younger Students
- paper
- crayons

Older Students
- journals
- pens

Closing Prayer

Gather the students together in a circle. Give them a few minutes to reflect on the following: What is one thing you would change about yourself if you could? What is one thing you would change about the world if you could? After a few minutes, ask for volunteers to share their thoughts. Hold hands as you conclude the session with the Lord's Prayer, the Hail Mary, and the Glory to the Father.

If you are choosing a student for next Sunday's opening prayer, do so now.

Making God's Word Our Own

This week seek out God. Keep your minds, hearts, and eyes open for burning bushes. Burning bushes are things that happen to us or ways God calls us into a relationship. Take time to look around you. Jesus reveals himself to you every day. Spend fifteen minutes every day this week looking for him. You just might be surprised where you find Jesus.

Fourth Sunday *of* Lent

Readings

Joshua 5:9a, 10–12
2 Corinthians 5:17–21
Luke 15:1–3, 11–32

Theme

God wants us to come back. Now is the time to reconcile.

Scripture *Background*

The readings for this Sunday focus on the notion that, with love and forgiveness, new beginnings are possible.

The first reading recounts Israel's rebirth in the land of promise. As the people crossed the Jordan River, they celebrated Passover, just as they had when they crossed the Red Sea. The period of wandering in the wilderness, of need and murmuring, of dependence and testing, was over. Now the Israelites had a home of their own and no longer needed manna, the wilderness food. They had arrived in the promised land.

In the gospel passage, Jesus answers the outraged Pharisees and scribes who are present with the story of the prodigal son. He tells the story of two sons, the elder reliable and obedient, the younger adventurous and irresponsible. The younger son took his share of the family estate, squandered it, and ended in abject poverty. Realizing that he had also lost his father's care and his place in the family, he returns, not as a son, but as a servant. New beginnings are always possible.

The father does not even wait for the apology of his wandering child. He runs to meet him and prepares a great feast in celebration. The elder son was scandalized that the father would do such a thing and grew jealous of his father's attention to the younger son.

Jesus did not interpret the parable; it needed no interpretation. The Pharisees could see their reflection in the elder son, scandalized and jealous. Jesus was telling them that not only did he eat with sinners but that God even throws a party at the return of sinners. Like the older brother, the Pharisees and all people are invited to the party. The price of admission is to rejoice in the return of lost brothers and sisters.

In his letter, Paul described the reconciliation that results in new creation, an even greater scandal to the unbeliever. Christ serves as an ideal model for the elder brother, who rejoices in the reconciliation of his other brothers and sisters with God. He also took their guilt upon himself, to the point of becoming sin himself. In this way, we sinners are able to reconcile with God.

Irene Nowell OSB

PART I: Gathering *for God's Word*

Opening Prayer **Alternative:** *Ask one of the students to lead the opening prayer.*

Open the session by saying: **God's peace to each and every one of you. Welcome. I invite the Church to stand. How are we going to begin our prayer?** (Let the students lead you in the sign of the cross. Ask them to explain it's connection to our Baptism into God's family.)

> *Jesus, let these children and adults always remember that no matter what sins we have committed, you will welcome us back if we are sorry in our hearts. There is nothing that can separate us from your love and mercy. We are all prodigal sons and daughters; may we also turn our hearts to you and come home to your loving arms. Bless us this Lent, and grant us the grace to turn to you for everything. Thank you for loving and forgiving us. We ask all this in your name.*

The students respond enthusiastically: **Amen!**

Song "Save Us, O Lord" by Bob Dufford from *Today's Missal* (OCP), *Journeysongs* (OCP), *Glory & Praise* (OCP [NALR]).

"The Cry of the Poor" by John Foley from *Today's Missal* (OCP), *Journeysongs* (OCP), *Glory & Praise* (OCP [NALR]).

"We Come to Ask Forgiveness" by Carey Landry from *Hi God! 3* (OCP [NALR]), *Glory & Praise* (OCP [NALR]).

Announcements
- parish news
- birthdays
- other

PART II: Remembering *God's Word*

Review last week's session using the following questions.

1. What happened in last Sunday's readings? What did you hear God saying to you about the Scripture passage?
   - Let the students respond openly and honestly.

2. What did God tell Moses God's name is?
   - God said, "I am who am."

3. What did you learn about God from last Sunday's readings?
   - Let the students respond openly and honestly.

4. What burning bushes did you find last week? How did God reveal himself to you?
   - Let the students respond openly and honestly.

PART III: Understanding *God's Word*

Scripture

Choose from two options.

Materials Needed

All Students
- recording of "I Know" by Jude from the *City of Angels* soundtrack
- CD or tape player
- candle
- matches
- Bible
- five volunteers (option one)
- two adult or older-student volunteers (option one)

Younger Students
- paper
- crayons

Older Students
- journals
- pens

Option One

Proclaim the parable of the prodigal son in Luke 15:1–3, 11–32. Have the class role-play the situation of the father on trial for having a favorite son and for being an unfair parent. Ask for two adult or older-student volunteers to role-play the father and the prosecuting attorney. Also choose a panel of judges from student volunteers. Give both the prosecutor and the father ample time to prepare their cases. To reinforce his or her case, the prosecutor should reread the gospel reading and pick out things that the father does differently from what the Church teaches us today about love, forgiveness, and mercy. Have fun with this activity; the more you get into it, the more you and your students will get out of it. After the prosecutor states his or her case against the father and the father has explained his actions, have the panel of judges render a verdict. Do they find the father guilty of playing favoritism between the two sons? Is the father fair or not?

Option Two

Proclaim the gospel. As you read, stop at the appropriate places and ask the students what they would do in this situation. For example, use the following questions after the Scripture quotation "The younger of them said to his father, 'Father, give me the share of the property that will belong to me.'"

- What would you do if you heard your younger brother say that to your parents?
- Would you ever ask your parents such a question?
- If you were the father, what would you say if your son or daughter asked you for his or her inheritance?
- Would you give your son or daughter the money if you were the father?

Reflection

Use the following questions and activities to discuss the gospel further.

Younger Students

1. Have you ever had to ask forgiveness from your mom, dad, brother, or sister? Was it easy or hard to ask for forgiveness?
2. Distribute to the students paper and crayons. Instruct them to draw a picture of the prodigal son coming home and meeting the father.
3. The father said, ". . . let us eat and celebrate; for this son of mine was dead and is alive again; he was lost and is found!" What did the father mean? Explain your answer.

Older Students

1. In the parable of the prodigal son, there are three main characters—the father, the younger son, and the older son. To which of these characters can you best relate? Why?
2. What is the main point or lesson learned from this parable?
3. What are you going to ask God for this Lent?

Closing Prayer

Turn out the classroom lights, and light a candle. Gather the students together, and have them sit in a circle. Play the song "I Know" by Jude from the *City of Angels* soundtrack. Say: **Quietly listen to this song. Imagine that God is speaking to you.** After the song, ask the students to silently examine their consciences. After a few moments of silence, hold hands and recite together the Act of Contrition.

> *O my God, I am sorry for my sins. In choosing to sin and failing to do good, I have sinned against you and your Church. I firmly intend, with the help of your Son, to do penance and to sin no more. Our Savior, Jesus Christ, suffered and died for us. In his name, my God, have mercy.*

Optional: Use the examination of conscience "Jesus, Heal Us" by David Haas from the *Walking by Faith* CD (GIA, Harcourt Religion Publishers).

Making God's Word Our Own

If you are choosing a student for next Sunday's opening prayer, do so now.

Reread the parable of the prodigal son (Luke 15:1–3, 11–32) every day this week. Spend fifteen minutes each day reading and asking Jesus to help you see the deeper meaning of this parable. What meaning does this parable have in your life today? Read it each morning, and think about it during the day. With Jesus' help, you will see something new in the parable each day.

Fifth Sunday *of* Lent

Readings

Isaiah 43:16–21
Philippians 3:8–14
John 8:1–11

Theme

Jesus' love and forgiveness offer true freedom.

Scripture *Background*

After exile in Babylon, the Jews were allowed to return to Jerusalem. However, not everyone wanted to return. Life during the Babylonian exile was not difficult. The trip back to Jerusalem would be arduous and lead the people to a devastated country in need of rebuilding. In today's first reading, the prophet encourages the people to accept deliverance in this new exodus. God had delivered their ancestors from Egypt centuries before. Now God was delivering them from Babylon. The trip to Jerusalem, like the trip through the desert, would be difficult, but God had a mission for them. As their ancestors in the first exodus had done, so they were to reestablish God's people in the land of promise. God would deliver them and care for them on the way. The people would witness divine power and love, announcing God's praise to the whole world.

In his letter, Paul speaks of a different kind of liberation. Jewish Christians in Philippi insisted that Christians, including Gentiles, could be saved only by keeping all the prescriptions of Jewish law. Paul insists that salvation comes not through scrupulous observance of the law but through faith in Christ and his resurrection. Salvation is a gift from God. Everything else is useless compared to the gift of Christ's death and resurrection. Even as we strive to share in Christ's sufferings in order to share in his resurrection, we know it is God who delivers. It is God who saves.

The gospel passage is a typical example of Jesus' mercy toward sinners and of his wit when dealing with the self-righteous. The Pharisees, intending to trap Jesus, presented a woman accused of adultery to him. In a sense, both the woman and Jesus were trapped. The woman was trapped by her guilt; Jesus was trapped by the demand for a merciless judgment. The woman made no defense. Jesus did not contradict the law nor declare the woman guiltless. Instead, he faced her judges with their own guilt. The self-righteous who condemned the woman ended by condemning themselves. The woman accepted her guilt and was forgiven. Jesus passed true judgment. He forgave the repentant and condemned the self-righteous. The trap was broken. God gives freedom.

Irene Nowell OSB

PART I: Gathering *for God's Word*

Opening Prayer **Alternative:** *Ask one of the students to lead the opening prayer.*

Open the session by saying: **Welcome, and may the peace of Jesus' forgiveness be with all of you. Thank you for joining us again. Today we are going to be detectives, so listen carefully for clues—especially when we proclaim the gospel. Jesus is up to something, and we need to find out what it is. To put ourselves into the proper state of being, I invite the Church to stand as we begin our opening prayer. We begin by embracing the fact that we are children of God because we have been baptized** (make the sign of the cross) **in the name of the Father, and of the Son, and of the Holy Spirit.**

> *Jesus, grant us the grace and wisdom to experience your forgiveness.*
> *Remind us that you don't condemn, and help us not condemn others.*
> *Help us share forgiveness with others through the forgiveness we receive*
> *from you. No matter who they are or what they did, teach us to forgive*
> *everyone as you forgive—to love as you love. We ask all this in your name.*

The students respond: **Amen!**

Song "Canticle of the Sun" by Marty Haugen from *Gather (Comprehensive)* (GIA), *Glory & Praise* (OCP [NALR]), *We Celebrate* (J.S. Paluch Co., Inc.), *Today's Missal* (OCP).

"Prayer of Saint Francis" by Sebastian Temple from *Today's Missal* (OCP), *We Celebrate* (J.S. Paluch Co., Inc.).

"Seek the Lord" by Roc O'Connor from *Glory & Praise* (OCP [NALR]), *Today's Missal* (OCP).

Announcements
- parish news
- birthdays
- other

PART II: Remembering *God's Word*

Use the following questions to review last week's session.

1. What does the word *reconciliation* mean?
   - turning back to God, being in relationship with the Father

2. What did the father of the prodigal son say when his son returned?
   - Bring him the finest robe and put it on him; put a ring on his finger; put shoes on his feet; kill the fatted calf. Let's celebrate!

3. What did the father mean when he said, ". . . let us eat and celebrate; for this son of mine was dead and is alive again; he was lost and is found"?
   - Let the students answer openly and honestly.

4. What did you learn about God and God's forgiveness?

  • Let the students respond openly and honestly.

5. What did you experience when you reflected on the story of the prodigal son last week? What did you learn?

  • Let the students share openly and honestly.

PART III: Understanding *God's Word*

Scripture

Materials Needed

All Students
  • Bible
  • prize(s)
  • small rock for each student
  • detective costume and props (optional)

Older Students
  • journals
  • pens

This activity can be done in a large group or in small groups. Only one prize is needed if done in large group. A prize for each group member is needed if done in small groups.

Optional: Dress as a detective. Wear a long trench coat and hat. Carry a large magnifying glass. If you know a parishioner who is a police officer, ask him or her to help conduct the activity to make the search more exciting.

Show the students the prize(s). Say: **This/These prize(s) will be presented to the student(s) who can solve the mystery. Listen closely to the gospel. It mentions that Jesus twice writes something in the dirt. The mystery is: What did Jesus write? Listen closely to the gospel for clues. Pay attention to what happens before Jesus writes, and listen to what happens to the gathered scribes and Pharisees and the woman after Jesus writes in the dirt. Again, the mystery is: What did Jesus write in the dirt?**

Proclaim the gospel slowly and reflectively twice. State the mystery again between readings.

*Many Scripture scholars have tried to answer this question over the years. There are just as many answers as there are scholars. In other words, no one really **knows** what Jesus wrote in the dirt. One common assumption of many Scripture scholars is that Jesus wrote the sins of the gathered scribes and Pharisees in the dirt. That is why everyone, starting from the elders, drifted away—they saw that Jesus knew of their own sins.*

No one is 100 percent certain what Jesus wrote in the dirt. Have the students share their answers. Choose the answer that comes closest to the answer stated above or the one that sounds theologically correct based on written and oral traditions of the Church.

Reflection

Use the following questions to help the students process the gospel reading further.

Younger Students

1. Have you ever done something that was not right and needed to be forgiven? (Do not let the students reveal their sins.)

2. How did you feel inside before you were forgiven and after you were forgiven?

3. Jesus wants us to live in freedom and love. How can we thank Jesus for the gift of forgiveness and freedom that he offers us?

Older Students

Allow ample time for the students to respond in their journals to the last question.

1. How do you think the woman felt after being dragged in front of everyone? How do you think she felt when Jesus did not condemn her but forgave her?

2. Ask the students to list all the sins that Jesus won't or couldn't forgive. Ask them to explain their responses. When they are finished listing sins, say: **Jesus forgives all of these sins and more. Jesus forgives all sin if we are truly sorry.**

3. What stops you from asking Jesus to forgive your sins? What prevents you from receiving Jesus' forgiveness?

Closing Prayer

If you are choosing a student for next Sunday's opening prayer, do so now.

Invite the students to gather in a circle. Take a moment of silence. Ask the students to think about someone whom they have condemned or not forgiven. Have them pray for that person and for themselves.

Distribute to the students small rocks. Invite them to carry their rocks as reminders that we all need Jesus' forgiveness and that Jesus wants us to live in the freedom of his love. Their rocks will also remind them not to throw stones at (judging and condemning) other people.

Conclude the session by holding hands and reciting or singing the Lord's Prayer.

Making God's Word Our Own

Find some pocket crosses to exchange for the rocks that are brought to next week's session. The pocket cross will replace the rock as a symbol of Jesus' love and forgiveness. Don't tell the students that they will be exchanging their rocks next week.

Take your rock everywhere you go this week. When it gets in the way, ask Jesus for his gift of forgiveness and healing in your own life or in the life of another person you know who may need Jesus' forgiveness and healing. Take this challenge seriously, and you will experience the power of Jesus' love. Remember to bring your rock with you to class next week.

Passion Sunday

Readings

Luke 19:28–40
Isaiah 50:4–7
Philippians 2:6–11
Luke 22:14–23:56

Theme

Jesus shows us how much he truly loves us.

Scripture *Background*

When Jesus entered Jerusalem the week before his death, he received a hero's welcome. The people waved palm branches and carpeted his path with their cloaks. The crowds praised God for the mighty deeds they had seen Jesus perform. They acclaim him "king." We hear the story of Jesus' final entry into Jerusalem in the first part of today's liturgy.

The glory of this entry into the city contrasted sharply with the shameful death by crucifixion Jesus endured at the end of the week. We also read that story today. As he told the story of Jesus' passion, Luke highlighted Jesus' fidelity to his Father. Jesus remained faithful to his mission. When some of the Pharisees protested the acclamation of those who followed him, Jesus was undaunted. In the face of torment, he brought healing (22:50–51; 23:39–43). In the face of betrayal, he was forgiving (23:34a). In the face of ultimate loss, he entrusted himself to the Father (22:42; 23:46). Luke's words challenged the disciples of his time (and ours) to be faithful to Jesus' way and to their commitment to God.

Today's gospel begins with Luke's account of Jesus' celebration of the Passover meal with his disciples. Luke's account of Jesus' table conversation with his disciples (22:21–38) is unique among the synoptic Gospels. Jesus' farewell words to his disciples emphasize the importance of fidelity (verses 21–33), service (verses 24–27), perseverance (verses 28–34), and mission (verses 35–38). Jesus himself is the model for the disciples' life and ministry.

As the faithful Son of God, Jesus gave his life as "food" for others. To describe Jesus' offering of himself for the sake of others, Luke used language often used to describe a sacrifice. In the Old Testament, sacrifices were sealed or ratified by a covenant offering. Luke's reference to a "new covenant" recalled the words of the prophet Jeremiah: "The days are coming, says the Lord, when I will make a new covenant with the house of Israel and the house of Judah" (see Jeremiah 31:31–34).

Like the servant in today's first reading (Isaiah 50), Jesus willingly gave his life in fidelity to his mission. This reading from Isaiah is one of four passages that focus on the "servant" of God (Isaiah 42:1–4; 49:1–6; 50:4–9; 52:13–53:12). Scholars are uncertain whether it was an individual or the nation as a whole who is the subject of these passages. Perhaps it is both. In all examples, the servant was faithful, even in the face of suffering.

In today's passage from Isaiah, the servant is described as one who will faithfully listen to God's word and who will prophetically speak that word to others. Throughout the Gospel of Luke, Jesus was depicted as the faithful prophet who speaks God's word. Even in the midst of his own sufferings, he announced good news and brought healing (22:42, 51).

Similar to the description of the servant of Isaiah, Jesus willingly accepted the suffering and anguish that can be the price of fidelity. Jesus trusted in the God who was his help. Like the servant of Isaiah, Jesus was not disappointed in his hope.

As Luke told the story, at his dying moment Jesus entrusted his spirit into the hands of the Father (Luke 23:46). Through his death, resurrection, and ascension, Jesus completed his journey to the Father.

We also find the journey theme echoed in today's second reading. Scholars believe that this passage was a familiar early Christian hymn. Paul wanted the Philippians to model their behavior and attitudes (verse 5) on Christ who "emptied himself" (or poured himself out) on behalf of others (verse 7).

The first part of the hymn (verses 6–8) describes Christ's journey from the divine realm to the human realm. Christ did not cling to the divine glory that was his. He was born in human likeness and assumed the status of a slave. (The Greek word for *slave* is also the word for *servant*.)

Jesus was known as the friend of outcasts: tax collectors, sinners, the poor, and all those who were scorned by others. Jesus was obedient to the Father throughout his life, even when it cost him his life. In his death by crucifixion, as well as in his life of humble obedience to the Father and ministry to others, Jesus maintained the status of servant.

Today we begin a special time of remembering the last days of Jesus' earthly life, the end of his journey to the Father. In this season we recall that we, too, are on a journey to the Father in Christ. We are reminded that it is not human acclaim we seek but the will of the Father. As we enter into the spirit of these days, let us take the time to focus ourselves on Jesus. He has shown us his compassionate concern for others, willingness to forgive, and obedience to the Father.

Anne Marie Sweet OSB

PART I: Gathering *for God's Word*

Opening Prayer   **Alternative:** *Ask one of the students to lead the opening prayer.*

Open the session by saying: **Welcome to Holy Week. This week we remember, reflect on, and celebrate the depth of God's love for us in Jesus. I invite the Church to stand as we remember that in our Baptism, we died with Jesus, with all that his death implies. Likewise we will rise with him, with all that his resurrection implies. Therefore, we begin** (make the sign of the cross) **in the name of the Father, and of the Son, and of the Holy Spirit.**

Lord Jesus, long ago you entered into Jerusalem in glory and honor. Everyone claimed you as Lord and King. May we remember today that you are Lord and King of our lives. May our actions praise you and our hearts shout for joy because of the love you have shown us. Open our hearts to experience your risen Spirit this Holy Week and every day of our lives. We ask this in your name.

The students respond: **Amen!**

Song   "Lord of the Dance," Shaker song from *Today's Missal* (OCP), *Gather* (GIA).

"Song of the Body of Christ"/ "Canción del Cuerpo de Cristo" by David Haas, Spanish Trans. by Donna Peña, from *Gather (Comprehensive)* (GIA), *Walking by Faith* (Harcourt Religion Publishers, GIA).

"The King of Glory" by Willard F. Jabusch from *Today's Missal* (OCP), *Gather (Comprehensive)* (GIA).

"We Remember" by Marty Haugen from *Gather (Comprehensive)* (GIA), *Today's Missal* (OCP), *Celebrating Our Faith* (Harcourt Religion Publishers, GIA).

Announcements
- parish news
- birthdays
- other

PART II: Remembering *God's Word*

Use the following questions to review last week's session.

1. What was the message in last Sunday's gospel reading?
- Forgiveness; don't condemn others

2. What did you learn from Jesus in the gospel?
- Jesus doesn't condemn us; rather he wants us to receive his forgiveness and love.

3. Did you carry your rock all week? How did it remind you of Jesus' forgiveness? What did you learn about yourself and Jesus?
- Let the students share openly and honestly.

Call forward all the students who have their rocks with them. Exchange each rock with a pocket cross. Say: **The rock stood for the weight of sin and guilt that we carry every day. This cross that I am giving you stands for light. Carry this with you as a reminder that Jesus loves and forgives you.**

Invite those who didn't bring their rocks this week to bring them to the next session and exchange them for Jesus' cross of love and forgiveness.

PART III: Understanding *God's Word*

Materials Needed

All Students
- Bible
- four 8" X 11" signs (each should read one of the following: *Palm Sunday, Holy Thursday, Good Friday, Easter Sunday*)
- table
- palms
- bowl of water
- towel
- bread and wine
- bag of coins
- kneeler
- crown of thorns
- crucifix
- cutout of a heart
- white cloth
- Easter candle
- gold/white vestment

Younger Students
- red construction-paper hearts with "Jesus Loves Me" printed on each one (one per student)
- red strands of yarn (one per student)
- crayons or markers
- paper punch
- paper

Older Students
- journals
- pens

Arrange on a table the following items: palms, bowl of water, towel, bread and wine, bag of coins, kneeler, crown of thorns, cross, cutout of a heart, white cloth, Easter candle, Bible, gold/white vestment. Pick students one at a time to go to the table and match a sign that has a day of Holy Week printed on it with an item that symbolizes that particular day of Holy Week. Ask the student to share what he or she knows about that day of Holy Week and the connection between the item and the day.

- palms—Palm Sunday
- bowl of water—Holy Thursday
- towel—Holy Thursday
- bread and wine—Holy Thursday
- bag of coins—Holy Thursday/Good Friday
- kneeler—Holy Thursday
- crown of thorns—Good Friday
- crucifix—Good Friday
- heart cutout—Good Friday and Easter
- white cloth—Easter
- Easter candle—Easter
- Bible—Easter
- gold/white vestment—Easter

Read Philippians 2:6–11 after all the items have been matched up to the proper day. Ask the students which day of Holy Week this reading symbolizes (Easter).

Use the following questions and activities to discuss Holy Week further.

Younger Students

1. Distribute to the students paper and crayons. Have them draw a picture of Jesus' entrance into Jerusalem as the people proclaimed him king.
2. What can you do this Holy Week to help make it special for you and your family?
3. Pass out crayons or markers and red construction paper hearts with "Jesus Loves Me" written on them. Have the students draw a cross and write their names on the heart. Use a paper punch to punch holes in the hearts. Thread yarn through the holes, and tie the ends to make a necklace. Let the students wear their necklaces.

Older Students

Allow time for the students to respond in their journals to the first question.

1. Jesus cared for us so much that he died for us. And then he rose from the dead to show us the depth of his love that he has for each of us. Because Jesus cared enough to die for us, are you willing to live for him? How would your life change if you lived it for Jesus?

2. What is your favorite day of Holy Week? Why? What is your least favorite day? Why?

3. Reread Philippians 2:6–11. What word, phrase, or idea about Jesus stands out? Why?

Closing Prayer

Gather the students in a circle. Take a moment of silence. Ask the students to think about what Jesus did for them. Pass a crucifix around the circle of students. Invite the student holding the cross to thank Jesus (aloud or silently) for something or someone in his or her life. Hold hands as you conclude the session with the Lord's Prayer.

Making God's Word Our Own

Give a schedule of the Holy Week services to the students. Encourage them to try to attend all the Holy Week services—Holy Thursday, Good Friday, and the Saturday Easter Vigil. Go celebrate our faith! Give Jesus this week of your life. He gave his life to save you.

If you are choosing a student for next Sunday's opening prayer, do so now.

Easter Sunday

Readings

Acts 10:34a, 37–43
Colossians 3:1–4
John 20:1–9

Theme

We are a resurrection people!

Scripture *Background*

The center of our story is Jesus of Nazareth. To celebrate the mystery of Christ's life and of our lives as Christians, we gather in the darkness of the Easter Vigil to watch and wait. With Christ, we pass through the darkness into light. This is as he himself passed over from death into life. His resurrection was the ultimate victory over the power of sin and death. In his resurrection, we find life in all its fullness.

The gospel readings for the Vigil (Luke 24:112) and Easter Sunday (John 20:1–9) narrate for us the first Easter. In both gospels it was the faithful women who visited the grave. In Luke, these were the same women who accompanied Jesus on his journey. In John, Mary Magdalene came alone. Neither of the passages narrate an appearance of the risen Jesus.

Both gospels present the women as the first to announce the events of the resurrection. In Luke, the women come to faith as they "remembered" the words of Jesus. In John, the "beloved disciple" believed when he saw the tomb. This disciple later serves as a model for us to "see" and believe.

"All who believe" are forgiven of their sins, said Peter to the Gentile household of Cornelius (Acts 10:34a, 37–43). The disciples' witness to all they had seen and heard is the subject of the Acts of the Apostles. Their witness brought the good news to the far ends of the earth. Today's reading summarizes their proclamation. Our presence here, as Christians, bears witness to the powerful word of the gospel that has gone forth through all generations.

The Easter Sunday reading from Paul (Colossians 3:1–4) calls us to focus on our journey of faith. In Baptism we have "passed over" from death to life. Paul calls for a new way of life. We must "seek what is above." Baptism is the beginning. We must focus our hearts on the journey's end and on the glory the Lord will reveal when he comes in glory at the end of time. While we wait, we move forward, alive in Jesus' life.

Anne Marie Sweet OSB

PART I: Gathering *for God's Word*

Opening Prayer

Alternative: *Ask one of the students to lead the opening prayer.*

Open the session by saying: **Welcome. May the Spirit of our Risen Christ fill all of your hearts with laughter and love. This is it! Today we celebrate why we gather week after week; it's the reason we can sing, dance, laugh, and celebrate true life. Jesus' resurrection from the dead shows us how much God loves us. Jesus is alive! Sin and death no longer have power over us. It's right here at Easter where our faith begins. Jesus was raised from the dead so that we can live with him forever.**

I invite the Church to stand for our opening prayer. We begin by remembering that we are baptized in Jesus' death, resurrection, and life eternal (make the sign of the cross) **in the name of the Father, and of the Son, and of the Holy Spirit.**

Jesus, thank you for the gift of new life in you and freedom from sin. Open our hearts and minds to help us understand more deeply your resurrection and its meaning for us. May Easter excitement, joy, and surprise stay in our hearts all year long. Bless these students and their families with the Spirit of resurrection and new life. Thank you, Jesus, for hearing our prayers.

The students respond enthusiastically: **Amen!**

Song

"I Am the Resurrection" by Jim Anderson from *Today's Missal* (OCP).

"Jesus Christ Is Risen Today" (traditional) from *Gather (Comprehensive)* (GIA), *Today's Missal* (OCP), *We Celebrate* (J.S. Paluch Co., Inc.), *Lead Me, Guide Me* (GIA).

"People of God" by David Haas and Fintan O' Carroll from *Walking by Faith* (GIA, Harcourt Religion Publishers).

"Sing to the Mountains" by Bob Dufford from *Today's Missal* (OCP), *Glory & Praise* (OCP [NALR]), *Gather (Comprehensive)* (GIA).

Announcements

- parish news
- birthdays
- other

PART II: Remembering *God's Word*

Review last week's session using the following questions.

1. What was your favorite experience during Holy Week (Palm Sunday, Holy Thursday, Good Friday, Easter)?

- Let the students respond openly and honestly.

2. What did you learn about Jesus this Holy Week?

- Let the students respond openly and honestly.

3. What did you learn about yourself this Holy Week?

- Again, let the students respond openly and honestly.

PART III: Understanding *God's Word*

Materials Needed

All Students
- Bible
- three large balloons—one not inflated, one filled with air, and one filled with helium (attach a string and a small weight to the balloon so it doesn't float away)
- three volunteers
- table
- helium balloons with scrolls of the Nicene Creed tied to them (one per student)

Younger Students
- paper
- crayons

Older Students
- journals
- pens

The Nicene Creed

We believe in one God,
the Father, the Almighty,
maker of heaven and earth,
of all that is seen and unseen.

We believe in one Lord, Jesus Christ,
the only Son of God,
eternally begotten of the Father,
God from God, Light from Light,
true God from true God,
begotten, not made, one in Being with the Father.
Through him all things were made.
For us men and for our salvation
he came down from heaven:
by the power of the Holy Spirit
he was born of the Virgin Mary, and became man.

For our sake he was crucified under Pontius Pilate;
he suffered, died, and was buried.
On the third day he rose again
in fulfillment of the Scriptures;
he ascended into heaven
and is seated at the right hand of the Father.
He will come again in glory
to judge the living and the dead,
and his kingdom will have no end.

We believe in the Holy Spirit, the Lord, the giver of life,
who proceeds from the Father and the Son.
With the Father and the Son he is worshiped and glorified.
He has spoken through the prophets.
We believe in one holy catholic and apostolic Church.
We acknowledge one baptism for the forgiveness of sins.
We look for the resurrection of the dead,
and the life of the world to come. Amen.

Scripture Place three balloons (one not inflated, one filled with air, one filled with helium) on a table in front of the room. Invite three volunteers to come up to the front of the classroom and pick a balloon. After the volunteers have chosen a balloon, have each volunteer answer the following questions in front of the large group.
- What is the balloon made of?

- What makes that particular balloon different from the other two?
- Which of the three balloons symbolizes your life and the way you would like to live? Why?
- Which balloon symbolizes your faith and the way you live your faith? (flat, filled with air, or filled with helium) Why?

If time allows, invite the rest of the students to respond to these questions.

Say: **Because Jesus rose from the dead, he now pours out the Holy Spirit on the world. Now the Holy Spirit is offered to all of us, freely, without cost. This gift of the Holy Spirit makes our life different—just as the balloons were the same, yet very different. The gift of Jesus' resurrection is like the helium that frees us, allows us to fly, and brings great joy. It transforms the world.**

Reflection

Use the following questions and activities to explore the gospel reading further.

Younger Students

1. Distribute to the students paper and crayons. Instruct them to draw a picture of Jesus' disciples finding the empty tomb. Encourage the students to include themselves in their pictures.

2. Because Jesus was raised from the dead, all those who believe in him and follow his law of love will also be raised from the dead and live with him forever. This is our faith! How do you feel knowing that you can live with Jesus forever?

3. As a class, list all the things we don't have to worry about or fear anymore because of Jesus' resurrection.

Older Students

Allow ample time for the students to respond to the last question in their journals.

1. Reread John 20:1–9. Why do you think the wrappings are mentioned twice? Why are they important, and what do they represent?

2. Does Jesus' resurrection change anything in your life? If so, how? If not, why?

3. What keeps you bound or wrapped up in your life? How can Jesus' resurrection free you from your own wrappings?

Closing Prayer

Gather the students in a circle, and give each one a helium-filled balloon with a scroll of the Nicene Creed attached. Unfold the scroll, and pray together the Nicene Creed slowly and reflectively. Inform the students that this proclamation of faith was written in the fourth century.

Making God's Word Our Own

This week make a list of how Jesus' resurrection can or has changed your life. Each day, add one or more ways you are more free to live life because of Jesus' resurrection. Bring your lists to our next gathering.

If you are choosing a student for next Sunday's opening prayer, do so now.

Second Sunday *of* Easter

Readings

Acts 5:12–16
Revelation 1:9–11a,
 12–13, 17–19
John 20:19–31

Theme

Jesus sends us forth.

Scripture *Background*

The reading from the Acts of the Apostles is one of three summaries that describe the ideal Christian community. Two of those summaries (see Acts 2:42–47; 4:32–35) describe the inner life of the community. The summary in Acts 5 describes the witness of the community to outsiders. People regarded the Christians with reverence and approached them to be healed. The healing ministry of the Risen Christ continued through the ministry of the Christian community. Jesus was alive and active through those who believed in him.

The reading from Revelation recounts the first vision of the book. The author was apparently exiled on the island of Patmos because of his witness to Jesus. He writes to encourage other persecuted Christians to maintain their faith. Here he describes a vision of the victorious Christ holding all power, even over death. He presents the Risen Christ with divine attributes and titles. Christ is the beginning and the end. His power endures beyond all persecution, beyond even death. He has risen and lives forever. Those who believe in him will share in his life and resurrection.

The gospel passage narrates two appearances of the risen Jesus. In both stories his first words are "Peace be with you." The gift of peace was given to the disciples to share with the community. As Jesus was sent to bring healing and forgiveness, so he sends the disciples. His first gift was peace; his first commission was forgiveness. Peace and forgiveness would be the signs of Jesus' presence.

The second appearance involves the apostle Thomas. He was not present on the first occasion and could not believe the witness of the other disciples. He needed evidence of Jesus' resurrection. Jesus ministered to Thomas's need by showing him his wounded hands and side. Thomas then made a greater leap of faith than the others by calling Jesus "God." Jesus then proclaimed a beatitude on those who believed without evidence. The initial disbelief of Thomas strengthened his witness and helped strengthen the faith of all future believers.

Irene Nowell OSB

PART I: Gathering *for God's Word*

Opening Prayer

Alternative: *Ask one of the students to lead the opening prayer.*

Open the session by saying: **Welcome, and happy Easter! Remember, Easter is not a one-day celebration; it is a way of life. We celebrate the Season of Easter for fifty days.**

I invite the Church of the resurrection to stand for our opening prayer. We begin (make the sign of the cross) **in the name of the Father, and of the Son, and of the Holy Spirit.**

Jesus, our Savior and friend, thank you for your resurrection from the dead, which shows us how loved we are by God. Bless us and continue to breathe the gift of your Spirit upon us. May we freely go wherever you send us and do whatever you ask us to do because we believe in you. We ask all this in your name.

The students respond enthusiastically: **Amen!**

Song

"This Is the Day" by Marty Haugen from *Gather (Comprehensive)* (GIA).

"Walking by Faith" by David Haas from *Walking by Faith* (Harcourt Religion Publishers, GIA).

"We Walk by Faith" by Marty Haugen from *Gather (Comprehensive)* (GIA), *Today's Missal* (OCP).

Announcements

• parish news
• birthdays
• other

PART II: Remembering *God's Word*

Review last week's session using the following questions.

1. What did you learn about Jesus from last week's gospel?

   • Jesus is God. Jesus was raised from the dead. Jesus conquered sin and death.

2. What did you add to your lists last week?

   • Let the students share their lists from last week's prayer challenge.

PART III: Understanding *God's Word*

Scripture   Choose from two options.

Materials Needed

All Students—Option 1
- Bible
- TV
- VCR
- Jesus of Nazareth video, directed by Franco Zeffireli (Ventura, CA: Gospel Light Publications)

All Students—Option 2
- Bible
- dry-erase board or chalkboard
- dry-erase markers or chalk
- five or six volunteers

Younger Students
- paper
- crayons

Older Students
- journals
- pens

Option One

Show the students the Easter morning scene from the video *Jesus of Nazareth* (tape 3, 1:46:00 to 1:49:18). Discuss the video as needed.

Option Two

Have the students name places they have been sent to or chores they have been asked to do. Write their responses on a dry-erase board or chalkboard.

Use the newly created list to discuss what "being sent" means. There is a goal or purpose to be achieved by the sending forth. Examine the list, and help the students determine the purpose for each action of being sent.

Ask the students to listen carefully to the gospel, because Jesus does something very strange. Tell them you are going to ask them what strange thing Jesus did and the purpose of Jesus sending his disciples.

Call five or six volunteers forward. Ask them to stand up front while the gospel is being proclaimed (John 20:19–31). At the appropriate place in the reading, go over to the students and *breathe* on them. Don't blow on them, but *breathe* on them one at a time. Have the volunteers return to their seats. Ask:

- What strange thing does Jesus do to his disciples? (He breathes on them, giving them the Holy Spirit.)
- What is the purpose of Jesus sending his disciples? (to go out to tell others the good news of Jesus)

Reflection   Use the following questions and activities to review the gospel reading further.

Younger Students

1. Distribute to the students paper and crayons. Direct them to draw a picture of Thomas examining Jesus' wounds, his hands and his side.
2. What would you do if Jesus suddenly appeared to you and breathed on you, giving you the Holy Spirit?
3. Jesus sends us out in faith to share the good news with others and to tell them of God's forgiveness. What could you do to share the good news and forgiveness with others?

Older Students

Allow time for the students to respond in their journals to the last question.

1. "As the Father has sent me, so I send you." What does this mean for you personally?

2. Would you allow Jesus to breathe on you so that you could receive the Holy Spirit? Why or why not?

3. Jesus said to Thomas, "You became a believer because you saw me. Blest are they who have not seen and have believed." Do you consider yourself a Thomas or one who believes without seeing? Why?

Closing Prayer

Gather the students together in a circle, and reread John 20:19–23. Conclude by inviting the students to hug each other as a sign of peace.

Making God's Word Our Own

This week, at the top of a piece of paper, write "I believe in Jesus because . . ." Every day, ask one new person this question, and write down his or her response. Ask yourself this same question once every day, and write down your answer. Bring your written responses to the next session.

If you are choosing a student for next Sunday's opening prayer, do so now.

Third Sunday *of* Easter

Readings

Acts 5:27–32, 40b–41
Revelation 5:11–14
John 21:1–19

Theme

Jesus feeds us so that we can feed and serve others.

Scripture *Background*

The trial of the disciples described in Acts 5 was their second trial before the Sanhedrin (the highest court of justice in Jerusalem). The disciples had been interrogated and warned never to speak in Jesus' name again. They were arrested for disobeying this order and jailed. They were delivered from jail by an angel of the Lord, and they then returned to the temple to teach in Jesus' name. Again, they were brought in for interrogation.

The angry members of the Sanhedrin wanted to kill the disciples. A wise Pharisee named Gamaliel warned them that if they fought the disciples they might be fighting against God. Even so, the Sanhedrin ordered the disciples to be whipped. They repeated the order not to speak of Jesus. But the disciples immediately went out and continued their witness to the good news of Jesus.

The gospel is another story of an appearance of the risen Jesus. After the resurrection, the disciples returned to their homes in Galilee and to their former occupation of fishing. They appeared to be without direction. Even their fishing was unsuccessful. Suddenly everything was changed by the presence of Jesus. He told them where to catch the fish. The disciples were transformed by this appearance. John, the beloved disciple, recognized the presence of the Lord. Peter, the leader of the disciples, plunged into the sea to come to the Lord. The others landed the sizable catch. All the disciples shared a meal with the Lord.

We find the transforming presence of Jesus in the ordinary aspects of the apostles' daily life—in their work and in their sharing a meal. Three times Jesus asked Peter a simple but essential question: "Do you love me?" Three times Peter answered, "Yes." Three times Jesus gave Peter the commission to take care of his flock. Finally, Jesus warned Peter of the cost of discipleship. But the cost no longer seemed to matter. The presence of the Risen Christ had transformed the disciples.

The vision from Revelation presents the heavenly witness to the Risen Christ. The hymn of praise begins with the voices of angels, all living creatures, and the elders. The response comes from every creature in heaven and on earth, everything in the universe. The good news of the resurrection brings all creation together to praise the living God.

Irene Nowell OSB

PART I: Gathering *for God's Word*

> Wear an apron and a white chef's hat. Invite the students to guess why you are dressed this way. They will not be able to guess. Tell them they will have to wait until they hear the gospel to figure it out.

Opening Prayer

Alternative: *Ask one of the students to lead the opening prayer.*

Open the session by saying: **Welcome, and happy Easter to all of you. Yes, we are still celebrating the greatness of the resurrection of Jesus. In the faith of the resurrection of Jesus and in the hope of our own resurrection, I invite the Church to stand for our opening prayer. We begin** (make the sign of the cross) **in the name of the Father, and of the Son, and of the Holy Spirit.**

> *Jesus, our risen Lord, fill our hearts with faith to realize that you were raised from the dead so that we may live eternally in freedom with you. May the food of life that you give us strengthen us to feed others. We ask all this in your name.*

The students respond: **Amen!**

Song

"City of God" by Dan Schutte from *Glory & Praise* (OCP NALR), *Gather (Comprehensive)* (GIA), *Today's Missal* (OCP), *Journeysongs* (OCP).

"Do You Really Love Me" by Carey Landry from *Hi God!* (OCP [NALR]).

"I Am the Living Bread" by David Haas from *Today's Missal* (OCP), *Journeysongs* (OCP), *Glory & Praise 2* (OCP [NALR]).

"The Bread That Gives Life" by David Haas from *Walking by Faith* (Harcourt Religion Publishers, GIA).

Announcements

- parish news
- birthdays
- other

PART II: Remembering *God's Word*

Review last week's session.

1. What happened in last Sunday's gospel reading?

   - Jesus appeared again to his disciples. Jesus breathed on his disciples and gave them the Holy Spirit. Thomas put his hand in Jesus' wounds (in Jesus' hands and side).

2. What was the first thing Jesus said to his disciples when he appeared? (Hint: He said it to them three times.)

   - Peace be with you.

3. What responses did you receive to the statement "I believe in Jesus because . . ."? How did you respond?

   - Allow ample time for the students to share their lists with the class.

PART III: Understanding *God's Word*

Scripture

Materials Needed

All Students
- Bible
- three volunteers
- small dinner rolls (one per student)
- apron
- white chef's hat

Younger Students
- paper
- crayons

Older Students
- journals
- pens

Choose three student volunteers prior to the session. Ask them to be thinking about responses to these two questions: If Jesus asked you if you love him, what would you say? If Jesus asked you to feed his people, how would you do it?

Ask the following questions before you proclaim the gospel.

- When your parents repeatedly ask you to do something, three or four times, what does that usually mean?
- If someone repeatedly asks you to do something, how important do you think it is to him or her?

Say: **Listen carefully to what Jesus does in the gospel. Not only does Jesus feed his disciples, he cooks for them, too. See if you can figure out the connection between the gospel reading and our Sunday liturgy.**

Proclaim the gospel reverently, with feeling and excitement. Then discuss the following question.

- What does Jesus' feeding his disciples have to do with our Sunday liturgy? (*Jesus feeds his friends just like he feeds us in the Eucharist—to give them and us strength and energy to go out and feed others.*)

Invite the three student volunteers to come forward. Reread John 21:15–17. Then go to each of the volunteers and say:

> *[Student's name], do you love me? (The student should respond loudly.)*
>
> *[Student's name], go feed my sheep.*

- If Jesus asked you to "feed" his people, how would you go about it? (If time allows, open this question up to all.)

Reflection

Use the following questions and activities to help the students process the reading further.

Younger Students

1. Distribute to the students paper and crayons. Direct them to draw a picture of Jesus cooking fish for his disciples. Encourage the students to include themselves in the picture.
2. How could you help Jesus feed his sheep?
3. Who are Jesus' sheep?

Older Students

Allow ample class time for the students to respond in their journals to the last question.

1. "Feed my lambs. . . . Take care of my sheep . . . feed my sheep." What is Jesus really saying to Peter? What is Jesus saying to us?
2. Who are Jesus' lambs and sheep?
3. How many times would Jesus ask you if you love him? Why?

Closing Prayer

Gather the students together, and have them sit in a circle. Give them a few moments to reflect quietly on the fact that Jesus continues to feed us. In the Holy Eucharist, Jesus offers himself to us, feeds us, and strengthens us so that we may strengthen others. After a few moments of silent reflection, give each student a dinner roll. Invite them to share the rolls with their families when they get home. Hold hands as you conclude the session with the Lord's Prayer.

Making God's Word Our Own

This week tell Jesus that you love him. Look for ways to feed his people with the food of kindness, forgiveness, generosity, respect, and love. Jesus will show you what food needs to be shared (physical, emotional, spiritual), but you have to look for those who are hungry.

If you are choosing a student for next Sunday's opening prayer, do so now.

Fourth Sunday *of* Easter

Readings

Acts 13:14, 43–52
Revelation 7:9, 14b–17
John 10:27–30

Theme

Jesus knows us and calls us.

Scripture *Background*

The passage from the Acts of the Apostles describes the first missionary outreach of the early Church. Paul and Barnabas had been set apart by the Holy Spirit. Together they went forth to spread the good news. They began their preaching in the synagogue, preaching to the Jews. Initially the message was received with interest. The two missionaries were asked to return, and many Jews began to follow the new way. The following week, however, some of the Jews created dissension, and Paul and Barnabas were expelled from the town. Paul and Barnabas then decided to take the message to the Gentiles (non-Jews).

A major theme of Luke, both in his Gospel and in Acts, is universal salvation. Luke's audience was comprised mainly of Gentiles, and he emphasized the fact that the good news was for Gentiles as well as Jews. Conversely, Jews were not excluded. Faithful Jews also become devout believers in Christ. The missionaries began their preaching with the Jews and then moved to Gentiles.

The passage from Revelation was part of a grand vision in which all of God's faithful were gathered. First the multitudes from the tribes of Israel are described. Then comes the great crowd (described in today's reading) from every nation and race. There were no restrictions to join this immense group. The only requirement was fidelity to Christ. The crowd was dressed in white and redeemed and made holy through the blood of Christ. They became united with him in his death and were sustained in life by him.

The gospel is Jesus' description of himself as the Good Shepherd. The sheep hear his voice and follow him. They live because they do this.

Paradoxically, Christ the Shepherd is also Christ the Lamb. In the exodus event, the firstborn of Israel were shielded from the destroyer by the blood of the lamb on the doorpost. The servant of the Lord, described in Isaiah, went to death like a lamb to slaughter. We are saved from sin and death by the blood of the Lamb, Jesus. According to the Gospel of John, Jesus died at the time the Passover lambs were being slaughtered.

Irene Nowell OSB

PART I: Gathering for God's Word

Opening Prayer

Alternative: *Ask one of the students to lead the opening prayer.*

Open the session by saying: **Happy Easter. I am glad you are here today! Does anyone know what the very first image or picture of Jesus for the early Church was?** (Invite the students to respond.) **Most people don't know this; the very first image the early Church had of Jesus was that of the Good Shepherd. Today we are going to examine why the early Church knew that this image was important. Before we begin, I invite the Church to stand for our opening prayer. We begin** (make the sign of the cross) **in the name of the Father, and of the Son, and of the Holy Spirit.**

Good Shepherd, thank you for knowing us and calling out to us. May we all recognize your voice and come to you when you call. It is you who protects us, feeds us, and watches out for us. May we trust you in everything and have the wisdom to allow you to hold us when we are scared or hurt, love us when we feel unloved, and forgive us when we wander away from you. Thank you for being our Good Shepherd and friend. We ask all this in your name.

The students respond enthusiastically: **Amen!**

Song

"Are Not Our Hearts" by Carey Landry from *Hi God!* (OCP [NALR]), *Young People's Glory & Praise* (OCP [NALR]).

"Here I Am, Lord," by Dan Schutte from *Glory & Praise* (OCP [NALR]), *Gather (Comprehensive)* (GIA), *Today's Missal* (OCP), *Lead Me, Guide Me* (GIA), *Journeysongs* (OCP).

"Like a Shepherd" by Bob Dufford from *Glory & Praise* (OCP [NALR]), *Today's Missal* (OCP), *Gather (Comprehensive)* (GIA), *Journeysongs* (OCP).

"Shepherd Me, O God" by Marty Haugen from *Gather (Comprehensive)* (GIA), *Today's Missal* (OCP), *Celebrating Our Faith* (Harcourt Religion Publishers, GIA).

Announcements

- parish news
- birthdays
- other

PART II: Remembering *God's Word*

Review last week's session using the following questions.

1. What did you learn about Jesus from last Sunday's gospel passage?

   • Let the students respond openly and honestly.

2. Name the two items Jesus served his disciples.

   • fish and bread

3. How many times did Jesus ask Peter if he loved him and to feed his sheep?

   • three

4. Who do you think are the sheep and lambs Jesus refers to in the gospel reading?

   • All people of every nation and nationality.

5. Last week you were invited to go out and look for ways to feed Jesus' people with the food of kindness, forgiveness, generosity, respect, and love. Whom did you feed? What did you experience?

   • Let the students respond openly and honestly.

PART III: Understanding *God's Word*

Scripture

> **Materials Needed**
>
> **All Students**
> • Bible
> • dry-erase board or chalkboard
> • dry-erase markers or chalk
> • tape player
> • cassette tape with pre-recorded messages
>
> **Younger Students**
> • paper
> • crayons
>
> **Older Students**
> • journals
> • pens

Prior to the session, create an audiotape of the following scenarios (no longer than thirty or forty seconds):

• Mother telling a child to clean her or his room.

• DRE explaining something briefly about class.

• Catechist briefly explaining a lesson.

• Pastor or associate saying something briefly about faith.

• Yourself giving a brief message.

Play the recording you created, and ask the students if they recognize the people speaking. If they name the right people, ask them how were they able to recognize each individual. (They will say they recognized the voice.)

Proclaim John 10:27–30. Just as we are able to recognize human voices, we can also recognize God's voice. How can we learn to listen and recognize Jesus' voice? (Write the students' responses on the dry-erase board or chalkboard.)

Use the following questions and activities to help the students process the gospel reading further.

Reflection

Younger Students

1. Distribute to the students paper and crayons. Direct them to draw a picture of Jesus as the Good Shepherd with his sheep around him. Encourage the students to include themselves among the sheep.

2. What does it mean that Jesus knows his sheep?

3. Jesus said, "My sheep hear my voice. I know them, and they follow me." Where do you think Jesus will lead you?

Older Students

Allow ample time for the students to respond in their journals to the last question.

1. We are invited to follow Jesus. What is the way of Jesus? Where does he lead us?

2. Jesus says that the sheep who follow him will never perish nor be snatched out of his hand. What do you think would or could happen if one of his sheep stops listening or decides not to follow the Good Shepherd?

3. Jesus is very clear: "My sheep hear my voice. I know them, and they follow me." How do you feel knowing that Jesus knows us (the good, the bad, and the ugly—our strengths and weaknesses) and still loves us and offers us his friendship?

Closing Prayer

Gather the students in a circle. Reflectively read Psalm 23, followed by a few moments of silence. Then read John 10:27–28, and follow with a moment of silence. Hold hands as you conclude the session with the Lord's Prayer.

Making God's Word Our Own

If you are choosing a student for next Sunday's opening prayer, do so now.

This week's prayer challenge could change your life. Spend the week listening. Turn off the TV and radio, the computer and video games, and other distractions. Spend fifteen minutes each day listening to the Good Shepherd's voice. You could go for a walk, visit a church, read the Bible, or just sit in silence and ask the Good Shepherd to speak to you. It's easy but difficult. Give it a try! You just might learn something about the Good Shepherd and about yourself.

Fifth Sunday
of Easter

Readings

Acts 14:21–27
Revelation 21:1–5a
John 13:31–33a, 34–35

Theme

Jesus commands us to love one another!

Scripture *Background*

The reading from Acts describes the return of Paul and Barnabas to Antioch to report on the success of their missionary efforts. As they return to Antioch, they revisit the little churches that began as a result of their preaching. They help these new Christians organize their small communities. They encourage them to persevere in spite of the suffering that their new faith might bring them.

The gospel passage presents the heart of Jesus' message: "Love one another as I have loved you." The center of Jesus' life was his love for the disciples. Their love for one another would be the primary sign of their identity. This passage comes at a critical point in the Gospel. Jesus had just washed the disciples' feet and told them that they must do for one another what he had done. Immediately surrounding this passage were two descriptions of weak disciples. Before the passage, Judas left to betray Jesus; after the passage, Jesus told Peter that he would disown Jesus. The whole section moves steadily toward Jesus' death. In this context, Jesus told his followers: "As my love has been for you, so must your love be for each other. Even for the weak and faithless, you must be ready to die. This is how all will know you are my disciples: your love for one another, even to death."

The vision from Revelation is a description of God's final victory over evil and the establishment of the kingdom in its fullness. A new creation emerges where there is no sea, no dwelling place for evil. Jerusalem, the city of God and God's people, comes from heaven and is made new by God. The covenant between God and the people is a marriage; the new Jerusalem is the bride coming to meet her husband. A voice announces the marriage vow: God will be their God, and they will be God's people. God will remain forever with this people. Therefore, there will be only life. All the signs of death—crying out, pain, tears, sorrow—will disappear along with the sea, full of evil. The new community is represented by love for God and for one another. God on his throne announces the good news: "I make all things new."

Irene Nowell OSB

PART I: Gathering *for God's Word*

Opening Prayer **Alternative:** *Ask one of the students to lead the opening prayer.*

Open the session by saying: **Welcome, and happy Easter! That's right, we are still celebrating the mystery of Jesus' resurrection. I invite the Church to stand for our opening prayer. As we step into the light of Jesus' resurrection, we begin** (make the sign of the cross) **in the name of the Father, and of the Son, and of the Holy Spirit.**

> *Jesus, today we are going to hear of a new commandment that you want us to follow. This new commandment of yours will be costly and dangerous for us. You showed us how God will lift us up if we trust in your new commandment and follow it to the end. With the power of your Holy Spirit, we can do it! Bless these students and their families; open their hearts and minds to the love and strength you offer all of us. We ask all this in your name.*

The students respond: **Amen!**

Song "Do You Really Love Me?" by Carey Landry from *Hi God!* (OCP [NALR]).

"I Am the Resurrection" by Jim Anderson from *Today's Missal* (OCP), *Journeysongs* (OCP).

"Living and Loving and Learning" by Carey Landry from *Hi God! 3* (OCP [NALR]), *Young People's Glory & Praise* (OCP [NALR]).

"Love Can Do" by Amy Grant from *The Collection* (Word Music).

"Love that Is Kept Inside" by Carey Landry from *Hi God!* (OCP [NALR]), *Young People's Glory & Praise* (OCP [NALR]).

"They'll Know We Are Christians by Our Love" by Peter Scholtes from *Today's Missal* (OCP).

Announcements
- parish news
- birthdays
- other

PART II: Remembering *God's Word*

Review last week's session.

1. What was the first historical image or picture of Jesus?
- Jesus the Good Shepherd

2. What did you learn about Jesus or yourself from last Sunday's gospel reading?
- Let the students respond openly and honestly.

3. What will happen to all who hear the Good Shepherd's voice and follow him?
- The Good Shepherd will give them eternal life. They shall never perish.

4. Was it hard to listen to the Good Shepherd last week? What did he tell you?
- Let the students respond openly and honestly.

PART III: Understanding *God's Word*

Have the students write a last will and testament, either individually or in groups of three. Use the following scenario: You just found out that you have only one day to live. Write the three most important things you want to tell your family and friends. After you have written the three things you want to tell your family and friends, pick the one that is the most important to you, the one that you really want them to know and remember.

Give the students four to five minutes to reflect silently on the most important messages they want to leave with others. Then allow ample time for them to write and prioritize their messages. Choose three or four volunteers to share their most important message with the class.

Explain to the students that Jesus shared a message with the community of believers just hours before he died. Say: **Do you think what you will hear in this passage was important to Jesus? Yes, I think Jesus believed this message was very important and needed to be shared with the community. Let's listen to what Jesus asks of us.**

Proclaim John 13:31–33a, 34–35. Ask: **What is Jesus' new commandment for us?**

Reflection

Discuss the lesson further using the following questions.

Younger Students

1. Jesus loves us very much. How can we show Jesus that we love him?

2. Jesus has given us a new commandment, to love one another as he loves us. How does Jesus show his love for us? Name five ways you can share Jesus' love with your family, friends, and other students.

3. What stops us from following Jesus' commandment to love others? What can we do about it?

Older Students

1. What does "love in action" look like? What does it really mean?

2. Why is this one commandment so costly and dangerous to all who are willing to abide by it?

3. What does the Holy Spirit have to do with Jesus' commandment to love others? Does the Spirit have any connection at all to following this commandment?

Closing Prayer

If you are choosing a student for next Sunday's opening prayer, do so now.

Gather the students together, and form a circle. Tell the students that a good way to start loving others is to pray for others and their needs. Invite the students to offer prayers for those they need to love more. Those who don't feel comfortable praying in front of others can offer prayers of love silently in their hearts. Jesus will know and hear both prayers. Conclude the session by singing together a favorite hymn.

Making God's Word Our Own

This week's prayer challenge has two steps. We can truly love others only because Jesus first loved us. So this week, spend fifteen minutes alone with Jesus, and let him love you. Let him love all of you, from your head to your toes—especially your heart. Then, during the day, share the love you received from Jesus with others. Try it, and feel the power of love!

Sixth Sunday *of* Easter

Readings

Acts 15:1–2, 22–29
Revelation 21:10–14,
 22–23
John 14:23–29

Theme

*The Holy Spirit
instructs us in
everything we do.*

Scripture *Background*

As Gentiles began to join the Christian community, a controversy arose regarding requirements of the Jewish law. Some Christians were convinced that converts to Christianity must keep the prescriptions of the Jewish law. Others were equally convinced that Baptism, faith in Jesus, and good works were sufficient. Each of these groups was represented by major leaders in the early Church. Dissension and harsh judgment of one another threatened to split the new community.

In Paul's Letters and in the Acts of the Apostles, there are varying descriptions of the controversy and solutions. The solution described in Acts 15 imposed four regulations on Gentile believers. Three regulations dealing with food would allow all Christians to eat together. The fourth regulation applies to sexual morality. Some Gentile practices were forbidden by Jewish law and were also not appropriate for believing Christians. The early Church worked to solve these and other controversies through the peace and wisdom of God in the Spirit.

The gospel passage is Jesus' promise of the presence of God with the disciples. Both Jesus and the Father will dwell forever with those who love him and are true to him. This presence of God in the believer and in the community of believers bears much fruit. First, the presence of God is the source of peace in the individual and in the community. Second, the presence of God is their source of wisdom. Jesus' word comes from God.

The reading from Revelation continues to describe a vision of the new Jerusalem. The city was surrounded by twelves, the number for the fullness of Israel (twelve tribes) and the number for the fullness of the Church (twelve apostles). The city had no temple. The temple functioned originally as the sign of the presence of God. Such a sign was now no longer necessary. God the Father and the Lamb were present in the midst of the city. Jesus and the Father dwell in the midst of the community. The presence of God is its peace, its wisdom, its light, and its life.

Irene Nowell OSB

PART I: Gathering *for God's Word*

Opening Prayer

Alternative: *Have one of the students lead the opening prayer.*

Open the session by saying: **Welcome. May the Spirit of our Risen Lord fill our hearts with wisdom, laughter, and love. Happy Easter to you and your families. That's right, we are still celebrating Easter. Today we are going to examine the gift of the Holy Spirit—offered to us because Jesus rose from the dead. I invite the Church to please stand. We begin, as always, by remembering that we are sons and daughters of God** (make the sign of the cross), **in the name of the Father, and of the Son, and of the Holy Spirit.**

Lord Jesus, thank you for giving us the Counselor, the Holy Spirit, to lead and guide us. May we accept your gift of the Holy Spirit with open arms and an open heart. Grant that your Spirit will show these students and their teachers and catechists the true peace that only you can give, and may they share that peace with their families, friends, and everyone they meet. We ask all this in your name.

The students respond enthusiastically: **Amen!**

Song

"Great Things Happen When God Mixes with Us" by Carey Landry from *Glory & Praise* (OCP [NALR]), *Today's Missal* (OCP).

"Send Us Your Spirit" by David Haas from *Gather (Comprehensive)* (GIA), *Today's Missal* (OCP).

"Sing a New Song" by Dan Schutte from *Glory & Praise* (OCP [NALR]), *Today's Missal* (OCP).

Announcements

- parish news
- birthdays
- other

PART II: Remembering *God's Word*

Review last week's readings.

1. In last week's gospel reading, what commandment did Jesus give us?

- Love one another.

2. What does Jesus mean by "Love one another"?

- Let the students respond openly and honestly.

3. Why do you think this commandment is important to Jesus and important for us?

- It must be of great importance because Jesus gave us this commandment hours before he died. It is important for us because it is how we live this commandment that determines whether we are true followers of Jesus or not.

4. Who helps us live this commandment?

    • The Holy Spirit helps and shows us how to live Jesus' commandment of love.

5. What was it like to feel Jesus' love last week?

    • Let the students respond openly and honestly.

PART III: **Understanding** *God's Word*

Easter Quiz

1. On Easter Sunday, we heard in the Gospel of John that the stone was moved away from the tomb and the tomb was empty. Who was the first to see the empty tomb: Mary the mother of Jesus, Mary Magdalene, Simon Peter, the other disciple (the one Jesus loved), or Andrew and his brother?

2. On the Second Sunday of Easter, we heard in the Gospel of John that Jesus suddenly appeared to his disciples and did something really strange (but nice) for them. What did Jesus do for the disciples?

3. On the Third Sunday of Easter, we heard about Jesus appearing to his disciples after his resurrection. What did Jesus serve his disciples for breakfast, and what did he tell Peter (and us) to do?

4. On the Fourth Sunday of Easter, what did Jesus say about his sheep?

5. On the Fifth Sunday of Easter, Jesus said that all will know that we are his disciples if we do what?

Answers

1. Mary Magdalene

2. Jesus breathed on them, giving them the Holy Spirit so they could love and bring God's forgiveness to others.

3. Jesus prepared a breakfast of cooked fish and bread. He asked Peter and us to feed and care for his sheep (the Church) and to follow him.

4. Jesus' sheep will hear his voice. He will know them and they will follow him. He will give them eternal life.

5. Love one another.

Scripture

Goal: To show that the Holy Spirit helps us in all areas of our lives. The Holy Spirit helps us know Jesus better and actually opens our hearts and minds to the power of God that is all around us. All we have to do is be open to this gift in our everyday lives.

Arrange five chairs at the front of the classroom. Ask five volunteers to sit in the chairs. Explain that you will be giving them an oral quiz of five questions—one question from each Sunday of the Easter Season. Stress that there will be no talking and no cheating during the quiz.

After reading the first question, one student (who has been told beforehand) should immediately say a prayer aloud, asking for help. After the prayer, have an adult volunteer (wearing a sign that says Holy Spirit) come in and whisper the answer to the question in the ear of the student who asked for help. (Watch the other students go crazy saying that the student cheated!) Don't say anything. Watch to see if the other students will pray or ask for help from the Holy Spirit. If so, the "Holy Spirit" should whisper the answers to them as well.

Before you explain what just happened, proclaim John 14:23–29. Be sure to explain that the word *paraclete* is a Greek word that means "counselor."

After hearing the gospel, the remaining students should explain in their own words what happened with the quiz and the role of the Holy Spirit. You may have to reread verses 25–26: "I have said these things to you while I am still with you. But the Advocate, the Holy Spirit, whom the Father will send in my name, will teach you everything, and remind you of all that I have said to you."

If there is time, briefly discuss the answers to the quiz.

Reflection   Discuss the gospel reading further using the following questions and activities.

Younger Students

1. Jesus gives the Holy Spirit to all people so they might come to know that he is the Savior of the world and believe in him. How can the Holy Spirit help you get to know Jesus better?

2. Jesus said that the Holy Spirit will instruct us in everything. What would you like the Holy Spirit to teach you?

3. Distribute to the students paper and crayons. Direct them to write or draw a thank-you letter to Jesus for giving us the gift of the Holy Spirit. Collect the letters and pictures, and give them to the DRE or pastor.

Older Students

1. What does John 14:23–24 mean to you?

2. In what areas of life do people your age need the counsel of the Holy Spirit?

3. Jesus said he would send the Holy Spirit to teach and remind us of what we need to do. What do we need to do? Why?

Closing Prayer

Gather the students in a circle. Light a candle, and play reflective music. Place the candle in the middle of the circle as a symbol of the Holy Spirit. Invite the students to think about where they need the guidance of the Holy Spirit. After a few moments, hold hands and pray together the Prayer to the Holy Spirit.

Come, Holy Spirit, fill the hearts of your faithful,
And kindle in them the fire of your love.
Send forth your Spirit and they shall be created.
And you will renew the face of the earth.

Lord, by the light of the Holy Spirit
you have taught the hearts of your faithful.
In the same Spirit
help us relish what is right
and always rejoice in your consolation.

We ask this through Christ our Lord.
Amen.

Making God's Word Our Own

If you are choosing a student for next Sunday's opening prayer, do so now.

This week spend fifteen minutes each day with Jesus in quiet prayer. Ask Jesus to fill you with the gift of Holy Spirit. It's that easy; all we have to do is ask, and Jesus will take care of the rest.

Ascension *and the* Seventh Sunday *of* Easter

Theme

Jesus gives us spiritual gifts.

Scripture *Background*

The first reading for the Seventh Sunday of Easter describes the death of the first martyr. The Greek word for *testimony* is the word from which we get the English word *martyr.* A martyr is the ultimate witness; martyrdom is the ultimate testimony. Stephen, filled with the Holy Spirit, had preached too well. His words had stung and angered his listeners. The description of his death parallels and contrasts Luke's description of the trial and death of Jesus. Stephen saw the vision of the Son of Man as Jesus had announced at his trial; Stephen saw Jesus. Jesus commended his spirit to the Father; Stephen commended his spirit to Jesus. Jesus asked the Father to forgive his executioners; Stephen asked Jesus to forgive his executioners. Jesus announces that his testimony is true. Jesus' witness was sealed by his death and resurrection. Stephen gave witness to Jesus and the gift of resurrection.

The reading from Revelation mirrors the vision from the beginning of the book. Again, Jesus says, "I am the Alpha and the Omega, the First and the Last, the Beginning and the End." Those who wash their robes in the blood of the Lamb reappear. They have free access to the tree of life. Jesus now holds the keys of death. Death cannot conquer life. They have free access to the glorious city that is the bride of God.

The gospel passage is Jesus' prayer for his followers, to whom he bore witness. He had asked them to love as he loved, even to death. He had promised them the presence of God, the Spirit who gives wisdom and peace. Now he prayed that they may be one in love, in the presence of God. He prayed that they might share his glory. He had revealed God to them; now they must bear witness to the world, even to the point of martyrdom.

In the final paragraphs of the Book of Revelation, everyone cries out, "Come!" The Spirit, who is the presence of God and source of peace and wisdom, cries "Come!" The Bride, who is the city of God, the covenant partner of God, and the community of believers, cries "Come!" All who hear answer "Come!" The author of the book cries "Come!" And the One who gives witness at the price of his blood answers "Yes, I am coming soon! Come!"

Irene Nowell OSB

PART I: Gathering *for God's Word*

Opening Prayer

Alternative: *Ask one of the students to lead the opening prayer.*

Open the session by saying: **Welcome, and happy Easter to all of you. You may be asking yourselves "Will Easter ever end?" The answer is NO. Easter is a way of life. It never ends for those who believe that Jesus rose from the dead. However, the Easter liturgical season does end. Who knows when the liturgical Easter Season ends?** (Fifty days after Easter, Pentecost) **I invite the Church to stand for our opening prayer. We begin by remembering who we are in Christ. We are God's sons and daughters because we have been baptized** (make the sign of the cross) **in the name of the Father, and of the Son, and of the Holy Spirit.**

Jesus, before you freely gave your life, you prayed for us. Now that you have been raised from the dead, live with us in our hearts. May the prayer you prayed for us come to pass for each person here today and for their families. Thank you for all the good things you have given to us—life, faith, our relationship with you, our families and friends. We ask all this in your name.

The students respond enthusiastically: **Amen!**

Song

"Abba, Father" by Carey Landry from *Glory & Praise* (OCP [NALR]), *Young People's Glory & Praise* (OCP [NALR]), *Today's Missal* (OCP).

"Glory and Praise to Our God" by Dan Schutte from *Glory & Praise* (OCP [NALR]), *Today's Missal* (OCP).

"Oh, How I Love Jesus" by Carey Landry from *Hi God!* (OCP [NALR]).

"Send Us Your Spirit" by David Haas from *Gather (Comprehensive)* (GIA), *Today's Missal* (OCP).

"Sing a New Song" by Dan Schutte from *Glory & Praise* (OCP [NALR]), *Today's Missal* (OCP), *Journeysongs* (OCP).

Announcements

- parish news
- birthdays
- other

PART II: Remembering *God's Word*

Review last week's session.

1. What is the meaning of the Greek word *paraclete*?
   - It is translated as "counselor" and refers to the Holy Spirit as our guide and counsel.

2. What did you learn from last week's gospel?
   - Let the students respond openly and honestly. If needed, reminded them of the focus of last week's gospel: The Holy Spirit will help us if we ask and are willing to listen.

3. Last week, Jesus said two things will happen to those who love him and keep his commandments of love. What are these two things?

   • The Father will love them. The Father and Jesus will come to his followers and dwell with them always.

4. What happened last week when you asked Jesus to fill you with the gift of the Holy Spirit?

   • Let the students respond openly and honestly.

PART III: Understanding *God's Word*

Scripture

Proclaim John 17:20–26. After you proclaim the gospel to the students, ask them if they noticed anything strange and important in the passage. Distribute to each student a copy of John 17:20–26 and a set of three highlighters. Read the gospel a second time. Have them follow along with you and count and highlight the number of times Jesus uses the word *in* (eight times). Read the passage again and instruct them to highlight with a different color the word *love* or *loved* (five times). Read the passage a third time and direct the students to highlight with a different color the word *sent* (three times).

Ask: **What is Jesus asking for us in his prayer?**

Materials Needed

All Students
- Bible
- copy of John 17:20–26 (one per student)
- three different colored markers or highlighters (one set per student)

"I ask not only on behalf of these, but also on behalf of those who will believe in me through their word, that they may all be one. As you, Father, are in me and I am in you, may they also be in us, so that the world may believe that you have sent me. The glory that you have given me I have given them, so that they may be one, as we are one, I in them and you in me, that they may become completely one, so that the world may know that you have sent me and have loved them even as you have loved me. Father, I desire that those also, whom you have given me, may be with me where I am, to see my glory, which you have given me because you loved me before the foundation of the world.

"Righteous Father, the world does not know you, but I know you; and these know that you have sent me. I made your name known to them, and I will make it known, so that the love with which you have loved me may be in them, and I in them."

John 17:20–26

Reflection

Use the following questions to explore the reading further.

Younger Students

1. Who taught you the most about praying?

2. What was the first prayer you were taught?

3. Jesus prayed in John 17:20–26 that he would live in us. How does Jesus live in you? How do you know this?

Older Students

1. What's at the very heart of Jesus' prayer? What does Jesus want most?

2. Is there anything you have to do to allow Jesus to live in you?

3. Why do you think Jesus used the word *in* eight times in this one passage?

Closing Prayer

Gather the students in a circle. Invite them to pray spontaneously for others in their lives—as Jesus prayed for us. Hold hands as you conclude the session with the Lord's Prayer.

Making God's Word Our Own

If you are choosing a student for next Sunday's opening prayer, do so now.

This week read your highlighted copy of the gospel every day. Really think about the times Jesus uses the word *in* and what that means to you. Focus on the word *love* and how Jesus uses it. Decide what the word *sent* means to you. By the end of the week you will have a good understanding of what Jesus meant in his prayer.

Solemnity *of* Pentecost

Readings

Acts 2:1–11
1 Corinthians 12:3b–7,
 12–13
John 20:19–23

Theme

*God's breath—the Holy
Spirit—gives us true
life.*

Scripture *Background*

Today's celebration of Pentecost marks a season of new life. For the first disciples of Jesus, it marked the beginning of their life as a Church and the occasion of their empowerment to continue the mission of Jesus. For the people of Israel, Pentecost originally had been a festival celebrating the wheat harvest. Later it became associated with the covenant at Sinai and the exodus event. This event marked a new beginning in the history of God and his people. To remember this, Jews went to the temple in Jerusalem on this feast to offer sacrifices to God. That is why Jews from all parts of the world were gathered there in Jerusalem when the Spirit came upon the disciples (Acts 2:5).

Today's feast is more than a remembrance of beginnings that are sacred in our Judeo-Christian history. Today's feast reminds us that we have been gifted with God's Spirit. We are also reminded of the purpose for which we have been gifted. Today, Jesus gives us a mission: "**As** the Father has sent me, **so** I send you."

This theme of mission, of being sent, is found in each of today's readings. We read the story of the first Christian Pentecost from Acts 2. The disciples obeyed Jesus' instruction to wait for the coming of the Holy Spirit. In Luke's story, the group of disciples included the eleven disciples plus Matthias, Judas's successor (Acts 1:13, 26). Also present were the women who accompanied Jesus on his journey as he proclaimed the kingdom of God (Luke 8:1–3). Mary, Jesus' mother, and his brothers (a reference to extended family members; see Acts 1:14) were also part of the group.

The sign of the coming of God's Spirit was akin to a noise that sounded like wind. Another sign appeared like tongues as of fire (Acts 1:2–3). Fire was frequently associated with manifestations of God in the Old Testament. For example, God spoke to Moses from the midst of a burning bush.

In Acts, the sign of the coming of God's Spirit was akin to a "strong, driving wind." In Hebrew and Greek—the original languages of the Old and New Testament—the same root words are used for wind, breath, and spirit. God's gift of the Spirit was given for the benefit of others. Those Jews from other lands who gathered in Jerusalem that day heard the disciples preach about Jesus. Because each was able to hear the words in his or her own language, many believed and were baptized (Acts 2:41).

In today's gospel, we have the image of the Spirit as *breath* (John 20:19–23). Jesus "breathed" new life on the frightened disciples as he bestowed the gift of the Holy Spirit. The disciples were entrusted with the mission of forgiving sins. The disciples (literally, "followers" of Jesus) carried out this charge in various ways (see Matthew 5:23–24, Matthew 18:15–20, 1 John 5:16, James 5:16, 1 Corinthians 5:1–5, and 2 Corinthians 2:5–11). Clearly the followers of Jesus were gifted **for** and were sent to minister **to** others.

The purpose of gifts given to an individual or to the community was apparently sometimes misunderstood in Corinth. In his first letter to the community, Paul devoted three chapters to this subject (12–14). Paul made clear that God's gifts were given to serve and build the community: "To each individual the manifestation of the Spirit is given for some benefit."

Paul compared the Christian community to the human body. All the parts of the human body are needed for the body to function properly (see verses 14–26, verses not included in today's reading). So it is with the "parts" of the Christian community. All the gifts and ministries are needed if the "body" of the community is to live fully.

Furthermore, the community was called the *body of Christ*: "Now you are Christ's body, and individually parts of it" (1 Corinthians 12:27). A person becomes a member of this body in Baptism: "For in one Spirit we were all baptized into one body . . . and we were all given to drink of one spirit." Just as the breath of God animated the lifeless body of the first human creature (Genesis 2:7), so, too, the "breath" of God's Spirit gives life to the "body" of the Church.

It is the Spirit who initially leads the individual to faith. No one can acclaim Jesus as Lord except by the Holy Spirit (verse 3). Like the early Christians, we profess our belief in him as the source of our salvation. It is the power of the Spirit at work in our lives that enables us to do this.

The Easter Season, which concludes today, has been a time to focus on new life. We celebrated the new risen life of Christ. We renewed our baptismal commitment to die and rise with him. Today's feast reminds us that in this new life we are empowered by his Spirit. We are sent now, with different gifts and in many forms of service, as his body, his presence in our daily life.

Anne Marie Sweet OSB

PART I: Gathering *for God's Word*

Opening Prayer   **Alternative:** *Invite one of the students to lead the opening prayer.*

Open the session by saying: **Welcome. Happy Pentecost! Today, we celebrate the gift of all gifts—the gift of the Holy Spirit! The Holy Spirit makes us a Church, a people of God. And it is the gift of the Holy Spirit that gives us life in Jesus. I invite the Church to stand for our opening prayer. We begin by remembering who we are in Jesus** (make the sign of the cross), **in the name of the Father, and of the Son, and of the Holy Spirit.**

> *Jesus, it is through the gift and power of the Holy Spirit that we pray and hope in you. Thank you for generously pouring out upon those who accept your gift of the Spirit. Open our hearts and minds to receive your holy breath so we may truly live in you and you in us. May the Spirit shining within us light the world with our love. We ask this prayer and all the prayers in our hearts in Jesus' name.*

The students respond: **Amen!**

Song   "Holy Spirit" by Marianne Misetich from *Today's Missal* (OCP), *Journeysongs* (OCP).

"Send Us Your Spirit" by David Haas from *Gather (Comprehensive)* (GIA), *Today's Missal* (OCP).

"The Spirit Is A-Movin'" by Carey Landry from *Glory & Praise* (OCP [NALR]), *Young People's Glory & Praise* (OCP [NALR]), *Today's Missal* (OCP).

Announcements   • parish news
• birthdays
• other

PART II: Remembering *God's Word*

Review last week's session.

1. How many times did Jesus use the words *in, love* or *loved,* and *sent* last Sunday?

   • the word *in*—eight times; the word *love* or *loved*—five times; the word *sent*—three times

2. In last week's gospel, Jesus prayed for us. What was at the heart of Jesus' prayer?

   • The Father and Jesus live in us; Jesus and the Father love us. We are sent to live the good news of Jesus.

3. What did you learn last week about the meaning of the words *in, love,* and *sent*?

   • Let the students respond openly and honestly.

PART III: Understanding God's Word

Materials Needed

All Students
- Bible
- seven volunteers
- seven envelopes
- the seven gifts of the Holy Spirit and definitions written on seven index cards (one per card)
- handout listing the gifts of the Holy Spirit and the Prayer to the Holy Spirit (one per student)
- recording of or lyrics to the Taizé song "Veni, Sancte Spiritus" ("Come, Holy Spirit")

Younger Students
- crayons
- paper

Older Students
- journals
- pens

The Gifts of the Holy Spirit

Wisdom: ability to see things as they truly are in an open-minded manner

Understanding: having a heart that accepts, cares, listens, understands, and forgives

Right Judgment: ability to make good and wise decisions

Courage: strength to do what is right in spite of challenges

Knowledge: ability to comprehend important truths

Reverence: deep respect for God, others, and all creation

Wonder and Awe: sense of the greatness and majesty of God coupled with a deep realization of God's nearness

Prayer to the Holy Spirit

Come, Holy Spirit, fill the hearts of your faithful,
And kindle in them the fire of your love.
Send forth your Spirit and they shall be created.
And you will renew the face of the earth.

Lord, by the light of the Holy Spirit
you have taught the hearts of your faithful.
In the same Spirit
help us relish what is right
and always rejoice in your consolation.

We ask this through Christ our Lord.
Amen.

Scripture

Spiritual Charades

Prior to the session, write on seven index cards the seven gifts of the Holy Spirit and each gift's definition (one gift per card). Place each of the index cards in an envelope.

Invite seven volunteers to come forward. Proclaim John 20:19–23. As you proclaim "Jesus breathed on them," breathe on each volunteer as you hand him or her an envelope containing one index card with a gift of the Holy Spirit written on it.

After the gospel reading, tell the students to open the envelope without letting anyone see the spiritual gift they have been given. Have the volunteers pantomime their gifts. Give them a few moments to prepare. Encourage the other students to try to guess what gifts the volunteers are pantomiming.

Emphasize to the students that Jesus' gift to us is his Holy Breath, the Holy Spirit. The only way to understand the true power of these spiritual gifts is to use them to serve others—to give them away! Great things happen in us and around us when we use these gifts.

Reflection

Review the gospel reading further, using the following questions and activities.

Younger Students

1. Distribute to the students paper and crayons. Instruct them to draw a picture of Jesus breathing the Holy Spirit on his disciples. Encourage the students to include themselves in the picture.

2. What gifts of the Spirit do you like the best? How do you use that gift to help others?

3. How do you use the gifts of the Holy Spirit to help others?

Older Students

Allow ample time for the students to respond to the last question in their journals.

1. Which spiritual gifts do you have and which ones would you like to have? (Remind the students that they received the Holy Spirit and the gifts of the Holy Spirit at Baptism and, if they have celebrated it, Confirmation.)

2. Are there any gifts of the Holy Spirit you don't really want? Which one(s)? Why?

3. How can you use the gifts of the Holy Spirit to make needed changes in the world?

Closing Prayer

Gather the students together in a circle. Pass out a handout listing the seven gifts of the Holy Spirit and the Prayer to the Holy Spirit. Chant the Taizé song "Veni, Sancte Spiritus" ("Come, Holy Spirit"). While the students are chanting, invite them to open their hearts so Jesus may continue to pour fourth his Spirit on them.

After three or four minutes of meditative chant, invite the students to share any prayers they might have and pray for each other's needs.

Making God's Word Our Own

This week use a different gift of the Holy Spirit each day. Look for opportunities to use that gift each day. You will have used and lived all seven gifts of the Holy Spirit by the end of the week. Begin each day with the Prayer to the Holy Spirit that is found on your handout.

If you are choosing a student for next Sunday's opening prayer, do so now.

Trinity Sunday

Readings

Proverbs 8:22–31
Romans 5:1–5
John 16:12–15

Theme

God is love.

Scripture *Background*

The Old Testament personified Lady Wisdom and God's Spirit but never considered them distinct persons in God. The New Testament suggested the idea of Father, Son, and Spirit in some places but never clearly defined the idea. Therefore, the Scripture readings for the Solemnity of the Trinity do not speak directly of the Trinity. This concept can be understood through the later definition of three Persons in one God.

The reading from Proverbs was part of a hymn sung by Lady Wisdom. She was begotten and brought forth by God before all creation. She was present at creation as God's designer or engineer in the work of creation. The world was created through her.

The last four lines of the reading indicate Lady Wisdom's role as a link between humans and God. Two key words are *delight* and *playing*. Lady Wisdom is God's delight, and she delights in humans. Her play (lines 2 and 3) is surrounded by this delight (lines 1 and 4). She plays before God; she plays on the earth.

The description of Lady Wisdom became a model for the description of Christ. He serves (as did Lady Wisdom) as the bond between God and humans and as the one through whom God creates. Christ is the Wisdom of God.

The reading from the Letter to the Romans developed the idea of Christ as our mediator with God. Christ has reconciled us to God, and now we are at peace with God. This happened, not because of any efforts on our part, but because of the immense love of God. The Spirit of love that flows between Christ and God has been given to us. Therefore, our justification has happened through no merit of our own. We are strong because the Spirit of God lives in us.

The reading from the Gospel of John was part of Jesus' speech to the disciples the night before his death. Jesus promised to send the Spirit to the disciples to comfort and strengthen them after he had gone to the Father. Just as Jesus was the revealer of God, so the Spirit revealed God to the disciples.

Irene Nowell OSB

PART I: Gathering for God's Word

Opening Prayer

Alternative: *Ask one of the students to lead the opening prayer.*

Open the session by saying: **Welcome! Today we are blessed to have the opportunity to examine and embrace one of the most wonderful mysteries of our faith. We are baptized in it; we proclaim it; it is the blueprint for us. It is the Trinity. We have one God, but we experience God as Father, Son, and Holy Spirit. I invite the Church to stand for our opening prayer. Realizing that we were baptized into God, we begin** (make the sign of the cross) **in the name of the Father, and of the Son, and of the Holy Spirit.**

God the Father, protect us and show us your ways. Jesus, thank you for showing us the way to our Father. Holy Spirit, continue breathing life on all our students and their families, teachers, and friends. We ask all of our prayers in Jesus' name.

The students respond: **Amen!**

Song

"Abba, Father" by Carey Landry from *Glory & Praise* (OCP [NALR]), *Young People's Glory & Praise* (OCP [NALR]), *Today's Missal* (OCP).

"Send Out Your Spirit" by Tim Schoenbachler from *Today's Missal* (OCP), *Journeysongs* (OCP), *Glory & Praise 2* (OCP [NALR]).

"Send Us Your Spirit" by David Haas from *Gather (Comprehensive)* (GIA), *Today's Missal* (OCP).

"Sing of the Lord's Goodness" by Ernest Sands from *Today's Missal* (OCP), *Journeysongs* (OCP), *Glory & Praise 2* (OCP [NALR]).

Announcements

- parish news
- birthdays
- other

PART II: Remembering God's Word

Review last week's session.

1. What did we celebrate last week?

- the feast of Pentecost

2. What happened at the first Pentecost?

- The Holy Spirit was poured out on the followers of Jesus.

3. What are the seven gifts of the Holy Spirit?

- wisdom, understanding, right judgment, courage, knowledge, reverence, wonder and awe

4. How did you use the seven gifts of the Holy Spirit?

- Let the students respond honestly and openly.

PART III: Understanding *God's Word*

Scripture

The Mystery of Three

Remember the Trinity is a mystery and impossible to explain completely.
The goal of this activity is to demonstrate how one substance or object can
have three distinct parts.

Invite three volunteers to come forward to help answer a question. After they come forward, ask: **What is the Trinity?** After the students offer their insights, thank them for their input. Remind them that although there is much we do know in the world thanks to science and technology, our understanding of the one God in three Persons (the Trinity) is a mystery. The only way to truly understand the mystery is to embrace it and let God help us understand the richness of who God is. Invite the students to return to their seats.

Show an apple to the students, and then place it on a table in the front of the room. Ask the students how an apple can help us better understand the Trinity. Listen to their responses. Then take a knife and cut the apple in half, showing the students the three parts of one apple: the outer peel, the meat of the apple, and the apple core.

Draw a tree on the board, and ask the students to share what a tree has in common with the Trinity. The roots, the trunk and the branches, and the leaves are all different, but the three different parts together make up one tree. Invite the students to share other examples from nature that reflect the mystery of the Trinity.

Divide the large group into three small groups. Have the groups discuss ways we, as Christians, experience God as Father, God as Son, and God as Spirit. Allow ample time for sharing. Then ask the groups to share their examples, listing their responses on the chalkboard or dry-erase board. As a large group, examine all the examples and tie them together. Point out that the three groups in discussing the Trinity not only worked separately but also as one large group to better understand the Trinity. There were three aspects to the one discussion: individual reflection, small-group sharing, and large-group sharing. Conclude the activity by proclaiming Romans 5:1–5.

Materials Needed

All Students
- Bible
- three volunteers
- chalkboard or dry-erase board
- chalk or dry-erase markers
- apple
- knife

Younger Students
- paper
- crayons

Older Students
- journals
- pens

Reflection

Discuss the Trinity further using the following questions and activities.

Younger Students

1. Distribute to the students paper and crayons. Direct them to draw a symbol of the Trinity.
2. Do you know God more as the Father, Son, or Holy Spirit? Why?
3. What can you do to get closer to the other Persons of the Trinity?

Older Students

Allow ample time for the students to respond in their journals to the first question.

1. Do you pray more often to God the Father, God the Son, or God the Spirit? Why?
2. Why do we pray the Sign of the Cross?
3. What does it mean when we say "in the name of the Father, and of the Son, and of the Holy Spirit"?

Trinity Sunday **127**

Closing Prayer
Gather the students into a circle. Invite them to bless and sign each other in the name of the Father, and of the Son, and of the Holy Spirit. After everyone has been blessed, hold hands as you conclude the session with the Lord's Prayer.

Making God's Word Our Own
Each day this week ask God to help you understand the Trinity. Also arrange to meet with someone you admire to discuss the nature and richness of the Holy Trinity. Be prepared to discuss with the class at the next session what you discovered about the Trinity.

If you are choosing a student for next Sunday's opening prayer, do so now.

The Body and Blood of Christ

Theme

Jesus continues to offer himself to us and feed us in the Holy Eucharist.

Scripture *Background*

There are several implications for this Sunday. In addition to the physical body of Jesus, the *Body of Christ* connotes the presence of Christ in the Eucharistic bread and wine and the presence of Christ in the Christian community. This multilevel meaning is reflected in the readings.

The first reading describes Melchizedek, king and priest in what would later be called Jerusalem. Melchizedek met Abraham on his way home from a victory over a coalition of kings who had attacked Sodom and captured Abraham's nephew, Lot. Melchizedek blessed the victorious Abraham and offered him bread and wine. The bread and wine may have been simple refreshment or may have been a covenant ceremony. In the ancient Near East, to share food meant to share life. Those who ate together were responsible for each other's life. Thus Abraham and Melchizedek were bonded together. This foreshadowed the binding of Abraham's descendants to Jerusalem.

In the selection from 1 Corinthians, Paul is scolding the wealthy members of the community for having special dinners (before the Eucharistic meal) to which the poor were unable to come. The Corinthians misunderstood that their sharing in the Eucharistic meal made them one body with each other, the Body of Christ. At the center of his argument, Paul repeated the traditional story of the institution of the Eucharist. Paul reminded the Corinthians that Jesus was present whenever they told the story and shared the meal. This was the Body of Christ.

Today's gospel is Luke's version of the multiplication of the loaves and fishes. The telling of the story has been influenced by later liturgical practice. The crowd is assembled, not in the desert as in the other Gospels, but in the little town of Bethsaida. Luke's audience of city Christians recognized their own assembly that gathered to hear the word of the Lord and share the meal.

The words describing Jesus' actions reflect the telling of the Eucharistic story. The Greek word for the fragments, *klasma,* was a term used in the early Church for the Eucharistic bread.

Jesus does not feed the crowd but instructed the disciples to do so. This suggests the ministries in the Church of distributing the Eucharistic food and sharing meals with the hungry. The twelve baskets of leftover food indicate that God gives more than enough to nourish the Body of Christ.

Irene Nowell OSB

PART I: Gathering *for God's Word*

Opening Prayer

Alternative: *Ask one of the students to lead the opening prayer.*

Open the session by saying: **Welcome! God's peace be with all of you. Thank you for joining us. We are privileged to explore the wonders of God's love for us in the Eucharist! But before we embrace any of God's mysteries, we need to stop and ask God to open our minds and hearts. I invite the Church to stand for our opening prayer. We begin by remembering who we are** (make the sign of the cross) **in the name of the Father, and of the Son, and of the Holy Spirit.**

> *Jesus, you give yourself to us in the form of bread and wine. We thank you for these precious gifts of yourself; we ask that you open our hearts and minds so we might understand the depth of your love for us. You feed us so we have the strength to feed others. Bless these students and their families. Keep them strong and well nourished; cover them in your blanket of love. We ask all this in your name!*

The students respond enthusiastically: **Amen!**

Song

"I Am the Bread of Life" by Suzanne Toolan from *Glory & Praise* (OCP [NALR]), *Gather (Comprehensive)* (GIA), *Today's Missal* (OCP), *We Celebrate* (J.S. Paluch Co., Inc.), *Lead Me, Guide Me* (GIA), *Celebrating Our Faith* (Harcourt Religion Publishers, GIA).

"In the Breaking of the Bread" by Bob Hurd from *Today's Missal* (OCP).

"One Bread, One Body" by John Foley from *Today's Missal* (OCP), *Glory & Praise* (OCP [NALR]), *Gather (Comprehensive)* (GIA), *Lead Me, Guide Me* (GIA).

"The Bread That Gives Life" by David Haas from *Walking by Faith* (Harcourt Religion Publishers, GIA).

Announcements

• parish news
• birthdays
• other

PART II: Remembering *God's Word*

Review last week's session.

1. What feast did we celebrate last Sunday?

   • Trinity Sunday

2. What did you learn about the Holy Trinity?

   • Let the students respond openly and honestly.

3. How does an apple or a tree help us understand a little about the Trinity?

   • They are each one object, but they have three distinct parts.

4. What did you find out about the Trinity last week? To whom did you talk? How did Jesus help you understand the Trinity more fully?

   • Let the students respond openly and honestly.

PART III: Understanding *God's Word*

Scripture

Materials Needed

All Students—Option 1
- Bible
- VCR
- TV
- *Jesus of Nazareth* video, directed by Franco Zeffireli (Ventura, CA: Gospel Light Publications)
- bread
- fish-shaped crackers
- baskets or bowls

All Students—Option 2
- six volunteers to role-play Narrator 1, Narrator 2, Jesus, Peter, James, John
- seven copies of the role-play script (page 133)
- simple costumes (optional)
- bread
- fish-shaped crackers
- baskets or bowls

Younger Students
- paper
- crayons

Choose from two options.

Option One

Play for the students the "Feeding of the Five Thousand" scene from tape two of *Jesus of Nazareth* (0:55:00) by Franco Zeffireli. The scene, which runs about five minutes, is well done and a wonderful visual tool for the students. It will provoke many questions and a lively conversation.

Option Two

Invite six volunteers to come forward to perform in a short role-play. After assigning parts, allow ample time for the students to look over the script (page 133) and to get into costume. Place baskets of bread and fish crackers nearby on a table. Begin the role-play when the volunteers are ready and feel comfortable with their roles.

After the role-play, discuss the following questions.

- What had Jesus planned for the disciples when they came back from sharing the good news and healing others? What happened?
- How do you think the disciples felt about the crowd?
- What did Jesus do to show that he cared about the needs of the people?
- What message is Jesus telling us in this story?

Use the following questions and activities to help the students process the gospel further.

Younger Students

1. Distribute to the students paper and crayons. Direct them to draw a picture of Jesus feeding the five thousand people. Remind the students to include themselves in the picture.
2. Jesus shows his love and care for us by feeding us. How can you share Jesus' love and care with others in school? On the playground? At home?
3. How does Jesus feed us today?

Reflection

Older Students

1. What does this story in Luke 9:11–17 tell us about Jesus? About discipleship? About people?
2. How does Jesus continue to feed you today?
3. Jesus shares himself with us in the Word, in the Eucharist, and in the community. How do you share what you have received with others? Give examples.

Closing Prayer

Gather the students together. Play or sing one of the songs suggested for this session. Hold hands as the class concludes with the Lord's Prayer.

Making God's Word Our Own

This week bake some bread with your family. After you have cleaned up and the bread is baked, sit down with your family and share the bread together. As you eat, discuss how Jesus is the bread of life for us. This activity can be a lot of fun, yet challenging at the same time. This experience may change the way you see the world and yourself.

If you are choosing a student for next Sunday's opening prayer, do so now.

Role-Play Script—
Jesus Feeds Five Thousand

Narrator 1: Welcome. The title of this skit is "Jesus Feeds Five Thousand." This skit is based on the Gospel of Luke—chapter 9, verses 11 through 17. This is our cast of characters.

Introduce the students and the roles they are playing.

Narrator 2: Jesus had sent the disciples out to all the villages to preach the good news and heal people everywhere. When they came back, Jesus took them to an out-of-the-way place to rest.

Narrator 1: When the crowds heard about this, they followed Jesus and the disciples. Jesus welcomed them, spoke to them about the kingdom of God, and healed those who needed healing.

Narrator 2: When the sun had begun to set, the disciples approached Jesus with a concern.

Peter: Send the people away so that they can go to the villages and farms around here to find food and lodging. We are in the middle of nowhere!

Jesus: You give them something to eat.

James: All we can gather from the crowd is five loaves and two fish. Do you want us to go and buy food for the whole crowd?

Jesus: Make the people sit down in groups of about fifty.

The disciples ask the students to sit down. Jesus holds up the baskets of bread and fish.

Narrator 1: The disciples made them all sit down. Jesus took the five loaves and two fish. Looking up to heaven, he thanked God for the food, broke the loaves, and gave the food to the disciples.

Jesus: Go and feed the people.

The disciples distribute to the students the baskets of bread and fish. Allow a few minutes for the students to eat.

John: Lord, they have all eaten and had enough!

Jesus: Now pass through the crowd and gather anything that is left.

The disciples collect the baskets.

Narrator 2: The disciples took up twelve baskets of what the people had left over.

Twelfth Sunday
in Ordinary Time

Readings

Zechariah 12:10–11,
  13:1
Galatians 3:26–29
Luke 9:18–24

Theme

*The cross is a way of
life for Jesus' followers.*

Scripture *Background*

The first reading from Zechariah follows a section that describes the cataclysmic day of the Lord when the wicked would finally be destroyed and God's righteous ones would be victorious. The verses read for today promise that David's line and the city of Jerusalem would continue. The citizens of Jerusalem and the royal house would be filled with mercy and prayer. But they would also mourn deeply for someone who had been thrust through and apparently killed by them. The mourning would be as great as the mourning over Hadadrimmon in the plain of Megiddo.

Who was this person? Was it the Canaanite storm god? His worshipers mourned annually his dying and rejoiced over his rising. Was it King Josiah, killed by the Egyptian army at Megiddo in 609 B.C.? Is it Isaac, the only son, threatened with death? Was it the suffering servant described in Isaiah 52:13–53:12? Whoever it was, he was very dear.

During Jesus' time, there was a strong sense of anticipation for the messiah. John the Baptist had been martyred by Herod. Some expected him to return. Elijah, according to tradition, had not died but had been taken up in a fiery chariot. He was expected to return and bring the messiah. Jesus was identified with both of these and was also thought to be a prophet risen from the dead. In the gospel reading, Jesus asks Peter, "Who do people say that I am?"

Peter answered, "You are the Messiah." Jesus, however, would not accept that title without modifying the definition. People expected the messiah to come with royal power and majesty to defeat the enemies and establish the kingdom of David. Jesus clearly did not fit this image and did not intend to carry out this agenda. Jesus accepted the title of Messiah, but he interpreted it in terms of suffering. This idea contrasted with what was believed by the people. Then he added an even stronger statement: If the Messiah must suffer in order to come to glory, so, too, must his followers.

Paul's statement in his letter to the Galatians is a cry of liberation from discrimination. In Christ all are one, all are equal. Those considered superior are lowered to a level with everyone else. Those who are thought to be inferior are raised to the level of the others. All are one.

Irene Nowell OSB

PART I: Gathering *for God's Word*

Opening Prayer

Alternative: *Ask one of the students to lead the opening prayer.*

Open the session by saying: **Welcome. May God's peace be with you. We gather together in Jesus' name so we may gain strength and courage to embrace and carry our crosses. I invite the Church to stand for our opening prayer as we remember that we are baptized into the cross of Christ so we may share his life** (make the sign of the cross) **in the name of the Father, and of the Son, and of the Holy Spirit.**

> *Jesus, be with us today and every day of our lives. Give us the courage to embrace the crosses we are given and provide us with the strength to carry them. Help us remember that it is through the cross that we die to ourselves and are raised to new life with you. Sometimes it's not easy, Jesus, and we need your help. Give us the wisdom to call on your love to guide us. May your mercy heal us. Continue to bless these students and their families. We ask all this in your name.*

The students respond enthusiastically: **Amen!**

Song

"Gather Us In" by Marty Haugen from *Gather (Comprehensive)* (GIA), *Glory & Praise* (OCP [NALR]), *Today's Missal* (OCP), *We Celebrate* (J.S. Paluch Co., Inc.).

"Save Us, O Lord" by Bob Dufford from *Today's Missal* (OCP), *Journeysongs* (OCP), *Glory & Praise* (OCP [NALR]).

"You Are Near" by Dan Schutte from *Gather (Comprehensive)* (GIA), *Today's Missal* (OCP), *Glory & Praise* (OCP [NALR]), *Young People's Glory & Praise* (OCP [NALR]), *Journeysongs* (OCP).

Announcements

• parish news

• birthdays

• other

PART II: Remembering *God's Word*

Review last week's session.

1. What special feast did we celebrate last week?

• The feast of the Body and Blood of Christ

2. Jesus did three important things last Sunday to show us that God loves us and truly cares for us. He preached to the crowd about the reign of God, and he healed those who needed healing. What was the third?

• Jesus fed a crowd of five thousand by multiplying the loaves of bread and fish.

3. How many loaves and fish did Jesus start with to feed the five thousand? How much was left over?

   • Jesus started with five loaves of bread and two fish. There were twelve filled baskets left over.

4. You and your family were invited to bake some bread and think about Jesus being the Bread of Life. What did you experience? What thoughts did you have about the Bread of Life?

   • Let the students respond openly and honestly.

PART III: Understanding *God's Word*

Materials Needed

All Students
- Bible
- nine volunteers
- nine sheets of poster board with phrases written on each sheet (see box in text)
- reflective music
- tape or CD player
- candle
- cross
- matches

Younger Students
- paper
- crayons

Older Students
- journals
- pens

Poster Board Phrases

- "Whoever wishes to be my follower
- must deny his very self,
- take up his cross
- each day,
- and follow in my steps.
- Whoever would save his life
- will lose it,
- and whoever loses his life for my sake
- will save it."

Ask nine volunteers to come forward. Mix up the poster boards, and give one to each of the volunteers. Have them hold the poster boards so that all can see. Allow the volunteers three to five minutes to put them in the proper order. Then invite the rest of the students to help. The students really enjoy this activity. Involve as many students as possible. For example, have the younger students hold the poster boards and the older students put the boards in order.

Scripture

Once the poster boards are assembled in the order as shown in the box above, ask the students to explain the Scripture passage in their own words. Then proclaim Luke 9:18–24.

After the reading, invite volunteers to name some crosses that students their age may be asked to carry in their own lives. Discuss the crosses in terms of heavy, medium, and light.

Reflection

Use the following questions and activities to review the gospel reading.

Younger Students

1. Distribute to the students paper and crayons. Direct them to draw a picture of Jesus embracing or carrying the cross. Encourage the students to take their pictures home to share with their families.

2. Jesus asks us to follow him. What does that mean to you?

3. What cross is Jesus asking you to carry at this time in your life? How does Jesus help you carry it?

Older Students

Allow ample time for the students to respond in their journals to the second question.

1. What do the following statements mean to you: Deny your self; take up your cross daily; follow Jesus; lose your life to save it?

2. When did Jesus become more than just a name in the Bible for you?

Closing Prayer

Gather the students in a circle. Turn out the lights, and light a candle. Play some reflective music. Ask the students to think of crosses they have been asked to carry. After a few minutes, slowly pass a cross around the circle. Invite the students to pray quietly as they receive the cross for strength and wisdom to continue carrying their personal crosses. Ask the other students to pray quietly for the person holding the cross. Continue until everyone has held the cross. Then hold hands as you conclude the session with the Lord's Prayer.

Making God's Word Our Own

If you are choosing a student for next Sunday's opening prayer, do so now.

Each day this week look for a cross that Jesus has given you to carry. You may find a different cross facing you each day, or you may find little crosses that are always around you. Ask Jesus each morning to help you carry whatever cross you find during the day. Thank him before you go to bed for what you have learned through carrying that particular cross.

Birth *of* John the Baptizer, June 24

Readings

Isaiah 49:1–6
Acts 13:22–26
Luke 1:57–66, 80

Theme

All things are possible with God. Let God's will unfold!

Scripture *Background*

Zechariah and Elizabeth stand in the tradition of Israel's faithful ancestors. These parents of patriarchs and prophets, whose children's births were associated with special manifestations of God's care and concern, include Abraham and Sarah, the parents of Isaac (Genesis 15; 18:1–15), and Elkanah and Hannah, the parents of Samuel (1 Samuel 1:1–2:11). In each case, the child of extraordinary birth was destined for an extraordinary mission on behalf of Israel.

John's parents, Zechariah and Elizabeth, were elderly and childless. From the Jewish perspective at the time, childlessness was considered as a sign of God's disfavor or a punishment for sin. Yet the Gospel portrayed Zechariah and Elizabeth as a couple devoted to the Lord and careful to observe the commandments. To be childless must have caused deep anguish for them and been something about which they had prayed. When the angel announced John's birth, he told Zechariah, "Your prayer has been heard" (Luke 1:13). The name John means "God is gracious" and attests to the angel's pronouncement.

John's mission, according to the angel, was to *"turn many of the people of Israel to the Lord their God. With the spirit and power of Elijah he will go before him, to turn the hearts of parents to their children, and the disobedient to the wisdom of the righteous, to make ready a people prepared for the Lord"* (Luke 1:16–17). John was filled with the Holy Spirit from his mother's womb. He would prepare himself until the time when he would be consecrated to the Lord.

John was like the suffering servant of Isaiah, the subject of today's first reading. The image of the servant as a "sharp-edged sword" seems appropriate for John. His manner of speaking during his "public appearance in Israel" could certainly be described as "sharp."

Like the servant before him, John must have wondered at times if he had toiled in vain. Yet, like the servant, he must also have learned that his recompense was not measurable by human standards but would be found with God.

The second reading shows how similar John is to the Isaiah servant. Like that servant, John had come to bring Israel to repentance. John came to enlighten Israel in God's ways. John, like Isaiah's servant, is a prophet of the Most High, going before the Lord to prepare God's ways, bringing knowledge of salvation.

Anne Marie Sweet OSB

PART I: Gathering *for God's Word*

Opening Prayer

Alternative: *Ask one of the students to lead the opening prayer.*

Open the session by saying: **Welcome. Thank you for joining us on this wonderful day. Today we are going to examine the powerful mystery of God touching human history as we celebrate the birth of John the Baptizer. I invite the Church to please stand for our opening prayer. Recalling that John baptized with water and that we were baptized in water with the Holy Spirit, we begin** (make the sign of the cross) **in the name of the Father, and of the Son, and of the Holy Spirit. Amen.**

Jesus, open our minds and hearts so we may more clearly see and understand your will as it unfolds around us. You are so close to us that we fail to recognize you. Grant us the grace to know and trust you as you invite us to grow and follow in your footsteps. Continue to bless these students and their families and this community with the spirit of hospitality. Strengthen our religious leaders. We ask all this in your name.

The students respond loudly: **Amen!**

Song

"Center of My Life" by Paul Inwood from *Today's Missal* (OCP), *Gather (Comprehensive)* (GIA), *Journeysongs* (OCP), *Glory & Praise 2* (OCP [NALR]).

"Only in God" by John Michael Talbot from *Today's Missal* (OCP), *Journeysongs* (OCP), *Glory & Praise 2* (OCP [NALR]).

"Seek Ye First the Kingdom of God" by Karen Lafferty from *Worship* (GIA), *We Celebrate* (J.S. Paluch, Co.), *Gather* (GIA), *Today's Missal* (OCP), *Journeysongs* (OCP), *Glory & Praise 2* (OCP [NALR]).

Announcements

• parish news
• birthdays
• other

PART II: Remembering *God's Word*

Review last week's session.

1. What did Jesus ask Peter last week? How did Peter respond?

• Jesus asked, "Who do you say that I am?" Peter responded, "the Messiah of God."

2. What did Jesus say would happen to the Messiah?

• The Messiah will suffer, be rejected, put to death, and then be raised up.

3. Jesus said that the Messiah would be raised from the dead after how many days?

• three

4. What must someone be willing to do if they want to follow Jesus?

   • Jesus said, "Whoever wishes to be my follower must deny his or her very self, take up his or her cross each day, and follow in my steps. Whoever would save their life will lose it, and whoever loses their life for my sake will save it."

5. What crosses did you have to carry during the past week? How did Jesus help you carry them?

   • Invite volunteers to respond openly and honestly.

PART III: Understanding *God's Word*

Materials Needed

All Students
- Bible
- 20–30 sheets of white paper
- washable markers
- index cards with a variety of objects written on them (one object per card)
- copies of the Prayer of Abandonment
- a book of baby names

Younger Students
- paper
- crayons

Older Students
- journals
- pens

Prayer of Abandonment

Father,
I abandon myself into your hands—
Do with me what you will.
Whatever you may do, I thank you.
I am ready for all—accept all.
Let only your will be done in me—
And in all your creatures.
I wish no more than this, O Lord.

Into your hands, I commend my soul;
I offer it to you with all the love of my heart—
For I love you, Lord, and so need to give myself—
To surrender myself into your hands,
Without reserve, and with boundless confidence,
For you are my Father.

Brother Charles of Jesus

Scripture

The students really enjoy this activity. It's fun, easy, and gets everyone involved. The activity works along the same principle as the "telephone" game, only in this activity, the students are **not** allowed to speak. Only when all the groups are finished should anyone talk. The purpose of this activity is to illustrate that when we concentrate and pay close attention, we see God in our lives and in the lives of others.

Divide the students into equal-size groups of five or more students. Have each group sit in a vertical line so that the students are facing each other's backs. They need to sit close enough to draw on each other's backs. Distribute to the students paper and washable markers. Be sure the markers won't bleed through the paper.

Show the students at the end of each line one of the index cards. Each group should have a different object to draw. The student at the end of each line then places the paper on the back of the student in front of him or her and draws a picture of the object. He or she can't say a word and can only draw it once. Without saying a word, and without showing the next student the picture drawn, the next student must draw the same object on the back of the student in front of him or her and so on down the line. The students must draw from what they felt on their backs. Show the pictures to the students when all the teams are finished. Ask the students who drew first to share the name of the object they drew.

Repeat the activity as often as time permits, rotating the students so that as many as possible have an opportunity to be at the back and the front of the lines.

Proclaim Luke 1:57–66, 80. Ask the students how the previous activity relates to the gospel reading. *(Everyone in the gospel reading thought they fully understood what God was doing in their lives. But in reality, God was doing greater things; they just had to wait for God's plans to unfold and be completed—just like in our lives and in the activity. We think we understand, but we need to concentrate on God's movements in our lives and ask Jesus to help us more clearly see God's plans. And when we do, we will be wonderfully surprised—just like everyone in the Scripture passage was greatly surprised.)*

Reflection

Use the following questions and activities to help students further understand the gospel reading.

Younger Students

1. Distribute to the students paper and crayons. Direct them to draw a picture of Zechariah and Elizabeth holding their baby John, later known as John the Baptizer. Why was his birth a miracle?

2. Do you know why your parents chose your name? If so, explain. If not, ask your parents.

3. What does your name mean? (Have available a book of baby names through which the students can look.)

4. What are some miracles that have happened to you or someone you know?

Older Students

Allow time for the students to respond in their journals to the last question.

1. Why did Elizabeth name her child John?

2. What might be some of the hopes and dreams your parents had for you when you were born?

3. What would John the Baptizer be like today? Where would he live? What would he do? Would you be his friend? Why or why not?

4. What plans do you feel God has for you?

Closing Prayer

Gather the students in a circle. In the spirit of desiring to do God's will and in the spirit of John the Baptizer, give each student a copy of the Prayer of Abandonment.

Making God's Word Our Own

This week read the Prayer of Abandonment twice each day. You might be surprised at what happens when you put meaning and feeling into the prayer.

If you are choosing a student for next Sunday's opening prayer, do so now.

Thirteenth Sunday *in* Ordinary Time

Readings

1 Kings 19:16b, 19–21
Galatians 5:1, 13–18
Luke 9:51–62

Theme

We are all invited to "come follow."

Scripture Background

The first reading tells of Elijah's call of Elisha. Elijah announced God's call to Elisha by throwing his mantle over him. This signified the call to prophetic office. When Elisha wished to bid his parents farewell, Elijah asked, "Have I done anything to you?" Elisha had to make his own decision about the call and not rely on the presence of Elijah. Elisha closed the door to his former way of life by killing the draft animals with which he had been plowing, using the plow for firewood, and preparing a magnificent feast for the people. Then he abandoned all this and followed Elijah.

The gospel passage shows the price Jesus paid to follow his call. He "set his face" to go toward Jerusalem, where, eventually, his life would be demanded of him. At the beginning of the journey, he met rejection. Because he was on his way to Jewish Jerusalem, the Samaritans would not welcome him. Jesus was caught between two hostile forces. One group rejected him because he was going to Jerusalem. There, the other group would kill him. The disciples wanted to respond with violence. Jesus, however, accepted the cost of his call without resistance.

As the journey toward Jerusalem continued, other examples of responding to the call arose. The inherent message is that response to a call must be total. One must come and expect nothing but the reward of following Jesus, even to death. One must leave anything and everything that hinders the call.

In his Letter to the Galatians, Paul emphasized that this call was a call to freedom. The disciples were called to abandon all the things that enslaved them and to subject themselves to the spirit of love. That spirit brings joy and peace, kindness and generosity. It offers no resistance to the demands of the call because the rewards are those of love. Jesus set his face to go to Jerusalem, to answer the demands of the call, because of love for his Father and for us. We respond to the demands of being called in the same Spirit, the Spirit of the love of Christ.

Irene Nowell OSB

PART I: Gathering *for God's Word*

Opening Prayer

Alternative: *Ask one of the students to lead the opening prayer.*

Open the session by saying: **Welcome. God's blessing to everyone. I invite the Church to stand as we recall the gift of our Baptism and what that gift does for us as we begin our prayer** (make the sign of the cross) **in the name of the Father, and of the Son, and of the Holy Spirit. Amen.**

Today let's take a full minute of silence to listen to the world around us. Quietly stand with your eyes closed, concentrating on the sounds around you. Listen to as many sounds as you can. (Allow a full minute for this exercise.)

Jesus, may we hear your whispering words of love, encouragement, and invitation to follow you. Bless these students, their families, and their teachers with the life-giving presence of your Holy Spirit; guide them along the path of life. Help them realize that you walk beside them as they strive to follow in your footsteps. We thank you for hearing our prayer. We ask all of these things in your name.

The students respond loudly: **Amen!**

Song

"Come with Me into the Fields" by Dan Schutte from *Glory & Praise* (OCP [NALR]).

"God has Chosen Me" by Bernadette Farrell from *Today's Missal* (OCP), *Journeysongs* (OCP), *Glory & Praise 2* (OCP [NALR]).

"People of God" by David Haas and Fintan O' Carroll from *Walking by Faith* (GIA, Harcourt Religion Publishers).

Announcements

- parish news
- birthdays
- other

PART II: Remembering *God's Word*

Use the following questions to review last week's session.

1. Whose birth was celebrated in last Sunday's gospel reading?
   - John the Baptizer
2. After Zechariah agreed with Elizabeth that their son should be called John, he began to do what?
   - Zechariah, who was unable to speak prior to the birth of his son, began to speak, praising God.

3. How did the drawing activity from last week relate to the gospel reading?

- Everyone in the gospel reading thought they fully understood what God was doing in their lives. But in reality, God was doing greater things; they just had to wait for God's plans to unfold and be completed—just like in our lives and in the activity. We think we understand, but we need to concentrate on God's movements in our lives and ask Jesus to help us more clearly see God's plans. And when we do, we will be wonderfully surprised—just like everyone in the Scripture passage was greatly surprised.

4. What did you experience when you prayed the Prayer of Abandonment daily?

- Let the students respond openly and honestly.

PART III: **Understanding** *God's Word*

Materials Needed

All Students
- Bible
- copies of oatmeal raisin cookie recipe (one for each student)
- copies of disciple of Jesus recipe (one for each student)
- chalkboard or dry-erase board
- chalk or dry-erase markers
- bowl of holy water
- Paschal candle

Younger Students
- paper
- crayons

Older Students
- journals
- pens

Oatmeal Raisin Cookies

1 cup shortening	1/2 tsp. salt
1 cup brown sugar	1 tsp. baking powder
1 cup sugar	1 tsp. baking soda
3 eggs	3 cups oatmeal
1 tsp. vanilla	1 cup raisins
2 cups flour	

Directions: Cream shortening, sugars, eggs, and vanilla. Sift dry ingredients together, and gradually add to the cream mixture. Mix well. Stir in oatmeal and raisins. Drop by rounded spoonfuls onto an ungreased baking sheet. Bake at 350 degrees for 8–10 minutes.

Disciple Recipe

1 cup	1/2 tsp.
1 cup	1 tsp.
1 cup	1 tsp.
3	3 cups
1 tsp.	1 cup
2 cups	

Directions:

Scripture   Proclaim Luke 9:51–62. Distribute to the students the oatmeal raisin cookie recipe, and read it aloud to the class. Share with them that one can make really good cookies using this recipe. Explain that as there are many diverse ingredients that make up the cookies, there are also many ingredients that make up a follower of Jesus. Gather the students into small groups. Direct the groups to write a recipe for a disciple using the same measurements from the cookie recipe. After ten minutes, ask the groups to share their recipes with the entire class. List on the chalkboard or dry-erase board all the ingredients the groups used.

Reflection   Use the following questions and activities to help students process the readings.

Younger Students

1. Distribute to the students paper and crayons. Direct the students to draw a picture of Jesus calling them to come follow him. Invite volunteers to share their drawings with a partner or with the class.

2. Jesus invites us to follow him. Where do you think he will lead us?

3. What can you do each day to let Jesus and the world know that you are a follower of Jesus?

Older Students

Allow ample time for the students to respond in their journals to the last question.

1. Jesus expects a lot from his followers. If he came up to you right now and invited you to follow him, what would you say and do?

2. Jesus freely offered his life to show us his love for God and us. What are you willing to do to show Jesus you love him?

3. What stops people from following Jesus? What would enable you to follow Jesus freely?

Closing Prayer

Gather the students in a circle. Slowly read the disciple recipes that the students created. Remind them that through Baptism, we are all called to follow Jesus in our daily lives. With his help and grace, we can be great disciples. Allow the students a moment of quiet personal prayer.

Place a bowl of holy water and the Paschal candle in the center of the circle. Let each student individually bless himself or herself with the holy water and say a brief prayer, either silently or aloud. Then hold hands as you conclude the session with the Lord's Prayer.

Making God's Word Our Own

If you are choosing a student for next Sunday's opening prayer, do so now.

Bake two batches of cookies this week. Keep one batch for yourself and your family. Give the other to a neighbor, someone in a care center, or someone who lives alone. After you have cleaned up and are waiting for your cookies to bake, fill out the recipe for a disciple with your parent(s) or guardian(s). Post the recipe on the refrigerator. Throughout the week try to put into practice some of the ingredients of a good disciple.

Fourteenth Sunday
in Ordinary Time

Readings

Isaiah 66:10–14c
Galatians 6:14–18
Luke 10:1–12, 17–20

Theme

*We are called to
evangelize.*

Scripture *Background*

The passage from the Book of Isaiah belongs to the third section of the book (chapters 56–66). It was written to encourage those who had returned from exile in the sixth century B.C. Second Isaiah (40–55) had promised a glorious return and a wonderful restoration. In reality, those who returned faced an overwhelming task of rebuilding. This task was complicated by internal dissension and opposition from the outside.

One major theme of Third Isaiah was the continued promise of a glorious new Jerusalem. The people should not yield to the obstacles they faced. God had the power to fulfill promises and was faithful to those promises. The people should begin already to rejoice over the new Jerusalem. Their rejoicing would proclaim the good news. Jerusalem was presented as a mother, vibrant and healthy, rich in compassionate love for her children. Jerusalem, their mother, nourished them.

All three synoptics (Matthew, Mark, Luke) included a story of Jesus sending out the Twelve to teach. Only Luke included an additional story of the sending of the seventy-two. Twelve was the traditional number for all Israel because of the twelve tribes. Seventy-two (or seventy) was a number sometimes used to symbolize the Gentiles, since there were seventy-two (or seventy) nations listed in the genealogy of Genesis 10. It was fitting that Luke, who showed so much more interest in the Gentiles, should have a speech to suggest the mission to the Gentiles.

The instructions to the disciples were similar to those of other missionary speeches. Jesus instructed the disciples to take few material things with them. Possessions would slow their journey. The people they encountered would support them. They were told how to begin their teaching ("Peace to you"), what to preach (the kingdom of God), and how to deal with rejection ("Shake the dust from your feet").

The seventy-two disciples returned from their journey delighted with their success. Jesus congratulated and encouraged them. He also reminded them, however, that fidelity was worth more than success when he said, "Rejoice that your names are written in heaven."

This Sunday we read the conclusion of Paul's Letter to the Galatians. Paul's final statement concurs with Jesus' final statement in Luke. Paul was not as concerned over the success of his preaching as he was over his fidelity to Christ and his cross. Nothing else mattered. He had given his life to preach the good news of Christ: The cross of Christ had marked him. Now only Christ mattered.

Irene Nowell OSB

Fourteenth Sunday in Ordinary Time **147**

PART I: Gathering *for God's Word*

Opening Prayer

Alternative: *Ask one of the students to lead the opening prayer.*

Open the session by saying: **I welcome you in Jesus' name! Thank you for joining us as we grow in our faith and relationship with Jesus. Today we are going to examine ways to share the good news of the gospel—to evangelize. I invite the Church to stand for our opening prayer. We begin by remembering that we are sons and daughters of God** (make the sign of the cross) **in the name of the Father, and of the Son, and of the Holy Spirit. Amen.**

> *Jesus, be with us as you promised, for we are gathering in your name. Open our hearts and minds to your love and grace as we explore how we are called to evangelize and share your love and message with others. We lift these students, their families, and their teachers up to you so you may cover them in your blanket of love. We ask all this in your name.*

The students respond enthusiastically: **Amen!**

Song

"Anthem" by Tom Conry from *Glory & Praise* (OCP [NALR]), *Today's Missal* (OCP), *Gather (Comprehensive)* (GIA), *Journeysongs* (OCP).

"Here I Am, Lord" by Dan Schutte from *Glory & Praise* (OCP [NALR]), *Gather (Comprehensive)* (GIA), *Today's Missal* (OCP), *Lead Me, Guide Me* (GIA), *Journeysongs* (OCP).

"I Have Decided" by Michael Card from *Amy Grant, The Collection* (Word Music).

"Reach Out" by Carey Landry from *Hi God!* (OCP [NALR]), *Young People's Glory & Praise* (OCP [NALR]).

Announcements

- parish news
- birthdays
- other

PART II: Remembering *God's Word*

Review last week's readings.

1. What was the theme of last Sunday's gospel?

- discipleship

2. What do cookies have in common with last Sunday's gospel?

- As it takes a variety of ingredients to make a batch of cookies, it also takes a variety of qualities to be a follower of Jesus. Jesus' disciples come in all different shapes and sizes.

3. What did you experience when you made cookies with your family? With whom did you share your cookies? What ingredients did your family put in the disciple recipe? How did you use your recipe throughout the week?

- Let the students respond openly and honestly.

PART III: Understanding *God's Word*

Scripture

Materials Needed

All Students
- Bible
- index cards with occupations written on them (one per card): firefighter, nurse, lawyer, teacher, priest, artist, writer, computer programmer, police officer, singer
- bag or bowl
- volunteers

Younger Students
- crayons
- paper

Older Students
- journals
- pens

Place the index cards in a bag or bowl, and choose one student to pick a card. Have the student act out the occupation on the card without talking, using only gestures. Ask the other students to guess the occupation. Invite other students up to act out the remaining occupations.

Ask the students which occupation or vocation is best for evangelizing. Listen to their reasoning, but don't indicate whether it is right or wrong. (At this point, you have not given them the definition of the word *evangelist*.)

Define the word *evangelist*. (An evangelist is someone who shares Jesus' message with others.) Ask the students again which occupation or vocation is best for evangelizing. Proclaim Luke 10:1–12, 17–20.

Tell the students that every baptized person is called to be an evangelist—to share with others the good news of Jesus and his message. We can evangelize through all vocations if we follow Jesus and share his message with others. Evangelization is not a job; it is a way of life. When we believe and live our faith, we are sharing the good news of Jesus with others. Our actions speak louder than words.

Discuss the readings further, using the following questions and activities.

Younger Students

1. Distribute to the students paper and crayons. Invite them to draw a picture of themselves evangelizing.

Reflection

2. Have you ever prayed for someone who really needed Jesus' help in their lives?

3. Have you ever invited one of your friends to go to church with you? If yes, why? If no, why not?

Older Students

1. Who in your life helps you get to know and experience Jesus? Who evangelizes you?

2. Have you ever asked someone to pray with you or to go to church with you? If yes, why? If no, why not?

3. When you evangelize, you allow God to work through you and touch the lives of others. How can you share your faith (evangelize) in your home or school or on the playground?

Closing Prayer

Gather the students in a circle. Ask them to think quietly about the people in their lives who have shared the good news of Jesus with them. Offer a quiet prayer of thanksgiving. If there is time, allow the students to share with the large group the names of these special people.

Making God's Word Our Own

If you are choosing a student for next Sunday's opening prayer, do so now.

This week evangelize with your actions. Use your actions to bring the good news of Jesus to the people in your life—at home, at school, on the playground. If this assignment seems difficult, ask Jesus to help you. He will show you what to do! Evangelize your world!

Fifteenth Sunday *in* Ordinary Time

Readings

Deuteronomy 30:10–14
Colossians 1:15–20
Luke 10:25–37

Theme

"Go and do the same!"

Scripture *Background*

The Book of Deuteronomy, written in the seventh century B.C., was a long exhortation to God's people to turn from everything else and to love God with a single passion. The primary message was to love God with all your being.

Today's reading stresses that this command is not difficult to understand or remember. It is a very simple command; one that is already found in the hearts of God's people. The difficulty of keeping the command lies only with hardness of heart.

Jesus told the parable of the Good Samaritan as an interpretation of the two great commands of Judaism: love of God (Deuteronomy 6:5) and love of neighbor (Leviticus 19:18). The lawyer knew the heart of Jewish law but asked for an explanation. Jesus told a story to illustrate love of neighbor. As a typical parable, it allowed the listener to form a judgment about the story. Often this pronouncement left the reader uncomfortable and faced with an ironic situation. In this story, the two passers-by who ignored the wounded man were members of the religious establishment. The Samaritan was a hated outsider, one who would be suspected as the robber before he would be expected to be the example of virtue. Ironically, it was the Samaritan who did the right thing. A person was in need, and so he helped him. There was nothing complex or sophisticated about his action; it was simple kindness. This is Jesus' example of fulfillment of the Law.

The lawyer asked, "Who is my neighbor?" "Whom should I love?" Jesus' example of the parable tells us, "Everyone."

The passage from the Letter to the Colossians is an awe-filled hymn to Christ. The imagery and vocabulary are from the descriptions of Lady Wisdom in the Hebrew wisdom tradition, especially Wisdom 7. Christ is described as the image of God and the link between God and all creation. Through Christ, the Wisdom Word, God created and sustains everything. Through Christ, redeemer, all creation is reconciled to God. In Christ, head of the Church, everything lives. Jesus is the perfect revelation of God because he put no resistance in the way of God but embraced the will of God totally.

Irene Nowell OSB

PART I: Gathering *for God's Word*

Opening Prayer

Alternative: *Ask one of the students to lead the opening prayer.*

Open the session by saying: **Welcome! It's good to see everyone here again. Today we are going to go right to the heart of what it means to be a follower of Jesus. We will do this by answering the question "How do I treat my neighbor?" I invite the Church to stand for our opening prayer. We begin by remembering who we are and what we are called to be because we are baptized** (make the sign of the cross) **in the name of the Father, and of the Son, and of the Holy Spirit. Amen.**

> *Jesus, thank you for the gift of life and for the gift of our faith. Open our eyes and our hearts to see all people as our neighbors, and grant us the courage to love them truly as we also love ourselves. Bless these students and their families; keep them safe in your love. We lift up these spoken prayers and those unspoken that we hold in our hearts in Jesus' name.*

The students respond loudly: **Amen!**

Song

"God Has Chosen Me" by Bernadette Farrell from *Today's Missal* (OCP), *Journeysongs* (OCP), *Glory & Praise 2* (OCP [NALR]).

"They'll Know We Are Christians" by Peter Scholtes from *Today's Missal* (OCP).

"Whatsoever You Do" by Willard F. Jabusch from *Gather (Comprehensive)* (GIA), *Journeysongs* (OCP), *Glory & Praise 2* (OCP [NALR]), *We Celebrate* (J.S. Paluch Co., Inc.).

Announcements

- parish news
- birthdays
- other

PART II: Remembering *God's Word*

Review last week's session.

1. What was the theme of last week's Scripture readings?
   - evangelization
2. What is an evangelist?
   - An evangelist is someone who brings the message of Jesus to others.
3. What is the best way to share with others the good news of Jesus?
   - Let the students respond openly and honestly.
4. You were asked last week to evangelize your faith at home with your family, at school, and on the playground. What did you experience? How did Jesus help you?
   - Let the students respond openly and honestly.

PART III: Understanding *God's Word*

Scripture

Materials Needed

All Students
- Bible
- eight volunteers to role-play the gospel: lawyer, victim, three robbers, Samaritan, priest, Levite
- costumes (optional)
- a bag of coins
- sheet of paper, a pen, and tape

Younger Students
- paper
- crayons

The goal is to act out the gospel so that the message of the parable of the Good Samaritan comes to life for the students. The following activity is very powerful.

Choose eight volunteers, and assign the students the following roles: lawyer, victim, three robbers, Samaritan, priest, Levite. Before you proclaim the gospel, have the person playing the lawyer ask the question "What must I do to inherit everlasting life?" Let the rest of the students try to answer the question. (Listen carefully to their responses. This will give you insight into your students.)

Tell the students you need their help to answer the lawyer's question. Ask them to describe, in general terms, the most disliked group of people in their city, town, school, or parish. Write the name of the most disliked group on a piece of paper, and tape it on the Good Samaritan's back. Explain that the Samaritans were hated by the Jews. They were hated so much that if someone even stepped over the border and touched the ground of the Samaritans, that person could not worship in the Temple until they were purified.

Proclaim Luke 10:25–37, slowly and with emotion. Ask the volunteers to echo their parts after you read them. After the gospel is proclaimed and acted out, ask the students, "What must we do to inherit everlasting life?" *(Love God with all your heart, all your soul, all your strength, all your mind, and show compassion, forgiveness, and love to everyone and yourself.)*

Reflection

Use the following questions and activities to help students get to the heart of the gospel.

Younger Students

1. Distribute to the students paper and crayons. Ask them to draw two pictures—one picture of Jesus showing compassion to someone who needs it and the other picture of Jesus showing the students' and their families' compassion.

2. Has anyone showed you compassion and helped you when you needed it? What happened? How did you feel?

3. Who in your family, school, parish, or town do you need to reach out to and help like the Good Samaritan did?

Older Students

1. What can you do to show that you truly love God with all your heart, soul, strength, and mind? How can you love your neighbor as yourself?

2. Who lives this gospel in your life? How?

3. Who are the most feared or misunderstood in your city or town? Are they or aren't they your neighbors? Explain.

Closing Prayer

Gather the students into a circle. After a few moments of quiet prayer, invite the students to offer their own spontaneous petitions. Hold hands as you conclude the session with the Lord's Prayer.

Making God's Word Our Own

If you are choosing a student for next Sunday's opening prayer, do so now.

This week ask Jesus to show you who needs compassion and kindness and to show you ways to help these people. You will be able to do great things if you are truly willing to try with an open heart. Try it for one week, and watch what happens!

Sixteenth Sunday *in* Ordinary Time

Readings

Genesis 18:1–10a
Colossians 1:24–28
Luke 10:38–42

Theme

Hospitality—We welcome Jesus in our lives.

Scripture *Background*

Hospitality was valued among most ancient peoples. The host accepted responsibility for any guests who came. In today's reading from Genesis, Abraham offers hospitality with the generosity typical of a nomadic chief. He implored the passers-by to stay, washed their feet, and then prepared a magnificent meal for them. Even though the guests were unknown, Abraham entertained them lavishly. Through this, he earned the satisfaction of having entertained the Lord who had come to repeat his promise of a son to Abraham.

Hospitality is an important issue in the gospel, too. A statement concerning the status of women was made in the story of Martha and Mary. Martha exercised the role expected of women in her culture when she entertained her guest. It was an extremely important role. Conversely, Mary assumed the role of the disciple. She sat at the feet of the master to learn. This role was not only unexpected for a woman, it was strongly disapproved of or forbidden. Learning, especially of a religious nature, was limited to men. The story illustrated that Christian discipleship was open to both men and women. Jesus praised Mary for taking the role of disciple and referred to this role as "the better part."

Through this, Jesus was not disparaging the role of hospitality. The sharing of meals was one of the major images of sharing life with Jesus. This sharing was also an image of discipleship. Thus the duties of hospitality led to the table fellowship that eventually found expression in the Eucharist. Martha appeared to be an expert in hospitality, and Jesus loved to stay at her house. Both Martha and Mary, therefore, fulfilled the duties of discipleship.

The Letter to the Colossians presents a third image of discipleship. Paul was portrayed as a prisoner who suffered for preaching the good news of Christ. He had become a minister of the word. He hoped all would have the opportunity of "sitting at the Lord's feet," of "sharing at the Lord's table."

Irene Nowell OSB

PART I: Gathering *for God's Word*

Choose seven volunteers as the students arrive. Give them a piece of paper with the following questions on it. This will allow them ample time to prepare their responses.

1. Would you go see Jesus if he were passing through your town? Would you invite him home with you for dinner? Why?

2. List seven things you would do to make Jesus feel welcome if he were coming to your home for dinner tonight.

Also, as the students arrive, go out of your way to welcome them to the class; cover them with the "spirit of hospitality." Shake their hands, pat them on the back, smile warmly, and call each person by name. You know your students and their needs; be creative and sincere as you show them the gift of hospitality.

Opening Prayer

Alternative: *Ask one of the students to lead the opening prayer.*

Open the session by saying: **Welcome. Thank you for joining us today. I hope you all feel welcome and at home. It is my prayer that the peace Jesus offers us will be with you now. I invite the Church to stand for our opening prayer. We remember we are one family in God because we were baptized** (make the sign of the cross) **in the name of the Father, and of the Son, and of the Holy Spirit. Amen.**

> *Jesus, Martha welcomed you into her home and cared for you. Grant us the spirit of hospitality. May we learn to welcome others and care for their needs before our own. Martha's sister, Mary, shows us how important it is to welcome you into our hearts by resting in your presence and love. Grant us the wisdom to slow down and listen to your words so that we may discover your grace that is around us. Thank you, Jesus, for the gifts of life and faith. Bless these students, and keep them safe. Never let them forget that you will always welcome them in your arms and that they belong by your side. We ask all this in your name.*

The students respond: **Amen!**

Song

"Come to the Water" by John Foley from *Glory & Praise* (OCP [NALR]), *Today's Missal* (OCP), *Gather (Comprehensive)* (GIA), *Journeysongs* (OCP).

"Companions on the Journey" by Carey Landry from *Glory & Praise* (OCP [NALR]), *Today's Missal* (OCP).

"Taste and See" by James Moore from *Gather (Comprehensive)* (GIA), *Glory & Praise* (OCP [NALR]), *We Celebrate* (J.S. Paluch Co., Inc.), *Lead Me, Guide Me* (GIA).

Announcements

- parish news
- birthdays
- other

PART II: Remembering *God's Word*

Use the following questions to review last week's session.

1. Jesus told us last week what we must do to inherit everlasting life. What must we do?

    • We shall love the Lord our God with all our heart, all our soul, all our strength, and all our mind, and love our neighbor as ourselves.

2. Who is our neighbor, according to Jesus?

    • Everyone is our neighbor.

3. What did you learn about Jesus in last week's gospel? What did you learn about yourself? What did you learn about others?

    • Let the students respond openly and honestly.

4. Who needed your compassion and kindness last week? How did you reach out to these people? How did Jesus help you? What happened?

    • Let the students respond openly and honestly.

PART III: Understanding *God's Word*

Scripture

Materials Needed

All Students
- Bible
- seven volunteers
- seven copies of the questions on page 155 (one for each volunteer)
- seven pencils
- instrumental music
- CD or tape player
- small rocks (one for each student)
- bowl
- candle
- matches

Younger Students
- paper
- crayons

Older Students
- journals
- pens

Reflection

Invite the students to listen carefully to what Jesus says about the two sisters in the reading. Proclaim Luke 10:38–42.

Invite the seven volunteers to come forward. Ask them to respond to the two questions they were given prior to the session. Invite the remainder of the students to respond to the second question if time allows.

Proclaim the gospel again. Invite the students to reflect upon their willingness to invite Jesus into their hearts and homes. Are they truly willing to take Jesus' words of life to heart?

Use the following questions and activities to help students get to the heart of the gospel.

Younger Students

1. Distribute to the students paper and crayons. Direct them to draw a picture of themselves and their families showing Jesus hospitality in their homes.

2. How are the two sisters, Martha and Mary, alike? How are they different?

3. Are you more like Martha or Mary? Why?

Older Students

Allow ample time for the students to respond in their journals to the last question.

1. What are some of the positive and negative characteristics of Martha and Mary in this story?

2. What does Jesus mean when he says, "Mary has chosen the better portion, and she shall not be deprived of it"? What would you do if your were Martha?

3. What would Jesus say if he dropped in on your home today?

Closing Prayer

Place small rocks in a bowl. Ask each of the students to choose one rock.

Gather the students in a circle. Play some reflective music, and light a candle. Turn out the lights. Encourage the students to silently invite Jesus into their hearts. Tell them to listen for Jesus' words. Hold hands as you conclude the session with the Lord's Prayer.

Making God's Word Our Own

If you are choosing a student for next Sunday's opening prayer, do so now.

Ask Jesus into your heart this week. Place your rock next to your bed every night before going to sleep. Invite Jesus into your heart and home. When you get up in the morning, pick up your rock, and place it on your pillow. Again, invite Jesus into your heart and into your home. Do this for one week.

Seventeenth Sunday *in* Ordinary Time

Readings

Genesis 18:20–32
Colossians 2:12–14
Luke 11:1–13

Theme

The Lord's Prayer is a map for life.

Scripture *Background*

The reading from Genesis is a classic example of prayer in the Old Testament. It is from the Yahwist tradition of the Pentateuch and was written around the tenth century B.C. In the Yahwist tradition God was very close to humans and displayed human traits. In this passage, Abraham haggled with God in the Near-Eastern style, working God to the lowest possible price. Would God spare the city for the sake of as few as ten just people?

The story portrays Abraham as a friend of God. In characteristic human style, God decides not to hide plans from this friend. God is willing to discuss the decision with this friend and even seems willing to alter the decision. Abraham acts the role of the prophet interceding for the people.

The passage from the Gospel of Luke is a collection of Jesus' reflections on prayer. The first section (verses 1–4) is the Lucan version of the Lord's Prayer (see Matthew 6:9–13). The disciples observed Jesus praying and asked him to teach them how to pray. Jesus responded with the prayer we know as the Lord's Prayer. The version in Luke is shorter than the one in Matthew's Gospel. Matthew's version was possibly expanded by the worshiping community for whom Matthew wrote.

Following the prayer, Jesus offered a parable about the need for persistence. We respond to someone's persistence even when we won't respond to the request of friendship. Think how warmly God responded to someone like Abraham, who was a friend. Jesus continued to suggest that, though God always responds, the response will be warmer when we approach God lovingly.

The reading from the Letter to the Colossians attempts to explain why Christians can pray with such confidence. Baptism has united Christians with Christ in his death as well as his resurrection power. When we had no claim to God's love, when we were "dead in sin," God gave us new life. Christ has won our friendship with God. In Christ we can pray with absolute confidence.

Irene Nowell OSB

PART I: Gathering *for God's Word*

Opening Prayer

Alternative: *Ask one of the students to lead the opening prayer.*

Open the session by saying: **Welcome! I am glad you are here. We are going to have a lot of fun today as we look at a special prayer that Jesus gave us. I invite the Church to stand for our opening prayer. I will need your help with the opening prayer, so be thinking of special people or things you would like to offer up in prayer. We begin our prayer by remembering that, because of our Baptism, we are sons and daughters of God, and we can ask God for anything. We pray** (make the sign of the cross) **in the name of the Father, and of the Son, and of the Holy Spirit. Amen.**

Jesus, when your disciples didn't know how to pray, you taught them to pray to God the Father in confidence, intimacy, and love. Please grant us your Holy Spirit so that our hearts and minds will be open to understand that God, the creator of everything, wants to be in a loving relationship with us. Jesus, continue to bless these students and their families.

What would you like to say to God? (Let the students pray for their needs.)

Jesus, we place all these prayers and those we hold in our hearts at your feet.

The students respond enthusiastically: **Amen!**

Song

"Abba, Father" by Carey Landry from *Glory & Praise* (OCP [NALR]), *Today's Missal* (OCP).

"Only a Shadow" by Carey Landry from *Today's Missal* (OCP), *Glory & Praise* (OCP [NALR]).

"Unanswered Prayers" by Garth Brooks from *No Fences* (Capitol Records).

"You Are Near" by Dan Schutte from *Gather (Comprehensive)* (GIA), *Today's Missal* (OCP), *Glory & Praise* (OCP [NALR]), *Journeysongs* (OCP).

Announcements

• parish news
• birthdays
• other

PART II: Remembering *God's Word*

Use the following questions to review last week's session.

1. Who were the two sisters in last week's gospel?

• Martha and Mary

2. What did Martha do? What did Mary do?

• Martha invited Jesus over to dinner and showed him hospitality. Mary welcomed Jesus, sat at his feet, and listened to him.

3. How did your rock help you invite Jesus into your heart last week? What happened?

• Let the students respond openly and honestly.

PART III: Understanding *God's Word*

Scripture

Materials Needed

All Students
- Bible
- dry-erase board or chalkboard
- dry-erase markers or chalk
- timer or watch
- coin
- index cards with one sentence of the Lord's Prayer written on each card

Younger Students
- crayons
- paper

Older Students
- journals
- pens

Divide the class into two teams. Flip a coin to see which team goes first. Pick a student from the winning team to come forward. Give that person an index card with one of the lines of the Lord's Prayer written on it. Direct the student to draw pictures on the chalkboard or dry-erase board to help his or her team guess the sentence on the index card. No words can be spoken or written; the students can only draw pictures. Appoint a timekeeper and a scorekeeper. Each team is allowed one minute to guess. If the team cannot guess the sentence in the time allowed, the opposite team gets a minute to guess. Each correct answer is worth five points. If a team guesses incorrectly, they lose three points. Make sure the cards are mixed up well to make the game more fun and interesting. Play until all the cards have been guessed correctly.

Proclaim Luke 11:1–13. Focus on verses 9–13. Ask the students what they think Jesus means by asking, seeking, and knocking.

Use the following questions and activities to aid further discussion of the gospel.

Younger Students

1. Distribute to the students paper and crayons. Direct them to draw a picture of themselves praying to Jesus.
2. Recite the Lord's Prayer together. Is there a word or sentence you don't understand or like? Why might you dislike this sentence?

Reflection

Older Students

Allow time for the students to respond in their journals to the last question.

1. What does Jesus reveal to us about the kind of relationship God wants to have with us?
2. Do you know anyone who is an example of prayer by the way he or she lives? Describe this person.
3. When has God answered your prayers by giving you something better than that for which you prayed?
4. How could you improve the way you pray?

Closing Prayer

Gather the students in a circle. Have them quiet themselves. Invite volunteers to offer their own special prayers. Don't pressure the students to participate; reassure them that it is fine if they don't feel comfortable praying aloud. Hold hands as you conclude the session with the Lord's Prayer.

Making God's Word Our Own

If you are choosing a student for next Sunday's opening prayer, do so now.

Pray for someone different each day this week. Write that special person's name on a piece of paper or card, and carry it around with you all day as a reminder to pray for that person. It may be one of your grandparents, parents, siblings, friends, or someone you don't know very well. Pick a new person each day. Try this challenge, and experience the power of prayer!

Eighteenth Sunday *in* Ordinary Time

Readings

Ecclesiastes 1:2,
  2:21–23
Colossians 3:1–5, 9–11
Luke 12:13–21

Theme

*Everything is a gift
from God.*

Scripture *Background*

The Book of Qoheleth was written sometime in the third century B.C. Its author was a sage or a philosopher, someone who had spent much time reflecting on human life. Qoheleth was a realist and saw clearly the problems of life. The whole book was set under the title "Vanity of vanities; all things are vanity." The Hebrew word for *vanity* means "a puff of wind, a mere breath."

One pervasive human vanity is the inability to enjoy those things we earn. Qoheleth observed that people who worked hard and acquired property or wealth still had to die and leave everything to someone else. Instead of enjoying life, this person spent life working. But what was the profit? In the end, even the worker had nothing. Qoheleth's conclusion was that we have only the present moment, and that moment is a gift from God. The wisdom lay in making the best use of the present moment. This results from knowing that it is God's gift and avoiding worry about the future, over which we have no control.

The parable in the Gospel of Luke was based on the same observation. A wealthy man came to ask Jesus to settle a family inheritance squabble. Jesus told the parable of the fool who thought possessions guaranteed life. The fool did not know the wisdom that Qoheleth taught. Death would prevent him from enjoying the wealth that he had acquired. He had assumed that he controlled his own life. But possessions do not guarantee life. Only God has control of life. The present moment is our gift from God.

The wealthy man displayed his foolishness through another situation, too. He had not used his possessions and gifts in the service of God and neighbor. He had used them only for himself. Now God had judged him, and he had lost himself. He was indeed a fool!

The passage from the Letter to the Colossians describes the real wealth of the Christian. For the baptized, earthly possessions are meaningless. The one thing necessary is risen life with Christ. Only the possessions of the risen life are significant to the Christian. That is where true life resides.

Irene Nowell OSB

PART I: Gathering *for God's Word*

Choose seven volunteers as the students arrive. Give each of them an index card with the following question on it. Tell them to think about the question, and explain that they will be asked to share their responses later.

- If you had one minute, what three possessions would you try to save if your house caught on fire and your family and pets were safe? Why would you choose these things?

Opening Prayer

Alternative: *Ask one of the students to lead the opening prayer.*

Open the session by saying: **Welcome. I admire your desire to grow in faith. Our faith is a gift; our lives are gifts; everything is a gift from God. I invite the Church to stand for our opening prayer. Remembering that our Baptism into God's family is also a gift, we begin** (make the sign of the cross) **in the name of the Father, and of the Son, and of the Holy Spirit. Amen.**

> *Jesus, we thank and praise you. All good things come from you! Bless us with an appreciation of this truth. Help us realize that true happiness is being with you. Material possessions and money don't bring happiness. Open our minds and hearts so we may be truly free to follow you and share everything we have with others. We ask all this in your name.*

The students respond loudly: **Amen!**

Song

"Center of My Life" by Paul Inwood from *Today's Missal* (OCP), *Gather (Comprehensive)* (GIA), *Journeysongs* (OCP), *Glory & Praise 2* (OCP [NALR]).

"In This Place" by Tobias Colgan from *Today's Missal* (OCP), *Glory & Praise 2* (OCP [NALR]).

"Sing of the Lord's Goodness" by Ernest Sands from *Today's Missal* (OCP), *Journeysongs* (OCP), *Glory & Praise 2* (OCP [NALR]).

Announcements

- parish news
- birthdays
- other

PART II: Remembering *God's Word*

Review last week's session.

1. What was the theme of last week's readings?
   - prayer
2. Fill in the blanks: Jesus said, "Ask and you will _____, seek and you will _____, knock and the door will be _____.
   - receive, find, opened to you

3. Jesus said that the Father will give something to those who ask. What will the Father give?

  • the Holy Spirit

4. What did you experience when you prayed for someone different each day last week?

  • Let the students respond openly and honestly.

PART III: Understanding *God's Word*

Scripture

Materials Needed

All Students
  • Bible
  • seven volunteers
  • seven index cards with a question written on each
  • chalkboard or dry-erase board
  • chalk or dry-erase markers

Younger Students
  • paper
  • crayons

Older Students
  • journals
  • pens

Read to all the students the question you gave to the seven volunteers prior to the start of this session: *If you had one minute, what three possessions would you try to save if your house caught on fire and your family and pets were safe? Why would you choose these things?* Invite the volunteers to come forward and share their responses to the question. Invite other students to share if time allows.

Proclaim Luke 12:13–21. Ask the students to share ways we can "grow rich in the sight of God." List their responses on the chalkboard or dry-erase board. Include: following Jesus' commandments of love, imitating Jesus, forgiving others, caring for others, loving, showing mercy, praying, having faith in Jesus, and developing a relationship with Jesus.

Use the following questions and activities to expand upon the gospel reading.

Younger Students

1. How can we grow rich in material possessions and money? How can we grow rich in the sight of God?

2. Distribute to the students paper and crayons. Have the students draw a picture of all the riches God has already given them.

Reflection

Older Students

Allow ample time for the students to respond in their journals to the last question.

1. Was God's response to the rich harsh? Why or why not?

2. What does Jesus mean when he says "a man may be wealthy, but his possessions don't guarantee him life"?

3. What riches would you like Jesus to give to you? What would you do with them?

Closing Prayer

Gather the students in a circle. Ask them to think silently of all the gifts they have been given by God. Go around the circle, and invite volunteers to offer a prayer of thanksgiving. Hold hands as you conclude the session with the Lord's Prayer.

Making God's Word Our Own

If you are choosing a student for next Sunday's opening prayer, do so now.

Jesus told us to avoid greed in all its forms. Your challenge this week is to make a list of the different forms of greed in this world. Ask as many people as you can to contribute to your list. Bring the list you and others compiled to next week's gathering to share with the class.

Feast *of the* Transfiguration

Readings

Daniel 7:9–10, 13–14
2 Peter 1:16–19
Luke 9:28b–36

Theme

Jesus is human and divine.

Scripture *Background*

Today's gospel readings follow the story of Peter's profession that Jesus is the Messiah. Some of the disciples expected a messiah who would liberate Israel from its enemies and inaugurate a time of national independence. But the messiahship of which Jesus spoke involved suffering and death and resurrection. The disciples did not understand what he meant. The transfiguration follows to support Jesus' teaching.

The appearance of Moses and Elijah represents the law and the prophets. Their presence points to Jesus as the fulfillment of the Scriptures. Moses also typifies the Passover and Exodus experience of Israel. In the Gospels, the suffering and death of Jesus is depicted as a new Passover event. Jesus passes over from death to life. In the Lucan account of the transfiguration, Moses and Elijah speak with Jesus about his passage (*exodos* in Greek) in Jerusalem. In Jewish tradition, both Moses and Elijah are believed to have been mysteriously taken up into heaven. The transfiguration hints at a similar fate for Jesus.

The reading from Daniel reflects the belief that the crucified and risen Jesus was taken into heaven. In a vision, the prophet sees the heavenly throne (the Ancient of Days) of God described with apocalyptic imagery. We associate this imagery with the heavenly sphere that is defined by the color white, brightness, radiance, streams of fire, and a myriad of angels. There appears a "son of man" (a human). He is exalted by God while the enemies of God ("the beasts") are destroyed. This title, Son of Man, with its connotation of a human exalted by God, is applied to Jesus in the Gospels.

The disciples are enthralled by the glory of the experience and want to stay there forever. They have had only a brief view of Jesus' glory and final victory. For now, there is the journey that lies ahead, a way that leads through death to life.

The author of the Second Letter of Peter shares his experience of transfiguration with the Christians of his time. The account of Jesus' glory is not something imagined. It is rooted in the experience of those who journeyed with him.

Anne Marie Sweet OSB

PART I: Gathering for God's Word

Opening Prayer

Alternative: *Ask one of the students to lead the opening prayer.*

Open the session by saying: **Happy feast day! Today we, the Church, celebrate a special event that happened before Jesus suffered, died, and rose from the dead on Easter. The disciples get a glimpse of the human and divine existing together in Jesus in an event known as the Transfiguration. Jesus was revealed in his glory to strengthen the disciples' faith. I invite the Church to stand for our opening prayer. We begin by remembering that we also share in Jesus' glory and life because we were baptized** (make the sign of the cross) **in the name of the Father, and of the Son, and of the Holy Spirit. Amen.**

> *Jesus, share your glory and power with us as you did with your disciples. Grant us the same strength and hope that you granted them. Open our hearts so we might more clearly see your presence and glory that surrounds us. May we come to a deeper understanding of what awaits us when we allow you to embrace us more completely in your loving arms. Continue to bless these students, their families, teachers, and all those we hold in our hearts. We offer these prayers in your name.*

The students respond: **Amen!**

Song

"City of God" by Dan Schutte from *Glory & Praise* (OCP [NALR]), *Gather (Comprehensive)* (GIA), *Today's Missal* (OCP), *Journeysongs* (OCP).

"I Want to Walk as a Child of the Light" by Kathleen Thomerson from *Gather (Comprehensive)* (GIA), *Celebrating Our Faith* (Harcourt Religion Publishers, GIA).

"Tis Good, Lord, to Be Here" by Joseph H. Robinson from *Gather (Comprehensive)* (GIA).

"Transfiguration" by Carey Landry from *Abba! Father!* (OCP [NALR]), *Glory & Praise 2* (OCP [NALR]).

Announcements

- parish news
- birthdays
- other

PART II: Remembering God's Word

Review last week's session.

1. What was the main message in last week's readings?

- Wealth, power, and possessions don't guarantee happiness or eternal life. Jesus wants us to grow rich in God's sight, not in the sight of the world.

2. What are some ways we can grow rich in the sight of God?

   • Review the students' responses from last week. (Be open to new ideas that the students may have been thinking about during the week.)

3. What did you find out about greed last week? Whom did you ask about the different forms of greed in the world? What sources of greed did they share with you?

   • Let the students share their lists.

PART III: Understanding *God's Word*

Scripture

Materials Needed

All Students
- Bible
- large table with oversized tablecloth
- framed picture of a baby
- framed picture of an adult
- seeds
- small plant or tree
- grapes (real or plastic)
- a glass or bottle of grape juice
- flour
- loaf of bread
- popcorn kernels
- bowl of popped popcorn

Younger Students
- paper
- crayons

Older Students
- journals
- pens

Prior to the start of the session, place the baby picture, seeds, grapes, flour, and unpopped popcorn on top of the table at the front of the room. Place the picture of an adult, the small plant or tree, the grape juice, bread, and popped popcorn under the table, hidden by the oversized tablecloth.

Choose one student to come up and hold, touch, smell, or taste one of the objects on the table. Ask him or her to examine the object and share his or her findings with the class. Choose a new student for each object. Use the popcorn last, illustrating to the students that our hearts are just like popcorn. Our hearts can be just as hard as popcorn kernels. But if we open ourselves up to God's love and build a relationship with Jesus, God's love will transform us just as heat and oil change the hard kernels into soft and uniquely shaped popcorn puffs.

The purpose of this activity is to illustrate that there is a deeper reality within creation. With the proper disposition and conditions, things change—including our hearts. Connect Jesus' transfiguration to the objects. Show the students that there is a deeper reality hidden inside each of the objects.

After all the objects have been examined and discussed, one by one, bring out the adult picture, the plant, the grape juice, the loaf of bread, the bowl of popcorn. Do not explain or discuss the differences. Just place the items next to their corresponding objects.

Proclaim Luke 9:28b–36. Ask the students what the gospel tells us about Jesus, the objects on the table, and our own physical and spiritual lives. You will be astonished and truly amazed by the responses of the students.

Use the following questions to explore the reading further.

Younger Students

Reflection

1. Distribute to the students paper and crayons. Have them draw a picture of Jesus in his glory on one side of the paper and, on the other side of the paper, a picture of the wonderful person inside them waiting to be transformed by Jesus' love.

2. What does prayer have to do with Jesus' transfiguration? How does prayer help us become better persons?

3. What would you have done if you had been on the mountain with Jesus, Peter, John, and James when all this happened? How would that experience have changed you?

Older Students

Allow time for the students to respond in their journals to the last question.

1. God said, "This is my Son, my chosen one. Listen to him." What does this mean to you? In what ways do we listen to Jesus? Do you listen to him?

2. Reread the gospel. What does prayer have to do with the transfiguration? What does prayer have to do with your ability to change?

3. Describe a time when you have been overshadowed by the presence of God.

Closing Prayer

Gather the students in a circle. Pass around the group the bread and bowl of popcorn. Invite the students to eat some of each and to share what they hope to become one day. What changes might they like to make in their lives with the help of Jesus? Hold hands as you conclude the session with the Lord's Prayer.

Making God's Word Our Own

If you are choosing a student for next Sunday's opening prayer, do so now.

Spend fifteen minutes alone with Jesus each day this week. You don't have to say or do anything. Just close your eyes and sit with Jesus. Imagine that you are on the mountain with Jesus and the other disciples. Don't say a word; just be with Jesus on the mountain. A good time to try this is at night while you are lying in bed. If you do this with an open heart, watch out! You will experience Jesus' love, healing, and power. Jesus' love has a way of transforming lives. He invites you to take this prayer challenge.

Nineteenth Sunday *in* Ordinary Time

Readings

Wisdom 18:6–9
Hebrews 11:1–2, 8–19
Luke 12:32–48

Theme

*Do not live in fear.
Live, and be ready!*

Scripture *Background*

Today's reading from the Book of Wisdom reflects the experience of the Israelites during the exodus-wilderness period. It describes the Israelites as they prepare for the arrival of the "destroyer." They were celebrating Passover, "the divine institution," as they had been instructed to do. They held faith in God's promise. Moses said that the Egyptian firstborn would be slain and then the Israelites would be allowed to leave. Because they were ready, they were saved.

The passage from the Letter to the Hebrews presents the example of Abraham and Sarah. Abraham left his homeland for an unknown land promised to him by God. Sarah conceived a son, Isaac, through faith. Isaac was the tangible sign of God's covenant promise. Though Abraham and Sarah died without seeing the fullness of the promise, their faith in God held steady. Like the Israelites in Egypt, they believed God's promises and were ready for God's commands.

The first part of the gospel passage continues Luke's discussion of possessions. Disciples, as examples of faith, do not worry about possessions. In contrast to the rich fool, they build wealth where it could not be lost or destroyed. The disciples used their possessions to help others. In the parable that follows, thieves could not steal the treasure the disciples had amassed. However, the Son of Man, who would demand an account, would come like a thief. Therefore, the disciples should be prepared. Two other examples illustrate the need for readiness. First, servants should remain on call, ready for their master's return, no matter how late the hour. Second, homeowners should live in a state of preparedness, since they do not know when a thief might strike. There were great rewards for this preparedness. The faithful servants would be waited on by the master. This was a reward far beyond the wages they had earned. The homeowner had the intangible reward of security; possessions were not lost.

After Peter's question, the example of the servants was expanded. The servant who was faithful would be promoted, would receive added responsibility and greater rewards. The servant who took advantage of the master's delay, however, would be punished severely.

Examples from the past and examples from human experience illustrate the simple message: Be faithful. Be prepared.

Irene Nowell OSB

PART I: Gathering for God's Word

Opening Prayer

Alternative: *Ask one of the students to lead the opening prayer.*

Open the session by saying: **Welcome. May the Holy Spirit fill this place with peace, laughter, and love. Thank you for your determination to grow in your faith and your desire to learn more about our Lord. I invite the Church to stand for our opening prayer. How do we begin?** (Let the students respond—with the sign of the cross.) **What are we remembering?** (Let the students respond—our Baptism into God's family of faith.) **So we begin** (make the sign of the cross) **in the name of the Father, and of the Son, and of the Holy Spirit. Amen.**

> *Jesus, thank you for giving us everything we need: life, faith, forgiveness, love, and eternal life with you. Help us put aside all fear; cast away from us anything that is not of you. Continue to fill our hearts with the treasures of faith. We ask all this in your name as we continue to walk in faith.*

The students respond loudly: **Amen!**

Song

"Find Us Ready" by Tom Booth from *Find Us Ready* (OCP).

"Only a Shadow" by Carey Landry from *Today's Missal* (OCP), *Hi God!* (OCP [NALR]), *Glory & Praise* (OCP [NALR]).

"Walking by Faith" by David Haas from *Walking by Faith* (Harcourt Religion Publishers, GIA).

"You Are Near" by Dan Schutte from *Gather (Comprehensive)* (GIA), *Today's Missal* (OCP), *Glory & Praise* (OCP [NALR]), *Journeysongs* (OCP).

Announcements

- parish news
- birthdays
- other

PART II: Remembering God's Word

Review the Eighteenth Sunday in Ordinary Time.

1. What was the main message in last week's readings?

- Wealth, power, and possessions don't guarantee happiness or eternal life. Jesus wants us to grow rich in God's sight, not in the sight of the world.

2. What are some ways we can grow rich in the sight of God?

- Review the students' responses from last week. (Be open to new ideas that the students may have been thinking about during the week.)

3. What did you find out about greed last week? Whom did you ask about the different forms of greed in the world? What sources of greed did they share with you?

- Let the students share their lists.

> *This is a wonderful teaching moment, when the group examines and discusses ways to avoid greed and see how it destroys our relationship with Jesus and others.*

Review the session on the Transfiguration.

1. What feast did we celebrate last week?
   - the Feast of the Transfiguration

2. Who appeared while Jesus was praying?
   - Moses and Elijah

3. What did the voice from a cloud say?
   - This is my Son, my Chosen One. Listen to him.

4. What happened when you sat quietly with Jesus last week? What did Jesus share with you? How did this help you during the week?
   - Let the students respond openly and honestly.

PART III: Understanding *God's Word*

Scripture

Prior to class, write some clues on index cards. Each clue should lead to another clue hidden in the room. Also write on each card a verse from the gospel reading. The final clue should lead to Jesus. Jesus could be symbolized in a variety of ways—artwork, crucifix, candle, Bible, and so on. Be creative and have fun.

Divide the students into small groups. Give each group a clue. Explain that each clue leads to another clue. Their goal is to find the hidden treasure.

Once all the groups have finished the treasure hunt, read Luke 12:32–48. Discuss how the treasure hunt relates to the gospel. Some themes include journeying, being ready and looking for Jesus' return, realizing that Jesus is our treasure, and sharing your gifts.

Use the following questions and activities to help students process the gospel reading further.

Younger Students

1. Distribute paper and crayons to the students. Have them draw a picture of Jesus' return at the end of time. Remind them to include themselves in the picture. Then direct the students to draw a picture of their treasures on the back of the paper.

2. How can you better prepare for Jesus' return at the end of time?

Reflection

Older Students

Allow students ample time to respond in their journals to the last question.

1. What possessions could you not do without? Why?

2. What would you do to get ready if you knew Jesus was going to return in two weeks?

3. With what has God entrusted you as his manager? How are you taking care of this responsibility?

Closing Prayer

Gather the students in a circle. In the middle of the circle, place an old, used Bible and a lit candle on a nicely decorated table. Ask the students to sit quietly for a few moments. Then explain that the Sacred Scriptures are similar to a treasure map that reveals the most precious treasure of all—Jesus. Say: **God promised us that his word is alive. We encounter the living word in the Bible. Use it, explore it, follow it, and you will find life—wonderful clues into God, forgiveness, and love. Read the Bible daily. Jesus is waiting to lead you to God.**

Play some soft reflective music as the Bible is passed around the group. Invite each person to say a silent prayer as he or she holds the Bible. Hold hands as you conclude the session with the Lord's Prayer.

Making God's Word Our Own

If you are choosing a student for next Sunday's opening prayer, do so now.

Read the Bible for fifteen minutes every day this week. Read it with your parents, your guardians, or your entire family. Start with one of the Gospels or one of the Letters from Paul. Discuss the readings together. Write down any questions you may have, and bring them to the next session. Read the Bible on your own if you can't find someone to read with you.

Twentieth Sunday
in Ordinary Time

Readings

Jeremiah 38:4–6, 8–10
Hebrews 12:1–4
Luke 12:49–53

Theme

Sometimes following Jesus is not easy, but it is worth it!

Scripture *Background*

The first reading is from the prophet Jeremiah, who wrote at the end of the seventh century and the beginning of the sixth century B.C. During the time of Jermiah's ministry, the Babylonians overthrew the Kingdom of Judah, taking many of its citizens into exile. Jeremiah had repeatedly warned the people that the result of their sinful ways would be exile, but they failed to pay attention to him.

The Book of Jeremiah discusses the cost of preaching the word of God. Jeremiah was ostracized by his companions and friends. His family plotted against him, and he renounced marriage for the sake of the Word. He was put in stocks, imprisoned, and threatened with execution for preaching against the temple. In today's reading, he is thrown into a cistern, where he would certainly die. Because of the kindness of one of the king's courtiers, Jeremiah was pulled out of the cistern. He remained in custody until Jerusalem was taken.

In today's gospel passage, Jesus uses two images to discuss his moment of decision to complete his mission: fire and baptism. Both illustrate Jesus' longing for the work to be accomplished. He longed for the fire to be kindled, for the baptism to be done. He longed for the final conflict and victory.

The victory came at a price. His mission would cost him his life. Crucifixion must precede resurrection. The disciple could expect no less. Following Jesus meant following the difficult path. Division might even occur in the closest family units because one had chosen this path.

The selection from the Letter to the Hebrews continued to encourage disciples to follow Jesus. Jesus endured scorn, opposition, and the cross for the sake of the joy that followed. Christians had not begun to endure to the same degree. Christians should persevere without a thought for the cost. Discipleship is compared to a race in which the runner endures all things for the sake of the victory. Things passing by are ignored; attention remains fixed on the finish line. This analogy can be applied to discipleship. Attention is focused on Jesus. Whatever the passing cost, the goal is worth the price.

Irene Nowell OSB

PART I: Gathering *for God's Word*

Alternative: Ask one of the students to lead the prayer.

Open the session by saying: **Welcome. May Jesus send you the gift of peace. I affirm your determination to participate in class and your willingness to grow in your faith. I invite the Church to stand for our opening prayer. We begin by recalling the cool waters of our Baptism, where we were cleansed and given new life** (make the sign of the cross) **in the name of the Father, and of the Son, and of the Holy Spirit. Amen.**

Jesus, you are the way to true life, love, and happiness. Bless us this day, and refresh us with the cool creative power of the Holy Spirit. Open our minds and hearts to know and love you more each and every day. You have given us so many good things; help us take the time to stop and thank you for the miracles that surround us. Grant us your healing and peace. We ask all these prayers and those we hold in our hearts in your name.

The students respond enthusiastically: **Amen!**

Song

"Be Not Afraid" by Bob Dufford from *Glory & Praise* (OCP [NALR]), *Today's Missal* (OCP), *Gather (Comprehensive)* (GIA), *Lead Me, Guide Me* (GIA).

"Circle of Friends" by Point of Grace from *Life, Love, & Other Mysteries* (Word, Inc.).

"Ordinary Holiness" by Julie and Tim Smith from *A Eucharistic People* (Troubadour Productions).

"Jesus in the Morning," African-American folk song from *Gather (Comprehensive)* (GIA), *We Celebrate* (J.S. Paluch Co., Inc.), *Lead Me, Guide Me* (GIA).

Announcements

- parish news
- birthdays
- other

PART II: Remembering *God's Word*

Use the following questions to review last week's session.

1. What did you learn about Jesus from last week's gospel?

- Let the students respond openly and honestly. Reinforce: (1) Following Jesus is like a journey or a treasure hunt, challenging and fun. (2) Wherever your treasure lies, there your heart will be. (3) Jesus gives us responsibilities and wants us to fulfill them well. (4) Jesus is coming back at the end of time, and we will have to account for the way we lived and treated others.

2. Jesus said, "The Son of Man will come when you least expect him." If you were living at the time, what would you like to be doing when Jesus suddenly returns?

- Let the students respond openly and honestly.

3. What did you learn in your Bible reading last week? What did you experience when you shared the Bible with someone else?

• Let the volunteers respond openly and honestly.

PART III: Understanding *God's Word*

Scripture

Materials Needed

All Students
• Bible
• desk bell
• small desk or table
• scorekeeper

Younger Students
• paper
• crayons

Older Students
• journals
• pens

Place a bell on a small table at the front of the room. Divide the class into two teams. Appoint a scorekeeper. Choose a representative from each team to come forward. Have them face each other with the desk and bell in between them. Their hands must remain at their sides until the question has been read.

Read a question. The first student to ring the bell can either answer the question alone for five points or ask for help from the team for one point. If the question is answered incorrectly, the opposing student gets a chance to answer alone for five points or with the team for one point. Continue until all of the students have had a chance to answer in front of the class.

Questions

Jesus asked his disciples, "Who do you say that I am?" What was Peter's reply?

• the Messiah of God

Fill in the blanks: Jesus said to all, "If anyone wishes to come after me, he must _____ himself, take up his _____ daily, and follow _____."

• deny, cross, me

True or False: Jesus said, "No one who sets a hand to the plow and looks back to what was left behind is fit for the kingdom of God."

• True

Jesus appointed and sent out a certain number of disciples. He said to them, "Be on your way, and remember—I am sending you as lambs in the midst of wolves. Do not carry a walking staff or traveling bag, wear no sandals . . ." How many disciples did Jesus say this to? (a) 12, (b) 16, (c) 72, (d) 144

• (c) 72 (Some translations use 70.)

What does the word *evangelist* mean?

• Someone who shares the good news of Jesus by word and actions.

A scholar of the law asked Jesus, "What must I do to inherit eternal life?" And Jesus replied, "You shall love the Lord, your God, with _____."

• all your heart, all your being (soul), all your strength, all your mind, and love your neighbor as yourself

Jesus tells us a parable about a man who was robbed, beaten, and left for dead. Who helped this man and treated him with compassion? (a) a priest, (b) a Levite, (c) a Samaritan, (d) a family member

• (c) a Samaritan

Jesus is invited to Mary's and Martha's house for dinner. One sister is hospitable and cleans the house and prepares the food for dinner, while the other sister sits and listens to Jesus. **True or False:** Mary showed Jesus hospitality by cleaning the house and preparing the food.

- False. It was Martha.

Fill in the blanks: Ask, and you will _____. Seek, and you will _____. Knock, and the door will be _____.

- receive, find, opened

Jesus' disciples asked him to teach them how to pray. What is the name of the prayer Jesus taught his disciples?

- the Lord's Prayer

True or False: Jesus said, ". . . though one may be rich, one's life does not consist of possessions."

- True

Jesus took Peter, John, and James up a mountain to pray. Suddenly, Jesus changed, and two Old Testament men were talking with him. Who were these two Old Testament men who were talking to Jesus?

- Moses and Elijah

During Jesus' transfiguration, a cloud overshadowed those gathered, and a voice was heard from the clouds saying:

(a) This is my Son. Follow him to Jerusalem, and start a church.

(b) This is my beloved Son. Go fishing with him, and feed the poor with the fish you catch.

(c) This is my chosen Son; listen to him.

- (c) This is my chosen Son; listen to him.

Fill in the blanks: Jesus said, ". . . where your _____ is, there also will your _____ be."

- treasure, heart

Proclaim the gospel, Luke 12:49–53.

Reflection Use the following questions and activities to help students get to the heart of the gospel.

Younger Students

1. How does Jesus set the world on fire? Distribute paper and crayons to the students. Have them draw a picture of how Jesus sets the world on fire.

2. What baptism does Jesus refer to in the gospel reading?

3. Have you ever been in trouble because you were following Jesus' commandments? What happened?

Older Students

Allow time for the students to respond in their journals to the last question.

1. What is Jesus speaking of when he refers to "fire" in this passage?

2. Reflectively reread the gospel passage. What does Jesus seem to be feeling? Why?

3. How does Jesus bring division in your life? In your family? In the world?

Closing Prayer

Gather the students in a circle for silent prayer. After a few moments, invite volunteers to pray aloud for themselves or for someone who needs Jesus' healing and love. Hold hands as you conclude the session with the Lord's Prayer.

Making God's Word Our Own

Enjoy God every day this week for fifteen minutes. Go for a walk; find God in nature; go swimming or hiking; play cards with friends; read a good book; draw a picture; take a nap. Find God in everything you do. Enjoy God; take God everywhere you go. You just might find out something very special about God.

If you are choosing a student for next Sunday's opening prayer, do so now.

Twenty-First Sunday *in* Ordinary Time

Readings

Isaiah 66:18–21
Hebrews 12:5–7, 11–13
Luke 13:22–30

Theme

Following Jesus calls us to risk and not always take the easy road.

Scripture *Background*

Today's first reading is from the final chapter of the Book of Isaiah. After the return from the Babylonian exile, the people felt that they could remain faithful to the covenant by separating from peoples who were not chosen, who did not live according to God's law. The prophetic voice in Third Isaiah, however, stated that God's salvation extended to these other people. They would gather to see God's glory on the holy mountain of Jerusalem. Some of these Gentiles would even be taken as priests and ministers of the sanctuary—a thing unheard of in the religious belief of the time.

The gospel reading from Luke is a collection of sayings warning disciples to be faithful and prepared. Following Jesus is compared to entering through a narrow door. To follow Jesus is to choose the difficult means. The second image is also the image of a door, but now the master of the house will lock the door against those whom he does not know. The supposed guests claim to have eaten with Jesus. They have apparently been at the same dinners but missed the point. In Luke, table fellowship is a primary sign of discipleship. To eat with Jesus is to share his life; to share his life is to share his cross. The patriarchs knew what it meant to be faithful through trials. There are Gentiles, like those mentioned in Isaiah 66, who knew what it meant to take up the cross. But those who presume entry into the kingdom because of a passing acquaintance with Jesus will be greatly disappointed.

The author of the Letter to the Hebrews states the point directly. A good father disciplines his children to prepare them for life. God the Father disciplines his children to prepare them for eternal life. Discipline is not intended for immediate sorrow and pain but for everlasting joy. Through the cross, Jesus came to glory. Through sharing in the cross, the disciples come to share in the glory. The discipline, therefore, is truly a cause for joy. It should be accepted with courage. Discipline is a sign that we are truly children of God.

Irene Nowell OSB

PART I: Gathering *for God's Word*

Opening Prayer

Alternative: *Ask one of the students to lead the opening prayer.*

Open the session by saying: **Welcome, and thank you for joining us. I affirm your determination and steadfastness. In today's gospel, Jesus challenges us to believe in him and step out in faith. I invite the Church to stand for our opening prayer. We begin by recalling that, through our Baptism, we are sons and daughters of God; we pray** (make the sign of the cross) **in the name of the Father, and of the Son, and of the Holy Spirit. Amen.**

> *Jesus, open our hearts and minds to understand the free gift of salvation that you offer us. Remind us that we are resurrection people; we truly believe in your resurrection, that you are the savior of the world. By believing in you and following your law of love, we will live with you forever. Fill our hearts with so much joy and trust that we will want to be last so others can be first. You have called us to be your sons and daughters. Continue to bless these students, their families, and all they hold in their hearts. We ask this in your name.*

The students respond: **Amen!**

Song

"Anthem" by Tom Conry from *Glory & Praise* (OCP [NALR]), *Today's Missal* (OCP), *Gather (Comprehensive)* (GIA), *Journeysongs* (OCP).

"Deep Down I Know" by David Haas from *Walking by Faith* (Harcourt Religion Publishers, GIA).

"Only This I Want" by Dan Schutte from *Today's Missal* (OCP), *Glory & Praise* (OCP [NALR]).

"Reach Out" by Carey Landry from *Hi God!* (OCP [NALR]), *Young People's Glory & Praise* (OCP [NALR]).

Announcements

- parish news
- birthdays
- other

PART II: Remembering *God's Word*

Use the following questions to review last week's gospel reading.

1. In last Sunday's gospel passage, Jesus was excited. What did Jesus want to do?

- Jesus wanted to light a fire on the earth. He wished his blaze were ignited!

2. Is Jesus going to bring peace or division on earth? Why?

- Division. We must choose to follow Jesus and his teachings if we truly want to be his disciples. This may separate us from others who do not want to live according to Jesus' law of love.

3. How did you enjoy God last week? Where did you find God?

- Let the students respond openly and honestly.

PART III: Understanding *God's Word*

Materials Needed

All Students
- Bible
- two bowls (one marked "safe" and the other "risky")
- index cards on which "safe" and "risky" questions and actions are written
- reflective music
- tape or CD player

Younger Students
- paper
- crayons

Older Students
- journals
- pens

Questions and Actions

Safe
- What are your favorite foods?
- What do you do to relax and have fun?
- Share with us one fun experience you had this summer.
- Whistle the tune "Happy Birthday."
- Do ten jumping jacks.
- What is your favorite TV program?
- What do you think heaven is like?
- What would you choose if you were given three wishes?
- Turn around three times with your hands out-stretched.
- What is your favorite season of the year? Why?
- Where would you live if you could live anywhere in the world? Why?
- Shake hands with three people.
- What do you want to be when you grow up?
- What are the best things in life?
- If you could be any kind of animal, what would you be? Why?
- What is a true friend?

Risky
- When is it hard for you to follow Jesus?
- Describe a time when you were really scared.
- What really annoys you about life?
- What are some of the qualities you most like about yourself?
- Act like a monkey for thirty seconds.
- Sing any song you want.
- When have you felt especially close to your family?
- What three talents are you especially proud of?
- When is it hard to tell a family member you love him or her?
- When was the last time you cried? What happened?
- Run around the room three times making bird noises.
- What area of your life would you like to change?
- Why is it sometimes difficult to believe God loves you?
- Do five pushups.
- Shake hands with your teacher, and tell your teacher that you appreciate him or her.

Scripture

The students really like and are challenged by this activity. Allow them to choose the category ("safe" or "risky") with which they feel most comfortable. Jesus tells us in Luke 13:22–30 that following him would not be easy. To eat with Jesus was to share his life; to share his life is to share his cross—not always easy and often risky. It can be risky to put yourself last and allow others to be first.

Invite one brave volunteer to come forward, and have him or her choose from either the "risky" bowl or the "safe" bowl. Prior to their selection, let the students know that they will be expected to answer the question or do the action that is written on the card. Before the volunteer answers the question, ask him or her: Why did you choose safe/risky? (Remember that there is no right or wrong answer to this question.) Have the student do whatever the card asks. Choose as many volunteers to pick a card as time allows.

Proclaim Luke 13:22–30. Share with the students why following Jesus can be risky. Faith is a risky business, but by following Jesus and trusting in God, we find true life.

Reflection   Use the following questions and activities to help students process the readings further.

Younger Students

1. Distribute to the students paper and crayons. Have them draw a picture of the "narrow door" that Jesus talks about in the gospel.

2. What would you have to let go of to pass through Jesus' narrow door?

3. What does Jesus really mean when he says, "The first will be last and the last will be first"?

Older Students

Allow ample time for the students to respond in their journals to the last question.

1. If God wants all kinds of people (verse 29) to know him, why isn't the door wider?

2. Would it be easier to believe in Jesus' words if you were first in line or last in line? Why?

3. Often people believe that there is no room for second place, that it's important to be first at all costs, and that win, win, win is the name of the game. Jesus tells us that the first shall be last and the last shall be first. Whom do you believe—society or Jesus? Why? Whom do you often follow—Jesus or those who always have to be first? Why?

Closing Prayer   Gather the students together. Play some reflective music, and invite them to pray silently, asking Jesus to help them live the life our faith requires. After a few minutes, invite volunteers to share with the class one prayer for themselves or one for someone else.

Making God's Word Our Own   Allow someone else to go before you each day this week. Give it a try, and see how Jesus works through you. Watch what happens to others and to you. Ask Jesus to help you, and he will.

If you are choosing a student for next Sunday's opening prayer, do so now.

Twenty-Second Sunday *in* Ordinary Time

Readings

Sirach 3:17–18, 20, 28–29
Hebrews 12:18–19, 22–24a
Luke 14:1, 7–14

Theme

Give as God gives—in humility and love.

Scripture *Background*

Today's first reading gives us the wisdom of Ben Sira, a second-century Jerusalem sage. He speaks on the subject of "public relations." How does one live harmoniously with other people? Ben Sira observes that humility when dealing with others brings love and honor, whereas overweening pride brings hatred and disaster. One who is humble has a happier life. Not only will other people love the humble person; God, too, is pleased with humility. Greatness is God's domain; humility is the appropriate human response.

The final verses introduce another favorite theme of Ben Sira: the giving of alms. Almsgiving is a better remedy for sin than sacrifice. God remembers those who show kindness, and God repays.

In the gospel passage read for today, Jesus, like the wisdom teacher, was telling his disciples how to get along with others and how to receive honor rather than shame. It was the assumption that the lowest place allowed others an opportunity to offer increased status. To insist upon having the highest place is to risk embarrassment for being conceited.

The second part of the reading concerns the ordinary expectations of the host. When we invite people to dinner, we ordinarily expect that they will reciprocate the offer. This understanding of the social graces is part of our received wisdom. But Jesus instructs the disciples to invite those who could not possibly reciprocate. He suggests we should not invite them out of noble generosity. We are to invite them because God is the host who will assume the obligation. God will then invite **us** to dinner—the dinner of the kingdom.

The reading from the Letter to the Hebrews presents the kingdom of God in the image of the holy mountain. When God appeared at Mount Sinai, the signs of divine presence were lightning, thunder, fire, smoke, and trumpet blasts. The people responded with terror. God later manifested the divine presence in the new Jerusalem through the person of Jesus. Jesus sealed the new covenant in his own blood, as the Sinai covenant was sealed in blood. Jesus was willing to shed his blood so we could be covenant partners. Therefore, we should approach God's mountain without fear.

Irene Nowell OSB

PART I: Gathering *for God's Word*

Opening Prayer

Alternative: *Ask one of the students to lead the opening prayer.*

Open the session by saying: **Welcome. May God's peace be with all of you. Thank you for joining us again. I affirm your sense of responsibility and steadfastness to continue to nurture your faith and relationship with Jesus. I would like to do something special before we start today. Everyone sitting in the back row, please move to the front row; those in the front, please move to the back row.** (Organized chaos! Listen carefully to the reactions and responses of both groups. You will be able to use them in sharing after the gospel is proclaimed.)

We begin by remembering that by being called to the waters of Baptism, we were made anew in Jesus. Therefore we humbly and joyfully begin (make the sign of the cross) **in the name of the Father, and of the Son, and of the Holy Spirit. Amen.**

> *Jesus, thank you for bringing us into the Church. We have been given so much; show us how to give as God gives, to love as God loves, and to forgive as God forgives. Grant us the spirit of humility so that we will never forget from where and from whom all good things come. Continue to bless these students, their families, and their teachers. Continue to walk with them every day. We ask all this in your name.*

The students respond loudly: **Amen!**

Song

"Bless the Feast" by James Hansen from *Today's Missal* (OCP), *Gather (Comprehensive)* (GIA), *Glory & Praise* (OCP [NALR]), *Journeysongs* (OCP).

"Faith Walkin' People" by Brown Bannister and Amy Grant from *Amy Grant, The Collection* (Word Music).

"Give Me Jesus," traditional African American spiritual from *Today's Missal* (OCP).

"Here I Am, Lord," by Dan Schutte from *Glory & Praise* (OCP [NALR]), *Gather (Comprehensive)* (GIA), *Today's Missal* (OCP), *Lead Me, Guide Me* (GIA), *Journeysongs* (OCP).

Announcements

- parish news
- birthdays
- other

PART II: Remembering *God's Word*

Use the following questions to review last week's session.

1. True or False: Jesus wants his followers to take the safe road. Following Jesus is easy.

- False

2. True or False: To eat with Jesus was to share his life; to share his life was to share his cross.

   • True

3. What did Jesus say about being first and last in God's kingdom?

   • Those who are last will be first; those who are first will be last.

4. What did you learn about either God's kingdom or yourself from last week's gospel reading?

   • Let the students respond openly and honestly.

5. Whom did you put first last week? What did you experience?

   • Let the students respond openly and honestly.

PART III: Understanding *God's Word*

Scripture

For this activity, create a game show setting. Bring in someone from the parish to be the host of the show. The point is to have fun while you learn—so have fun. The students will get into it if you do.

   Divide the group into two teams. Each team will be asked a question about God and then have one minute to work together to answer it. The teams must answer these questions as if they know what God was, is, and will be thinking; they are to think with the mind of God. Give the teams a "ten seconds remaining" signal before time has expired. Each team gets 1,000 points if their answer is correct; they lose 1,000 points if they are incorrect. The correctness of the answer will be based on common sense, effort, and if the answer is theologically sound. If a team is unable to answer its question in the one-minute time allotted or if its answer is incorrect, the other team gets to try to answer the question.

Materials Needed

All Students
   • list of questions
   • game host (invite the pastor or priest, DRE, or a parishioner)
   • slips of paper with definition of the word *humility* (one per student)

Younger Students
   • paper
   • crayons

Older Students
   • journals
   • pens

Questions

   • Why did God make the world?
   • Why did God make women?
   • Why did God name Adam, Adam, and Eve, Eve?
   • Is God hurt or happy when we do something wrong? Why?
   • Why does God not always answer our prayers the way we think he should?
   • Why did God make us his sons and daughters?
   • Why does God enjoy giving us so many good things?
   • What are ten good things that God freely gives us?

Proclaim Luke 14:1, 7–14. After the reading, ask the following questions.

   • How does God want us to treat others?
   • How does God want us to share with others what we have been given?
   • How would God define the word *humility?*

Reflection   Use the following activities and questions to discuss the reading further.

Younger Students

1. Distribute to the students paper and crayons. Direct them to draw a picture of Jesus inviting them to move from the back of line to the front of line.

2. Why does Jesus say it is better to invite to lunch or dinner people who can't repay you?

3. Do you know anyone who is humble? How does a humble person act?

Older Students

Have the students respond in their journals to the last question.

1. Define the word *humility*.

2. What does the gospel reading say about Jesus' values versus society's values?

3. How could Jesus help you be more humble?

Closing Prayer   Gather the students into a circle. Divide the class into two groups by having the students count off "one" and "two." Sing in rounds "Humble Thyself" by Bob Hudson from Maranatha! Music. Once they are familiar with the song, it can be a very reflective and prayerful experience.

Group 2 starts singing. Group 1 joins in when group 2 sings "Lord." In chorus, group 2 sings their part where dots are on group 1 lines. (See below.) Everyone sings "you up" together.

Group 1: *Humble thyself in the sight of the Lord.*

Group 2: *Humble thyself in the sight of the Lord.*

Group 1: *Humble thyself in the sight of the Lord.*

Group 2: *Humble thyself in the sight of the Lord.*

Chorus

Group 1: *And He .... shall lift .... you up. (higher and higher)*

Group 2: *And He .... shall lift you up. (higher and higher)*

Group 1: *And He .... shall lift .... you up.*

Group 2: *And He .... shall lift you up.*

Making God's Word Our Own   Write on slips of paper the definition of the word *humility,* and distribute them to the students.

Humility means recognizing we are creatures made in God's image. Read this definition of the word *humility* each morning when you get up. Experience and look at the world through this definition. Spend about five minutes at the end of each day writing down in a notebook what you experienced with God that day. Try this challenge for one week. You may learn something about God, yourself, and the world!

> *If you are choosing a student for next Sunday's opening prayer, do so now.*

Twenty-Third Sunday
in Ordinary Time

Readings

Wisdom 9:13–18b
Philemon 1:9–10, 12–17
Luke 14:25–33

Theme

*Commitment is required
to follow Jesus.*

Scripture *Background*

The first reading is from a prayer for wisdom spoken by Solomon. The passage proclaims the superiority of God's wisdom over human wisdom. Simple concepts that humans should understand often escape us. How, then, can heavenly things be understood by earthly creatures? God sent Lady Wisdom to humans to offer understanding on how to live. Wisdom taught earthly concepts for earthly life and divine things for godly life. Thus she was the savior of humans who could not achieve true life without her.

In the New Testament, Jesus is the incarnation of God's wisdom, the teacher who taught humans how to live. He uses examples from human common sense to illustrate messages with deeper meanings. Just as a builder first calculates and assembles the resources necessary to complete the project, so also the disciple must understand and be prepared to pay the cost of following Jesus. The cost is beyond human calculation.

The disciple must be prepared to abandon all human possessions and all human ties, even those most dear. The disciple must be willing to sacrifice life itself for discipleship. Only one who is willing to pay the cost should attempt discipleship. One who does not believe that the rewards of following Jesus are greater than any cost does not understand discipleship. That person understands only human wisdom. Only through the gift of **God's** wisdom could anyone assume the cost of discipleship.

Paul's very short letter to his friend Philemon illustrates living by God's wisdom rather than human wisdom. Philemon owned a slave named Onesimus. Onesimus ran away and was baptized a Christian by Paul. Paul asks Philemon to avoid punishing his runaway slave and to treat him as a brother rather than as a slave. This was unthinkable in the social context of the era. Paul reminded Philemon of the debt he owed Paul. Philemon, a Christian because of Paul, owed his life to Paul. Now Paul asked Onesimus's life in return. It was absurd by human wisdom. By God's wisdom, it was the only choice.

Irene Nowell OSB

PART I: Gathering *for God's Word*

Opening Prayer   **Alternative:** *Ask one of the students to lead the opening prayer.*

Open the session by saying: **Welcome. God's peace to all of you. I affirm your commitment and loyalty. Following Jesus is a commitment; sometimes it is easy, but other times it is difficult. I invite the Church to stand for our opening prayer. We begin today by remembering where our commitment to Jesus started—at our Baptism.** (Make the sign of the cross) **In the name of the Father, and of the Son, and of the Holy Spirit. Amen.**

Jesus, we thank and praise you for the life and faith we have received. We offer to you our lives, this day and all of our days. Continue to walk with us, and show us the way to became strong and committed disciples. It's not easy, but with your help we can do it. Teach us to love, forgive, and serve others. Help us put aside anything that keeps us from you. Fill these students and their parents with your Holy Spirit so they may be free to embrace you with both arms. We ask all this in your name.

The students respond: **Amen!**

Song   "All That Is Hidden" by Bernadette Farrell from *Today's Missal* (OCP), *Glory & Praise 2* (OCP [NALR]), *Journeysongs* (OCP).

"Come with Me into the Fields" by Dan Schutte from *Today's Missal* (OCP), *Glory & Praise* (OCP [NALR]).

"I Have Decided" by Michael Card from *Amy Grant, The Collection* (Word Music).

"Only a Shadow" by Carey Landry from *Today's Missal* (OCP), *Glory & Praise* (OCP [NALR]).

Announcements
- parish news
- birthdays
- other

PART II: Remembering *God's Word*

Review last week's session.

1. What did Jesus share with us last week?
   - The last shall be first, and the first shall be last. Invite to dinner those who can't repay you.
2. When will we be repaid for helping those who are poor, disabled, ill, and blind?
   - At the resurrection
3. God has given us so much. How should we act in return?
   - We should be thankful to and humble before God.
4. How did the definition of the word *humility* help you see the world differently last week?
   - Let the students respond openly and honestly.

PART III: Understanding *God's Word*

Scripture

Objective: The only way to win is to let go of your puzzle pieces and share with others what you have. We win in our spiritual journey and are true followers of Jesus when we let go of what we have and share.

Mix together the pieces from a couple of different puzzles. Divide the students into small groups. Give each group an assortment of puzzle pieces. Provide the groups with a time limit in which they should complete the puzzle. Explain that the first group to finish the puzzle wins.

Once the groups begin working on the puzzles, they will soon discover that another group has the pieces they need to complete their puzzle and that they have pieces that other groups may need. **Don't tell them to share their pieces; let them figure it out themselves.**

Proclaim Luke 14:25–33. Discuss how the reading relates to last week's gospel reading.

Materials Needed

All Students
• Bible
• children's puzzles
• cross

Older Students
• paper
• journals
• pens

Reflection

Use the following questions to explore the reading further.

Younger Students

1. When have you started something but couldn't finish it? What was it? What happened?

2. What are you willing to give up and share in order to be a disciple of Jesus?

3. Jesus tells us that we need to be committed to being in relationship with God. What can you do to be more committed to being in relationship with God?

Older Students

Allow time for the students to respond in their journals to the first question.

1. Have you stopped and honestly calculated the cost to you personally to follow Jesus' law of love? Jesus gave his life for us; what will it cost you to follow him?

2. Have you ever started a project that you couldn't finish? What happened? How did you feel? What did others say?

3. Distribute to the students writing paper and pens. Direct them to write a letter either to the pastor, DRE, deacon, liturgist, parish priest, or catechist (teacher) thanking this person for his or her dedication and the sacrifices made in order to follow Jesus.

Closing Prayer

Gather the students in a circle. Slowly pass a cross around the circle. Invite the students to silently ask Jesus for assistance in giving up and sharing their possessions as they receive the cross. Invite the other students to pray silently for the person holding the cross. Hold hands as you conclude the session with the Lord's Prayer.

Making God's Word Our Own

If you are choosing a student for next Sunday's opening prayer, do so now.

Go through your possessions (clothes, shoes, toys, books, and toys), and box up what you don't need or use. Bring your items to church next week, and we will give them to someone who can use them. Ask other members of your family to join in and go through their things. Make sure you check with your parents or guardians before you bring your items to church next week.

Twenty-Fourth Sunday *in* Ordinary Time

Readings

Exodus 32:7–11, 13–14
1 Timothy 1:12–17
Luke 15:1–32

Theme

Come home. God's forgiveness is bigger than our sins.

Scripture *Background*

The story from Exodus occurred at Sinai, where God made a covenant with the people. Before the people ever left Sinai, they broke this covenant. Instead of trusting God to be faithful to them, they created a golden calf to attempt to control the presence of God. This breach of love and fidelity on their part broke the covenant. God responded by proclaiming to Moses his intention to destroy these people. Moses reminded God of the *unconditional* covenant with the patriarchs and of the danger to the divine reputation if God's people were destroyed in the desert. In response to Moses' prayer, God repents of the punishment.

The setting of this story at Sinai is significant. Though the people had broken the covenant, God does not deny the covenant but renews it. Within the initial covenant story, there is an implied hope for renewal. God's love is even greater than the covenant.

In response to the Pharisees' complaint that he ate with sinners, Jesus told the three parables we read today. The first two parables were simple examples of persons who rejoiced over a lost article that was found. Both the man and the woman held a party to celebrate the rediscovery. Both ate and drank to celebrate their joy.

The third parable was also a parable of lost and found. Regaining the lost son was more valuable to the father than any damage the son may have caused. To celebrate his find, the father held a party and ate and drank with the lost son. The elder son, however, was not happy about the party. Now the elder son grew distant in his heart and was lost. The father came out to the elder son and encouraged him to celebrate with them. Only if the elder son would join the celebration could the father have both his sons. Jesus told the parable to show the Pharisees that God also eats with sinners. If these Pharisees forgave sinners, then God would have all his children at the banquet. Then God would rejoice fully.

The passage from 1 Timothy presents Paul's thanksgiving prayer for having been forgiven when he was persecuting the Church. Paul is an example of God's forgiveness of sinners. We, too, can hope for forgiveness. God cannot bear to lose his children. He rejoices when they are found.

Irene Nowell OSB

PART I: Gathering *for God's Word*

Designate an area for the items the students bring from home as a result of last week's lesson. Invite a representative from Goodwill or the St. Vincent de Paul Society to come to the session and collect the students' donations. Have the representative explain to the students how their donations help others.

Opening Prayer

Alternative: *Ask one of the students to lead the opening prayer.*

Open the session by saying: **Welcome. Thank you for sharing your possessions with others. I invite the Church to stand as we begin our opening prayer. We are the Church, the people of God, because we have been baptized. We come together** (make the sign of the cross) **in the name of the Father, and of the Son, and of the Holy Spirit.**

> *Jesus, thank you for touching the hearts of the students who are sharing some of their material possessions with others. Remind us that you will take care of all our needs. Bless all of us here today, and open our hearts and minds to your tremendous love and forgiveness. Never let us forget that you will always take us back, love us, and forgive us if we turn to you in honesty and truth. Thank you for your wonderful gifts of forgiveness and love. We ask all these prayers in your name.*

The students respond loudly: **Amen!**

Song

"Abba! Father!" by Carey Landry from *Glory & Praise* (OCP [NALR]), *Today's Missal* (OCP).

"All I Ever Have to Be" by Gary Chapman from *Amy Grant, The Collection* (Word Music).

"Amazing Grace," Traditional from *Gather (Comprehensive)* (GIA), *Glory & Praise* (OCP [NALR]), *Today's Missal* (OCP), *We Celebrate* (J.S. Paluch Co., Inc.), *Lead Me, Guide Me* (GIA).

Announcements

- parish news
- birthdays
- other

PART II: Remembering *God's Word*

Review last week's session.

1. What did you learn about Jesus in last Sunday's gospel?
   - Let the students respond honestly and openly. Remind them that Jesus wants us to be committed to following him.
2. What did you learn about material possessions?
   - Jesus wants us to be free of anything that keeps us away from him. We need to let go of what we have been given and share it with others, especially those in need.

3. What did Jesus say about finishing something you started?
  - We need to stop and think about what we are doing and properly prepare to follow Jesus.

4. What is the cost of being Jesus' disciple?
  - It's free, but it costs everything—especially our hearts.

5. What did you learn about yourself as you went through your possessions and discarded what you didn't need? What items did you have a hard time letting go of? Why?
  - Let the students respond openly and honestly.

PART III: Understanding *God's Word*

Scripture

Materials Needed

All Students—Option 1
- Bible
- TV and VCR
- *Jesus of Nazareth* video, directed by Franco Zeffireli (Ventura, CA: Gospel Light Publications)
- reflective music
- tape or CD player

All Students—Option 2
- Bibles (one per group)
- chalkboard or dry-erase board
- chalk or dry-erase markers
- reflective music
- tape or CD player

Younger Students
- paper
- crayons

Older Students
- journals
- pens

Choose from two options.

Option One

Proclaim Luke 15:1–32. Then show the corresponding scene from tape 2 of the video *Jesus of Nazareth*. This ten-minute scene is very powerful.

Option Two

Divide the students into three groups, and give each group a Bible. Assign the groups the following Scripture passages. List the passages on the chalkboard or dry-erase board for easy reference.
- Group 1—Luke 15:1–7
- Group 2—Luke 15:8–10
- Group 3—Luke 15:11–31

After reading its passage, each group should decide upon the main point that Jesus wants us to know. Then give the groups ample time to prepare a short skit of the gospel story. Once prepared, have the groups present their skits for the entire class.

Use the following questions and activities to help students further understand the gospel reading.

Younger Students

1. Distribute to the students paper and crayons. Direct them to draw a picture of the father welcoming his son back home. Remind them to include themselves in the picture.
2. Have you ever lost something and spent a long time looking for it? Did you ever find it? How did you feel when you found it?
3. Who are the sheep that Jesus puts on his shoulders and carries back home?

Reflection

Older Students

Allow time for the students to respond in their journals to the last question.

1. What lessons did you learn in these three parables?

2. There are three main characters in the parable of the prodigal son: the father, the younger son, and the older son. Which character do you see yourself as? Why?

3. Compare your spiritual journey to the prodigal son's journey. Where are you now?

- at home, but not happy
- in a far-off country eating pig food
- coming to my senses
- on my way home, but not sure what I'll find
- at home enjoying the fatted calf and the party
- I've just arrived, and I feel my father's embrace. I feel great!

Closing Prayer

Gather the students in a circle. Play some reflective music, and invite the students to sit quietly for a few moments and think about the following question: **Is it more difficult to accept God's love and forgiveness or to forgive and love yourself? Ask Jesus to open your heart so that you may receive God's forgiveness and be able to forgive yourself.** Hold hands as you conclude the session with the Lord's Prayer.

Making God's Word Our Own

If you are choosing a student for next Sunday's opening prayer, do so now.

This week's prayer challenge is really going to help you walk the walk and not just talk the talk. You are invited to ask God's forgiveness for your wrongdoing. If you are old enough, you may want to do this by celebrating the Sacrament of Reconciliation. All of us can look into our hearts and ask Jesus' forgiveness for any actions that hurt our relationships with him. Ask Jesus for strength, forgiveness, and love. Then go to the people you have hurt in some way and ask their forgiveness. Promise them that you will try harder to be more loving and caring. If anyone asks your forgiveness, forgive with a generous heart.

Twenty-Fifth Sunday *in* Ordinary Time

Readings

Amos 8:4–7
1 Timothy 2:1–8
Luke 16:1–13

Theme

How do we use what God has given us?

Scripture *Background*

The prophet Amos preached during an era when division between the wealthy merchant class and the poorer rural class increased. At times, the merchants grew impatient for the religious holidays to end so that they could return to business. They reduced the size of their product and raised the price to increase their profit. They sold poor-quality merchandise and figuratively enslaved the poor for the price of a pair of sandals.

Amos proclaimed that, because the rich had neglected the poor, God would come in judgment and destroy the land. God cared for the poor, even if the rich did not. The day would come when both rich and poor would lose everything because of the exploitation that was occurring.

The passage from 1 Timothy called for God's faithful people to pray for those in authority to be good leaders. When there is a fair social structure, God's people can live in peace and be faithful to God's law. Therefore, they should pray for fair government and honest leaders. Through this, they prayed for the salvation of all people.

The manager in Luke's parable was probably a tenant farmer who managed an estate for an absentee landowner. The manager paid the creditor's accounts to the landowner. He earned his living by adding his commission to what the creditors had to pay. When the manager was about to lose his position, he found a clever solution. He changed the amount of the creditor's debts by subtracting his own commission. He used his salary to make friends who would look kindly on him when he was dismissed from his job. The landowner praised him for his cleverness.

This parable reflects the cleverness of the manager. Business people use possessions more cleverly than those who profess religion. Religious people should follow their example to gain *lasting* treasure. Possessions are useful, but they cannot be allowed to control the attention of disciples. The disciples should focus on service to God. To that end, possessions must be used.

Irene Nowell OSB

PART I: Gathering *for* God's Word

Opening Prayer

Alternative: *Ask one of the students to lead the opening prayer.*

Open the session by saying: **Welcome. May all of our eyes be open to the wonders of God's love that surrounds us. I affirm your generosity and idealism as we continue on our faith journey. I invite the Church to stand for our opening prayer. We begin by remembering what?** (Let the students respond.) **Our Baptism! We begin** (make the sign of the cross) **in the name of the Father, and of the Son, and of the Holy Spirit.**

> *Lord Jesus, we thank and praise you for all the good things you have given to us. We thank you for our families and friends, our homes, the food that nourishes us, and, especially, for your love and friendship. Bless those who do not have homes or enough food to eat. Please grant us the spirit of generosity and your gift of wisdom so we may be willing to share what we have with those in need. We ask all this in your name.*

The students respond loudly: **Amen!**

Song

"God of the Hungry" by Scott Soper from *Today's Missal* (OCP), *Glory & Praise 2* (OCP [NALR]), *Journeysongs* (OCP).

"Praise His Name" by Michael Joncas from *Today's Missal* (OCP), *Glory & Praise* (OCP [NALR]), *Journeysongs* (OCP).

"We Are the Light of the World" by Jean Greif from *Today's Missal* (OCP), *Glory & Praise 2* (OCP [NALR]), *Journeysongs* (OCP).

Announcements

- parish news
- birthdays
- other

PART II: Remembering *God's Word*

Use the following questions to review last week's session.

1. What three parables did Jesus tell last week?

- the parable of the lost sheep, the lost coin, and the prodigal son

2. Which parable did you like most? Why?

- Let the students respond openly and honestly.

3. What was the main point of all three parables?

- God loves us and will forgive us.

4. What did you experience as you asked forgiveness and forgave others?

- Let the students share openly and honestly.

PART III: Understanding *God's Word*

Scripture

Materials Needed

All Students
- Bible
- list provided
- bike
- bike helmet
- copies of "The Road to Life"

Older Students
- journals
- pens

Read each statement below. Those who choose one answer should gather on one side of the room, and those who choose the other answer should gather on the opposite side of the room.

> *I am more like hamburger or steak.*
> *I am more like a golfer or a skydiver.*
> *I am more like ice cream or hot sauce.*
> *I am more like the mountains or the ocean.*
> *I am more like a city or a small town.*
> *I am more like apples or oranges.*
> *I am more like morning or night.*
> *I am more like a helper or a receiver.*
> *I am more like a master or a servant.*
> *I am more like a server of God or a maker of money.*

Invite the students to spend a few minutes discussing with their group why they chose the response they did. Then allow each side to take turns explaining why their choice is best. Do this for each of the questions. Have the students move as their choice requires.

Proclaim Luke 16:1–13. Allow a few moments of reflection. Then ask: **Would you rather serve God or make a great amount of money?** Encourage the students to answer honestly. They should not be judged by you or by anyone in their class because of their responses.

Reflection

Use the following questions to help students process the readings.

Younger Students

1. Everything you have is a gift from God. How can you best use those gifts?

2. Would you rather be the richest person in the world or the holiest saint? Why?

3. What do you need to make you happy?

Older Students

Read the following verse, and then discuss the questions. Allow ample time for the students to respond in their journals to the last question.

> *"You cannot be the slave of two masters! You will like one more than the other or be more loyal to one than the other. You cannot serve both God and money." (Matthew 6:24)*

1. Do you believe this statement? Why?

2. How can we give ourselves to God? Give examples.

3. How can we give ourselves to money? Give examples.

4. Who is your master?

Closing Prayer

Gather the students together in a circle. Place a bike and a bike helmet in the middle of the circle. Read aloud the prayer "The Road to Life." After a moment of quiet reflection, give a copy of the prayer to each of the students. Hold hands as you conclude the session with the Lord's Prayer.

Making God's Word Our Own

Look around this week and see what you and Jesus can do to recycle and better reuse the materials of the earth—glass, plastics, paper, food, water, electricity, and so forth. Be thankful and aware of your environment; stop and take a good look around you. Ask Jesus to show you how you could best use your gifts and talents.

If you are choosing a student for next Sunday's opening prayer, do so now.

The Road to Life

At first I thought God was an observer, my judge, keeping track of the things I did wrong, so as to know whether I merited heaven or hell when I die. He was out there sort of like the president. I recognized his picture when I saw it, but I really didn't know him. But later on, when I met Jesus, it seemed as though life was rather like a bike ride, but it was a tandem bike, and I noticed that Jesus was in the back helping me pedal.

I didn't know just when it was that he suggested we change places, but life has not been the same since. When I had control, I knew the way. It was rather boring, but predictable. . . . It was the shortest distance between two points. But when he took the lead, he knew delightful long cuts, up mountains and through rocky places at breakneck speeds; it was all I could do to hang on. Even though it looked like madness, he said, "Pedal!"

I worried and was anxious and asked, "Where are you taking me?" He laughed and didn't answer, and I started to learn to trust. I forgot my boring life and entered into the adventure. And when I'd say, "I'm scared," he'd lean back and touch my hand. He took me to people with gifts that I needed, gifts of healing, acceptance, and joy. They gave me their gifts to take on my journey, my Lord's and mine. And we were off again. He said, "Give the gifts away; they're extra baggage—too much weight." So I did, to the people we met, and I found that in giving I received, and so our burden was light.

I did not trust him at first, in control of my life. I thought he'd wreck it. But he knows "bike secrets," knows how to make it bend to take sharp corners, jump to clear high rocks, fly to shorten scary passages. And I'm learning to be quiet and pedal in the strangest places, and I'm beginning to enjoy the view and the cool breeze on my face with my delightful constant companion, Jesus.

And when I'm sure I just can't do anymore, he just smiles and says, "Pedal!"

Author Unknown

Twenty-Sixth Sunday *in* Ordinary Time

Readings

Amos 6:1a, 4–7
1 Timothy 6:11–16
Luke 16:19–31

Theme

God cares for the poor and the oppressed, and we should too!

Scripture *Background*

On this Sunday another passage is read from the eighth-century prophet, Amos, concerning the appropriate use of possessions. Archaeological evidence points to great wealth in Samaria, the capital city of the northern kingdom of Israel. This wealth had been gained by exploitation of the poor. Worse, however, was that the plight of those who were poor did not stir any sympathy in the people of wealth. Because of their disregard, God announced that the wealthy would be the first to go into exile. They would lose their wealth and become the poorest of the poor.

The parable of Lazarus and the rich man has two main points. The first corresponds to the message from the prophet Amos. The relationship between Lazarus (the poor man) and the rich man was reversed in the kingdom of God. There, Lazarus rested in the arms of Abraham in everlasting delight. Conversely, the rich man was in eternal torment. The unconcern of the rich man led him to an eternal situation worse than that of Lazarus on earth. Despite his remorse, his situation could not be altered. Once, the rich man could have eased the misery of Lazarus; now even Lazarus was helpless to relieve the rich man's misery.

The second point of the parable begins here. The rich man asked Abraham to send Lazarus to warn his brothers. Abraham replied that his brothers had all the warning they needed. The Law (Moses) and the prophets clearly state that those in power are responsible for those who are poor and in need. If the brothers did not heed the word of God, Abraham reasoned, why would they pay attention to someone who had risen from the dead?

This final line of this parable is ironic. Those who will not believe the prophets will not believe the Risen Christ, either. Miracles do not compel faith. Even the greatest witness to God's love, the resurrection, does not compel faith. Those who will not live by the Law—that is, those who will not care for those who are poor and in need, as God cares for them—will also not believe the good news. Their complacency will, in the end, reduce them to absolute poverty, the loss of life with God.

Irene Nowell OSB

PART I: Gathering *for God's Word*

Opening Prayer

Alternative: *Ask one of the students to lead the opening prayer.*

Open the session by saying: **Welcome! I am happy and glad to see all of you here today. Today we are going to explore a side of God that many people are afraid to acknowledge. God really loves and cares for all those who are poor and those who suffer oppression in any of its forms. But before we do, I invite the Church to stand for our opening prayer. We begin by calling to mind our personal relationship with God because we were baptized** (make the sign of the cross) **in the name of the Father, and of the Son, and of the Holy Spirit.**

Jesus, you clearly told us how much God the Father cares for those who are poor and oppressed. Please grant us the spirit of compassion and the strength to reach out to those who are poor and to help, comfort, and love them as you do. Also grant us the wisdom to stand up to and stop anyone or any institution that oppresses people and takes their dignity away. May your justice and peace fill this room, faith community, and world. God, we ask all this and those prayers we hold in our hearts in Jesus' name.

The students respond enthusiastically: **Amen!**

Song

"Beatitudes" by Darryl Ducote from *Glory & Praise* (OCP [NALR]), *Today's Missal* (OCP).

"City of God" by Dan Schutte from *Glory & Praise* (OCP [NALR]), *Gather (Comprehensive)* (GIA), *Today's Missal* (OCP), *Journeysongs* (OCP).

"Cry of the Poor" by John Foley from *Today's Missal* (OCP), *Glory & Praise* (OCP [NALR]), *Journeysongs* (OCP).

Announcements

• parish news
• birthdays
• other

PART II: Remembering *God's Word*

Review last week's readings.

1. How many masters did Jesus say a person can have?

• One. "You cannot be the slave of two masters! You will like one more than the other or be more loyal to one than the other. You cannot serve both God and money." (Matthew 6:24)

2. Jesus was also clear about giving yourself to God or money. What did Jesus say about this?

• Jesus said, "You cannot serve both God and money."

3. In the past week, did you recycle and better reuse the materials of the earth—glass, plastics, paper, food, water, electricity, and so forth?

• Let the students respond openly and honestly.

PART III: Understanding *God's Word*

Materials Needed

All Students
- Bible
- four adults or older students
- four copies of the script (page 201)
- costumes (optional but recommended)
- table
- chair
- red sheet or cloth
- large rubber bands (one for each student)

Younger Students
- paper
- crayons

Older Students
- journals
- pens

Act out this very powerful gospel. It is recommended that four adults or older students play the parts, but younger students can also do a good job if they get into the roles and the message of the play. If you use the younger students, consider employing the following:

- Make a sign for each character to wear: Lazarus = poor and oppressed; rich man = wealthy and powerful; Abraham = faith.
- Instead of using a script, have the students echo their parts.

Distribute copies of the script to those participating. Give them a few minutes to prepare and, if you are using props, set the stage.

Allow ample time for the actors to perform. After the play, have the performers return to their seats. Ask the entire class the following questions:

- What is the main point of this parable?
- How does it apply to you?

Discuss the readings further, using the following questions and activities.

Younger Students

1. Distribute to the students paper and crayons. Have them draw a picture of Abraham comforting Lazarus. Encourage them to include themselves in the drawing.
2. Who helps you when you are in need?
3. Would you rather be Lazarus or the rich man in this parable? Why?

Reflection

Older Students

Allow time for the students to respond in their journals to the last question.

1. Think of a time in your life when you got the help you really needed. How did you feel?
2. Who needs your help? How can you help this person or these persons?
3. Do you understand that our faith in Jesus does not suggest but **demands** that we help others no matter who they are? What does this mean to you?

Closing Prayer

Have the students sit in a circle. Go around the circle, and give a large rubber band to each student. Direct the students to put the rubber bands around their wrists as a reminder that they are called to help those who are poor and oppressed. One at a time, have them say out loud as they place the rubber bands around their wrists, " I have been baptized; therefore I am called to serve those who are poor and in need." Hold hands as you conclude the session with the Lord's Prayer.

Making God's Word Our Own

If you are choosing a student for next Sunday's opening prayer, do so now.

Spend fifteen minutes this week sitting with Jesus. Ask Jesus to show how you can best help those who are in need. Make a plan, and put it into action. Do things that aren't normally expected of you, such as extra work around the house, or ask a neighbor if you could do odd jobs for some extra money. Then go to the store with the money you have earned and buy canned goods to donate to a food pantry that feeds people who are poor. Or give what you earned to the St. Vincent de Paul ministry at your parish; members of this group assist those who are poor and oppressed in your community. This challenge will take both prayer and action each day. Try it, and experience what God can do through you!

Role-Play Script—
The Rich Man and Lazarus

Narrator/Jesus: Once there was a rich man who dressed in purple and linen and feasted splendidly every day.

The rich man enters and wanders around while he or she eats. After the rich man sits in front of the table, continue with the narration.

Narrator/Jesus: A beggar named Lazarus lay in front of the rich man's gate. He was covered with sores.

Lazarus slowly hobbles in and sits on the floor by the rich man. The rich man looks at Lazarus but ignores him as he continues eating.

Narrator/Jesus: Lazarus longed to eat the scraps that fell from the rich man's table. The dogs came and licked his sores.

Lazarus makes a face of disgust and pain.

Narrator/Jesus: Eventually the beggar died. He was carried by angels to the bosom of Abraham.

Abraham enters and assists Lazarus to another location, where Abraham ministers and comforts him.

Narrator/Jesus: The rich man likewise died and was buried.

Two students move the rich man to the other side of the stage or room and lay him down roughly without compassion or care on a red sheet or red cloth.

Narrator/Jesus: From the abode of the dead where he was in torment, the rich man raised his eyes and saw Abraham afar off and Lazarus resting in his bosom. The rich man called out.

Rich man: Father Abraham, have pity on me. Send Lazarus to dip the tip of his finger in water to refresh my tongue, for I am tortured in these flames.

Abraham: My child, remember that you were well off in your lifetime while Lazarus was in misery. Now he has found consolation here, but you have found torment. And that is not all. Between you and us there is fixed a great abyss so that those who might wish to cross from here to you cannot do so, nor can anyone cross from your side to us.

Rich man: Father, I ask to send Lazarus to my father's house where I have five brothers. Let him be a warning to them so that they may not end in this place of torment.

Abraham: *(holding up a Bible)* They have Moses and the prophets. Let them hear them!

Rich man: But if someone would only go to them from the dead, then they would repent!

Abraham: If they don't listen to Moses and the prophets, they will not be convinced, even if one should rise from the dead.

Narrator/Jesus: This, my brothers and sisters, is the word of the Lord.

© Harcourt Religion Publishers

Twenty-Seventh Sunday *in* Ordinary Time

Readings

Habakkuk 1:2–3, 2:2–4
2 Timothy 1:6–8,
   13–14
Luke 17:5–10

Theme

Faith is the anchor and force of life.

Scripture *Background*

The prophet Habakkuk, a contemporary of Jeremiah, preached during a time of great turmoil. The Babylonians conquered the Assyrians in Mesopotamia. Egypt attempted to aid Assyria and failed but, in the process, had taken temporary control of Judah. Babylon then seized Judah from Egypt and began to collect payment from God's people. The social and political situation in Judah reflected the instability of the entire region. Dishonesty, exploitation, and intrigue permeated the culture.

Habakkuk complained to God that the wicked seemed to prosper while the righteous continued to suffer. God's response was that the Babylonians would serve as a divine instrument to punish the wicked. Habakkuk was horrified that God would use such a wicked instrument but waited for God's answer.

God instructed the prophet to write the vision clearly for all to read easily. God told the prophet that the faithful person must wait for God's promises. The **fulfillment** of the vision would come in **God's** time. The impatient person would not persevere, but the righteous person would be able to wait faithfully. The righteous person, because of this faith, would live.

The passage from 2 Timothy was an exhortation to Christian ministers to be faithful. When one accepts the call to ministry, one is gifted by the Spirit of God. The Spirit provides the necessary qualities for the task. The minister is required to be faithful, even in the face of hardship. The minister will live because of faith.

The gospel passage is from a collection of Jesus' sayings. The first saying discusses faith. The disciples asked for an increase of faith. Jesus told them that if they had the faith found in a mustard seed, they could do impossible tasks. They could demand that the mighty mulberry tree uproot and transplant itself, and the tree would obey. If small faith had such great results, then deep faith would have even greater results.

The second saying is about faithfulness of ministers. Workers must do their jobs without expectation of gratitude. They complete the task as a matter of duty. Likewise, ministers of the gospel and disciples are expected to be faithful. It is their job. They should not expect additional rewards for doing their duty. They are, after all, only servants of the gospel.

Irene Nowell OSB

PART I: Gathering *for God's Word*

Opening Prayer **Alternative:** *Ask one of the students to lead the opening prayer.*

Open the session by saying: **I welcome you with the simplicity and joy of Saint Francis. May the Spirit of our Lord fill our hearts with laughter, love, and peace! I invite the Church to stand for our opening prayer. It was because of faith in Jesus that you were baptized; it is in our faith in Jesus that we are called to live. Therefore, we gather** (make the sign of the cross) **in the name of the Father, and of the Son, and of the Holy Spirit.**

Jesus, we thank you for the wonderful and precious gift of faith. May we always treasure and appreciate the gift of faith. Grant us the wisdom to use our faith to reflect your love, forgiveness, and power by how we live our faith to the world. It is in faith that we stand before you; in confidence we ask that you bless us with your Holy Spirit and keep us safe in your love. Bless all those we hold in our hearts. We ask this in your name.

The students respond loudly: **Amen!**

Song "Center of My Life" by Paul Inwood from *Today's Missal* (OCP), *Gather (Comprehensive)* (GIA), *Journeysongs* (OCP), *Glory & Praise 2* (OCP [NALR]).

"Faith Walkin' People" by Brown Bannister and Amy Grant from *Amy Grant, The Collection* (Word Music).

"Walking by Faith" by David Haas from *Walking by Faith* (Harcourt Religion Publishers, GIA).

"We Walk by Faith" by Marty Haugen from *Gather (Comprehensive)* (GIA), *Today's Missal* (OCP).

Announcements
- parish news
- birthdays
- other

PART II: Remembering *God's Word*

Review last week's session.

1. What happened in last week's gospel?
   - Let the students recap the story about the rich man and Lazarus.
2. What did you learn about God from last week's gospel?
   - God cares for those who are poor.
3. Why was the rich man sent to a "place of torment" when he died? Was it because he was rich?
   - No. He was sent to a "place of torment" because he didn't share with or take care of those around him who needed help.

4. How can you share what God has freely given to you?

  • Let the students respond openly and honestly.

5. How did you help those in need last week? How did they help you?

  • Let the students respond openly and honestly.

PART III: **Understanding** *God's Word*

Scripture

Materials Needed
All Students
• Bible
• three volunteers
• copies of the Prayer of St. Francis (one per student)
Younger Students
• paper
• crayons
Older Students
• journals
• pens

Choose three volunteers. Call the first student to the front of the class to read scenario #1 to the group. Have the volunteer justify to the other students his or her actions, which were described in the scenario. Follow this procedure for each of the scenarios.

Scenario #1

An elderly neighbor, who is on a fixed income, asked me to come over and help him pick some oranges that were too high for him to reach. I told him I would be happy to help after I got permission from my parents. After getting their permission, I spent over two hours picking oranges. When I was finished, the neighbor gave me $15.00. I accepted the money graciously, thanked my neighbor, and went home.

Scenario #2

My mom asked me to rake up the leaves in the backyard, take out the trash, and clean my bedroom. I asked her what I would get in return for helping around the house. I suggested $10.00. I told her that (name of the student in scenario #1) told me that he/she got $10 for helping that old person down the street pick oranges. I asked her, "What will you give me?"

Scenario #3

My dad asked me to watch my younger brother and sister all Saturday afternoon so that he could finish a project that he had been working on. I said yes and helped take care of my younger brother and sister. I had fun with them and was not worried or concerned about what I would get in return. After dad returned home, I helped him cook dinner for the family.

Have the students vote: Which activity (not person) in the given scenarios best reflects the teaching of Jesus and is the work of a disciple of Jesus? Why?

Proclaim Luke 17:5–10. Say: **There is nothing wrong with receiving rewards, especially for a job well done. However, Jesus taught that we should follow his law of love and not look for immediate rewards when we are sharing the gifts that God has given to us. When we do what is right—what God expects of us—God rewards us in ways that are much better than we could ever imagine, all in God's time. We need to put our faith in God; God will take care of us and give us what we need at all times. The reward of faith is the gift of our friendship with Jesus.**

Reflection

Use the following questions and activities to help students get to the heart of the gospel.

Younger Students

1. Distribute to the students paper and crayons. Direct them to draw a picture of someone with faith the size of a mustard seed uprooting a large tree.

2. When were you rewarded for something you did? What happened?

3. Is it right to work and be helpful to others only when you expect to receive a reward? Why or why not?

Older Students

Allow time for the students to respond in their journals to the last question.

1. Have you ever seen real faith in action? Share what you saw or heard about the "power of faith."

2. What kind of reward will we get from God if we follow Jesus and live the gospel?

3. The gift and power of faith enable us to believe and follow Jesus. How has your faith helped you follow Jesus' law of love and live the gospel?

Closing Prayer

Gather the students in a circle. After a few moments of quiet prayer, distribute to the students copies of the Prayer of St. Francis. Reflectively pray the prayer together.

Prayer of St. Francis

Lord, make me an instrument of your peace.
Where there is hatred, let me sow love;
where there is injury, pardon;
where there is doubt, faith;
where there is despair, hope;
where there is darkness, light;
where there is sadness, joy;

O Divine Master, grant that I may not so much seek
to be consoled, as to console;
to be understood, as to understand;
to be loved, as to love.
For it is in giving that we receive;
it is in pardoning that we are pardoned;
and it is in dying that we are born to eternal life.

Making God's Word Our Own

If you are choosing a student for next Sunday's opening prayer, do so now.

Pray the Prayer of St. Francis each day this week. Pick a different phrase in the prayer each day and try to live it; put the prayer into action. Is there somewhere in your life that you can sow love or bring pardon, faith, hope, light, or joy? Can you console someone? Can you take time to understand someone? Can you love, give to, and pardon someone? This prayer is a great challenge for families to try. Invite your parents to do this activity with you for one week.

Twenty-Eighth Sunday *in* Ordinary Time

Readings

2 Kings 5:14–17
2 Timothy 2:8–13
Luke 17:11–19

Theme

We are Eucharistic people. We live in praise and thanksgiving.

Scripture *Background*

The story from 2 Kings is a part of the Elijah-Elisha cycle of prophetic legends. In this story, the Syrian army commander, Naaman, contracted leprosy. An Israelite slave girl assures Naaman and his wife that the God of Israel could cure his leprosy. When Naaman came to Elisha to request a cure, Elisha sent him to wash seven times in the Jordan River. This was a task that he resisted but eventually was persuaded to perform. Today's reading begins with the announcement that he had been cleansed. In gratitude, Naaman wanted to give Elisha a gift. Elisha refused, and Naaman left. He promised to worship the Lord, the God of Israel, for the rest of his life.

Today's gospel reading tells the story of a healing. Ten lepers came to Jesus for healing. He sent them to the priest for certification that they were clean and could again participate in community events. On the way there, they were healed. Only one, however, returned to thank God, and that one was a foreigner, a hated Samaritan.

The story followed the passage that was read last Sunday in which Jesus pointed out that servants who do their duty do not expect expressions of gratitude. However, gratitude is always due to God. This gratitude must be expressed publicly. In the biblical understanding, it was impossible to thank someone when there were only two people present. At least three people were necessary: the one to whom thanks was due, the one giving thanks, and a third party who could be told of the goodness of the person being thanked. Thus prayers of thanksgiving to God were addressed to those who are told of the great works of God. Naaman returned to Elisha to tell him of the great goodness of God. The Samaritan returned to Jesus for the same reason, to glorify God and to praise and thank Jesus.

The reading from 2 Timothy continues the series of exhortations for ministers of the gospel. The good news must be preached, no matter what the cost. The cost would be little compared to the reward of life with Christ in the kingdom. The fidelity of God was unchanging, and God would reward those who were faithful to him. This fact, in the end, was the true reason for gratitude.

Irene Nowell OSB

PART I: Gathering *for God's Word*

Opening Prayer

Alternative: *Ask one of the students to lead the opening prayer.*

Open the session by saying: **Thank you for joining us today. There truly are so many things for which to be thankful and give God praise; you are one of them. God has truly blessed this community! Look around. See the wonderful gifts God has give to us—YOU! Please stand for our opening prayer. We begin by thanking God for calling us to the waters of new life in Baptism** (make the sign of the cross) **in the name of the Father, and of the Son, and of the Holy Spirit.**

> *Lord Jesus, you have given us so much; sometimes we forget to stop and thank you. Today we are stopping to take an inventory of all the great things you have freely given us and to say thank you. May we use everything that you have given us to praise you and to enjoy the gift of life. Today we ask only one thing—please grant us the wisdom to share with others the gifts you have given us individually. May we freely share as we have freely been given. We offer this prayer of thanksgiving and praise in your name.*

The students respond: **Amen!**

Song

"All the Ends of the Earth" by Bob Dufford from *Gather (Comprehensive)* (GIA), *Lead Me, Guide Me* (GIA), *Today's Missal* (OCP), *Glory & Praise* (OCP [NALR]), *Journeysongs* (OCP).

"All the Ends of the Earth" by David Haas and Marty Haugen from *Today's Missal* (OCP).

"Make Us a Eucharistic People" by Tim and Julie Smith from *A Eucharistic People* (Troubadour Productions).

"This Is the Day" by Marty Haugen from *Gather (Comprehensive)* (GIA).

"This Is the Day (Psalm 118)" by David Haas from *Walking by Faith* (Harcourt Religion Publishers, GIA).

Announcements

- parish news
- birthdays
- other

PART II: Remembering *God's Word*

Use the following questions to review last week's session.

1. According to Jesus, what could happen if a person has faith the size of a mustard seed?

- That person could command a large tree to be uprooted and transplanted into the sea. In other words, with faith, anything can happen.

2. What did we learn about rewards from last week's gospel?

- Our reward is doing what we know Jesus wants us to do. God will take care of us in God's time and way.

3. What did you learn about Jesus or about yourself from last week's gospel?

   • Let the students respond honestly and openly.

4. How did you live out the Prayer of St. Francis last week? How did Jesus help you?

   • Let the students respond openly and honestly.

PART III: Understanding *God's Word*

Scripture

Choose from two options.

Option One

Invite someone from your parish community or local community who has been sick and healed to share his or her experience with the students. Have the person talk about what this week's gospel means to him or her. What has the illness and cure taught the person about thankfulness?

Option Two

Invite eleven volunteers to help act out the gospel. Assign parts (Jesus, ten cured lepers), and direct the students to echo their lines as the gospel is read.

Read Luke 17:11–19. At the end of the reading, have Jesus call the nine cured lepers over and ask them why they didn't return to give thanks. Each of the nine is given an excuse to tell Jesus. (They may also make up their own excuses or add to the ones provided in the text.) Jesus forgives each one and reminds them to be more grateful and thankful to God in the future.

Reflection

Use the following questions and activities to help students get to the heart of the gospel.

Younger Students

1. Distribute to the students paper and crayons. Direct them to draw a picture of Jesus healing the lepers.

2. For what are you thankful? How can you thank Jesus?

3. Who else in your life do you need to thank? What do they do for you? How can you thank them?

Older Students

Allow ample time for the students to respond in their journals to the last question.

1. Have your ever gone out of your way to do something extra special for someone, only to have that person not appreciate your gesture or show any gratitude? What happened? How did you feel?

2. Who are the lepers in your community? How would you feel about inviting them to dinner or being friends with them? How does being kind to others say "thank you" to Jesus?

3. Read Luke 17:17–18. What is the key to the healing in this event? Do you have enough faith for Jesus to heal you?

Materials Needed

All Students—Option 1
• guest speaker

All Students—Option 2
• Bible
• eleven volunteers
• nine copies of the excuses
• costumes (optional)

Younger Students
• paper
• crayons

Older Students
• journals
• pens

Closing Prayer

Gather the students in a circle. After a few minutes of quiet reflection, go around the circle, and invite each student to share that for which he or she is thankful to God. Conclude with a prayer of praise and the Lord's Prayer.

Making God's Word Our Own

If you are choosing a student for next Sunday's opening prayer, do so now.

This week's prayer challenge can be done alone or with your family. At the end of each day, reflect on the events of that day. List on a piece of paper what Jesus did for you that day for which you are thankful. Start by writing: "Today, I thank Jesus for . . ." Bring your list to the next session, and we will praise God by sharing some of your lists with the community.

Next week, put the students' lists in the Sunday bulletin for the whole faith community to witness God's goodness.

Excuses

Cured leper #1: I was so happy and excited. I just forgot to come back and thank you.

Cured leper #2: I was so happy. I immediately ran home to tell my parents and family.

Cured leper #3: Jesus, did you forget that you told us to go and show ourselves to the priests? That's what I did. Some of the others didn't, like the one who came back to you. I did exactly what you told me to do!

Cured leper #4: All my friends were hanging out, and I just wanted to be with them again now that I am cured. So I joined them for some fun.

Cured leper #5: I was going to come back and thank you, but some friends of mine were playing a game that I wanted to join. I was going to thank you when it was over.

Cured leper #6: I was not totally convinced that I was cured. I was going to wait and see if the leprosy returned before I fully believed that you healed me. Then I was going to thank you, if it was real.

Cured leper #7: Jesus, I was going to return, but I was so tired after walking all day. I stopped to rest for a short time and fell asleep. When I awoke, it was very late. Time just got away from me. Sorry. Thanks.

Cured leper #8: Jesus, why should I thank you? I did not ask to be sick. I follow all of God's laws; I do whatever the priests say without question, and I worship the Sabbath. This healing is my reward; I am a good, faithful person, and I am righteous in God's eyes, right?

Cured leper #9: Jesus, I am sorry. You cured me and made me whole. I didn't stop and think how wonderfully loving and powerful you are to do this for me. Please forgive me, and place in my heart the spirit of gratitude so that I will always remember to be thankful for everything you do for me every day of my life. Thank you, Jesus.

Twenty-Ninth Sunday *in* Ordinary Time

Readings

Exodus 17:8–13
2 Timothy 3:14–4:2
Luke 18:1–8

Theme

Never stop praying. Have faith and never give up!

Scripture *Background*

The Exodus story is part of the wilderness narrative. The Israelites had only recently left Egypt and were on the way to Sinai through the desert wilderness. One of the difficulties they encountered was conflict with the Amalekites, a nomadic people who warred against anyone who encroached on their territory or caravan routes. The Israelites decided to resist the Amalekites and, so, engaged them in battle. The story illustrates the principle that Israel's power came exclusively from God, not from human power or weapons. As long as Moses prayed, Israel won. When Moses stopped praying, Israel lost. "Some take pride in chariots, and some in horses, but our pride is in the name of the LORD our God" (Psalm 20:7).

The community nature of the prayer that won the battle should also be noted. Moses could not support the prayer alone. Only with the help of Aaron and Hur could he continue to pray for the people. It was the prayer of the community that saved the people.

The gospel story is a parable. Immediately preceding this story was Jesus' discourse on the coming of the Son of Man at the end of time. The final sentence of today's story refers again to the coming of the Son of Man. Another parable follows that also has to do with proper prayer.

In the parable of the Pharisee and the tax collector, the woman persists in her request until she finally wears down the judge. The judge grants the woman's request because of her perseverance. The point of the parable is perseverance in prayer.

The interpretation of the parable in verse 7 focuses attention on God and the judge. If such a dishonest judge acted in favor of the woman because of her persistence, won't God, who is good, act in favor of those who pray to him with perseverance? The judge delayed, but God will not delay.

The final sentence linked the parable to the preceding discourse on the coming of the Son of Man. It may seem that God is delaying. After all, the coming of the kingdom has not yet happened. Only those who have faith will be able to persevere to the end. Only those who have faith will continue to pray. They will persist like the widow and will be given justice in the end.

Irene Nowell OSB

PART I: Gathering *for* God's Word

Opening Prayer

Alternative: *Ask one of the students to lead the opening prayer.*

Open the session by saying: **Welcome! I thank and praise God for each and every one of you who are joining us again to grow closer to Jesus. Today we are going to learn more about faith, prayer, and ourselves. I invite the Church to stand for our opening prayer. We are the Church and stand together because of our common Baptism** (make the sign of the cross) **in the name of the Father, and of the Son, and of the Holy Spirit.**

Jesus, walk with us today and every day of our lives. Let these students know and experience your closeness and your desire to be in relationship with them. Teach all of us to pray, Lord; let us find the special place where we can go to you and be comforted, strengthened, and guided by your words. Listen now to the prayers of your children as they put their faith and trust in you. (Invite volunteers to offer a prayer from their hearts.) *Jesus, thank you for hearing the prayers of your children. Fill their hearts with faith and answer their prayers. We ask all this in your name.*

The students respond enthusiastically: **Amen!**

Song

"I Believe in the Sun" by Carey Landry from *Glory & Praise* (OCP [NALR]), *Hi God!* (OCP [NALR]).

"I Have Loved You" by Michael Joncas from *Glory & Praise* (OCP [NALR]), *Today's Missal* (OCP), *Journeysongs* (OCP).

"If God Is for Us" by Grayson Warren Brown from *Today's Missal* (OCP), *Glory & Praise 2* (OCP [NALR]).

Announcements

- parish news
- birthdays
- other

PART II: Remembering *God's Word*

Use the following questions to review last week's session.

1. What did you learn about Jesus last week?
   - He has the power to heal, and we should thank him daily for all he has done for us.

2. Only one leper returned to thank Jesus, although all ten were healed. What did the Samaritan have that the other nine didn't?
   - faith in Jesus and gratitude

3. Name some ways you can thank God for what he continues to give you.

   • Let the students respond openly and honestly. (Some examples are prayer, spending time with Jesus, doing nice things for others, taking care of what God gave us, trusting God, and singing at Sunday liturgy.)

4. What things did you thank God for last week? What did you list? How did Jesus help you see things in a new way?

   • Let the students respond openly and honestly.

PART III: Understanding *God's Word*

Scripture

Materials Needed

All Students
- Bible
- two large paper shopping bags
- two pairs of rubber gloves
- wrapped stick gum (one piece per student)

Older Students
- journals
- pens

This is a fun activity that the students really enjoy. The purpose is to show them to never give up; our prayers need to be constant and persistent. What may seem impossible and hard at first can be fulfilled if they have faith in Jesus.

   Divide the students into two or more teams. (For more teams, you will need more paper bags and extra pairs of rubber gloves.) Give each team a pair of rubber gloves and a paper bag containing wrapped sticks of gum (one for each person).

   When you give the signal, the first person on each team takes the pair of gloves, puts them on, grabs a piece of gum from the bag and unwraps it using only his or her hands and teeth. Then he or she begins chewing the gum and passes the gloves and bag to the next person. The first team to finish is the winner.

   Proclaim Luke 18:1–8. After the reading, ask the students what they think the message of Jesus' parable is. Then ask them what the activity has to do with the parable Jesus told in the gospel.

Reflection

Discuss the reading further using the following questions.

Younger Students

1. When you really want something, what do you do so your parents will give you what you want?

2. What did you learn from Jesus' parable about prayer and not giving up?

3. What are some ways of praying? Which way of prayer do you use the most? Why?

Older Students

Allow time for the students to respond in their journals to the last question.

1. What strategy do you use to get your way with your parents?

2. Are you more likely to give up or hang tough when you pray to God? Why? Give examples.

3. What does faith have to do with prayer? What does prayer have to do with faith? Which comes first—faith or prayer? Why?

4. How can you improve your prayer life?

Closing Prayer

Gather the students together; have them stand in a circle holding hands. Tell them that when it comes to prayer, we sometimes need the power of combined prayers. Say: **Jesus said that when two or more are gathered in his name, he will be among them.** (See Matthew 18:20.) **With one faith in Jesus, let us pray together for each other. If there is anything in particular for which you would like to pray, let's ask God together.** (Go around the circle, and let the students voice their needs before the Lord.)

Making God's Word Our Own

If you are choosing a student for next Sunday's opening prayer, do so now.

Spend fifteen minutes (or more) a day with Jesus this week. Pray in the way in which you are most comfortable. Ask Jesus for anything and everything. Ask him questions, or tell Jesus how you feel and what's going on in your life. What's important is that you spend time alone with Jesus. Talk with him, and listen to him. Try this for one week, and be persistent—never give up. Have faith! And if you don't know how to pray or what to pray for, Jesus will teach you.

Thirtieth Sunday *in* **Ordinary Time**

Readings

Sirach 35:12–14, 16–18
2 Timothy 4:6–8,
  16–18
Luke 18:9–14

Theme

God knows and sees our hearts.

Scripture *Background*

In the ancient Near East, it was the king's special duty to care for the most helpless members of the society. This included those who were orphaned, widowed, and oppressed. In Israel, God was the Most High King, and so these lowly people were the special concern of God. In turn, they also became a special concern of the Israelites' law. The basic principle of Israelite law was to be like God. Therefore, if God cared for oppressed and disadvantaged people, God's people should do so, too.

After his discussion of the benefit of almsgiving and the rewards one could expect from God, Ben Sira turned to the object of almsgiving—the helpless person. Even though God knows no favorites, attention is given to the lowly. God also hears the person who worships sincerely, whether that person has status in the eyes of society or not.

In the parable of the Pharisee and the tax collector, Jesus contrasts the attitudes of two people praying. The Pharisee's prayer was essentially a boast. He informed God of all the good works he did. He told the truth—the works he did were beyond the demands of the law. But somehow he thought that this put God in debt to him. The tax collector, on the other hand, had no good works to announce. He had nothing to bring to God but his sins. Therefore, he was in need of what God could give him. He had no illusions that he sustained his own life. He knew that whatever he received from God was a gift. The paradox here was that the prayer of the tax collector was preferred by God.

The section from 2 Timothy includes a description of Paul's expectation of reward for his faithful service. He knew that he had exercised his ministry well. But he also knew that what he had accomplished was a gift of God. Paul was aware of his absolute dependence on God. He anticipated a reward for his faithful service from a generous God.

Irene Nowell OSB

PART I: Gathering *for God's Word*

Opening Prayer

Alternative: *Ask one of the students to lead the opening prayer.*

Open the session by saying: **Welcome! I am glad you are here with us today. Once again, I wish to affirm your steadfastness and enthusiasm. Has anyone noticed that it's getting darker much earlier these days? It's a good reminder that we are children of the light and that there is nothing to fear as long as we stay in the** *light*—**stay in touch with Jesus. I invite the Church to stand for the opening prayer. Remember, we became "children of the light" at our Baptism when God placed the light of his life and love in our hearts. We confidently begin** (make sign of the cross) **in the name of the Father, and of the Son, and of the Holy Spirit.**

Jesus, we come before you today with a humble heart seeking your forgiveness, mercy, and love. Thank you for the gift of reconciliation, so that we may receive your forgiveness and healing. Bless these students and their families. Continue to help them grow strong in your light; keep them always close to you. Please watch over them, and keep them safe. We ask all this in Jesus' name.

The students respond loudly: **Amen!**

Song

"Be Not Afraid" by Bob Dufford from *Glory & Praise* (OCP [NALR]), *Today's Missal* (OCP), *Gather (Comprehensive)* (GIA), *Lead Me, Guide Me* (GIA), *Journeysongs* (OCP).

"Blest Are They" by David Haas from *Gather (Comprehensive)* (GIA), *Glory & Praise* (OCP [NALR]), *Today's Missal* (OCP), *Walking by Faith* (Harcourt Religion Publishers, GIA).

"Christ Be Our Light" by Bernadette Farrell from *Glory & Praise 2* (OCP [NALR]), *Journeysongs* (OCP), *Today's Missal* (OCP).

"Healing Waters" by Michelle Tumes from *Listen* (Sparrow Records).

Announcements

- parish news
- birthdays
- other

PART II: Remembering *God's Word*

Review last week's session.

1. Last week, Jesus told us a story about a lady who would not leave a corrupt judge alone. She bugged the judge until she got what she wanted. What was the moral of Jesus' parable?

   • God hears our prayers, and so we should not lose heart.

2. Jesus was concerned about not finding something when he returned. What was it?

  • faith on earth

3. What are some of the ways you like to pray?

  • Let the students share openly and honestly.

4. How did you pray with Jesus last week? What did you learn about Jesus? About yourself?

  • Let the students respond openly and honestly.

PART III: Understanding *God's Word*

Scripture

Proclaim Luke 18:9–14 using the script on page 219. The characters could proclaim their lines or echo them after you. Remind the students that a tax collector in Jesus' day was hated and considered unclean and evil by the people. When he collected taxes, he had to collect more for his payment; sometimes tax collectors got rich by collecting a great deal more than the taxes due. Prior to the reading explain that Jesus addressed this parable to those who thought they were better than everyone else.

After the reading, discuss the following questions.

• What was wrong with the Pharisee's thinking and actions?

• What was right about the tax collector's thinking and actions?

• Whose heart was open to God? How do you know?

Use the following questions and activities to expand upon the gospel reading.

Materials Needed

All Students
• Bible
• two volunteers
• costumes (optional)
• slips of paper
• box

Younger Students
• paper
• crayons

Older Students
• journals
• pens

Younger Students

1. Distribute to the students crayons and paper. Direct them to draw a picture of themselves praying to God for something very important.

Reflection

2. Have you ever thought that you were better than someone else? Explain, if you can, why you thought this way.

3. How do we know if we are humble? How can we humble ourselves before God and others?

Older Students

Allow ample time for the students to respond in their journals to the last question.

1. Why do you think the Pharisee acted the way he did? Why do you think the tax collector acted the way he did?

2. What does the word *humble* mean? How can we be humble?

3. Finish the following sentences: With the Pharisee, I could share . . . With the tax collector, I could share . . .

Closing Prayer

Place some slips of paper and a box on a table. Ask the students to write their names on the slips of paper and place the papers in the box. Then gather the students into a circle. Place the box in the middle of the circle. Take a few moments for quiet prayer. Invite the students to share with the group any prayers they would like to offer. Then pass the box around the circle, and have each student randomly take a slip of paper. Invite them to pray all week for the person whose name is on the slip of paper chosen. (In order that the students know for whom they are praying, go around the circle, and have the students introduce themselves if there are new students in the group.) Hold hands as you conclude the session with the Lord's Prayer.

Making God's Word Our Own

If you are choosing a student for next Sunday's opening prayer, do so now.

This week's prayer challenge has two steps. The first step is to sit down with your family and come up with a good definition for the word *humble*. Use the dictionary, or write the definition in your own words. The second step, which will be more of a challenge, is to live the definition of *humble*. In other words, live as humbly as you can for one week. Ask Jesus to help you if you have difficulties. Remember what Jesus said—those who humble themselves will be exalted.

Role-Play Script—
Luke 18:9–14

Narrator: Two men went up to the temple to pray; one was a Pharisee, the other a tax collector.

The Pharisee walks arrogantly into the room and stands to one side with head up in a proud way. After the Pharisee is in place, have the tax collector walk humbly in and kneel with head bowed in a humble position.

Pharisee: I give you thanks, O God, that I'm not like the other men and women—grasping, crooked, adulterous—like this tax collector (points to the tax collector). I fast twice a week. I pay tithes on all I possess.

Narrator: The other man kept his distance, not even daring to raise his eyes to heaven. All he did was beat his breast and say . . .

Tax Collector: (beating his breast and in a weak, broken voice) O God, be merciful to me, a sinner.

Narrator: Whom would you help if you were God listening to these prayers? Why?

Allow ample time for discussion of this question.

Narrator: This is what Jesus said: "Believe me, this man (place hand on the shoulder of the tax collector) went home from the temple justified, but the other did not. For everyone who exalts himself shall be humbled, while he who humbles himself shall be exalted."

All Saints/All Souls,
November 1 and 2

Readings for All Saints

Revelation 7:2–4, 9–14
1 John 3:1–3
Matthew 5:1–12a

Readings for All Souls

Texts may be chosen from a list of suggested readings.

Theme

Jesus shows us a way of staying connected to those who have died through faith and love.

Scripture *Background—All Saints' Day*

The gospel reading for All Saints' Day is Matthew's version of the Beatitudes. Here, Jesus offered guidelines for his disciples to follow. Jesus, the Teacher, set forth the principles by which they were to live. He also described the blessings that belong to those who live according to his teachings.

The disciples of Matthew's community were Jews who believed that Jesus was the Messiah. Because of this, they were rejected by their Jewish brothers and sisters. They were expelled from the synagogue. These Christians of Matthew's community knew well what it meant to be persecuted because of their belief in Jesus.

Despite this, the gospel says that those who are persecuted are "blessed." They had reason to be happy in spite of the pain they were experiencing. They could be happy because the kingdom of heaven was theirs. In verses one and ten, the present tense of the verb "to be" emphasizes that the kingdom is theirs **now.** In verses 4–9, the promises point to the future. Though the kingdom of God was here, it was not yet fully realized. We live "between the times."

The disciples were people who knew their need for God. That is what "poor in spirit" means. They were "pure in heart" because of their single-hearted service of God. They were gentle, patient, and merciful in their treatment of others. As they were to others, so God would be to them.

Two phrases from Matthew's Gospel occur in today's second reading from the letter of John: *children of God* and *see God.* Because of Christ's life within us, Christians are children of God **now.** We also recognize that there is a dimension of our life with God that will be realized in the future: ". . . what we will be has not yet been revealed. What we do know is this: when he is revealed, we will be like him . . ." (1 John 3:2). Then we will be transformed. We will be perfected in holiness. God's life within us will have been brought to maturity.

Our hope for the future also includes the expectation that we shall **see** God (1 John 3:2). The author suggests that there is a close relationship between our vision of God and our transformation in God's likeness. John's Gospel reminds us that our vision has begun: "Whoever has seen me has seen the Father" (John 14:9). Our "sight" now is our fellowship with the Father and with his Son, Jesus Christ (1 John 1:3). We are transformed if we walk in his light (1 John 1:7).

The first reading for the Solemnity of All Saints is from the Book of Revelation. The churches to whom the Book of Revelation was addressed had been persecuted for their faith. Some of their members had become martyrs. The biblical writer assured these churches of the reward awaiting the faithful in the age to come.

Today's reading describes John's vision of two great crowds before the throne of God. Among them are a select group of 144,000 who have been "sealed," or marked, as belonging to God. The number is not to be taken literally but rather is a symbolic number based on the twelve tribes of Israel. The second group includes people from all over the world. These people faithfully endured trials and have been perfected in holiness. As a result, they are privileged to stand before the throne of God. They praise God for the salvation that they have received from God and from the Lamb who is Jesus.

Scripture *Background—All Souls Day*

In the readings for All Souls, there are similar themes of reward in the age to come and the vision of God. The feast speaks directly of life beyond death.

Belief in life after death and of a resurrection of the dead developed gradually among the Jewish people. The first biblical evidence for a belief in resurrection is found in Daniel (12:1–3), a work that dates from the second century B.C. The wise would "shine like stars." This image drew upon a reference found in Daniel 8:10, where the angels of heaven were compared to stars. Daniel 12 suggests the just will be transformed to something like the angels. In the New Testament, in Mark 12:25, Jesus said something similar: ". . . when they rise from the dead, they . . . are like angels in heaven."

The Book of Wisdom also refers to the shining souls of the just after their death (3:7). The Book of Wisdom was a Jewish writing influenced by Greek philosophy. It is dated to the beginning of the common era. In Wisdom 3:4, one finds the first biblical use of the term *immortality*. As in Greek philosophy, immortality in the Book of Wisdom was understood in terms of the soul, not the body.

Christians base their belief in life after death, and in bodily resurrection, on the resurrection of Jesus. The New Testament tells us, ". . . God raised him on the third day and allowed him to appear" (Acts 10:40) and "for as all die in Adam, so all will be made alive in Christ" (1 Corinthians 15:22). Jesus' death and resurrection was the core of early Christian preaching (Acts 10:34–43). It is the reality to which we are called and in which we are transformed (Romans 5:5–11; 17–21).

When we commemorate the feast of All Saints and All Souls, we join a great crowd of holy ones. We look to the example of those who have gone before us.

Anne Marie Sweet OSB

PART I: Gathering *for God's Word*

Opening Prayer

Alternative: *Ask one of the students to lead the opening prayer.*

Open the session by saying: **Welcome. Happy Feast Day! The feast day of All Saints reminds us that we are all connected in God, and those who have died are still with us in a special way. Let's try something special for our opening prayer. Instead of standing, either kneel or sit. We will pray the Litany of the Saints. There are three responses in the Litany of the Saints. The first is "Pray for us," which is said after the name of a saint is proclaimed. The second response is "Lord, save your people," which is said after the next invocations requesting something from God. And the third response is "Lord, hear our prayer," which is said after special prayers are offered.**

We begin by recalling that our Baptism connects both the living and the dead together in Jesus. We pray (make the sign of the cross) **in the name of the Father, and of the Son, and of the Holy Spirit.**

After the first section of the Litany of the Saints, go around the room, and invite the students to say their names, using the word saint in front of their names, thus connecting them to the communion of saints.

Holy Mary, Mother of God, pray for us.

Saint Michael, pray for us.

Holy Angels of God, pray for us.

Saint John the Baptist, pray for us.

Saint Joseph, pray for us.

Saint Peter and Paul, pray for us.

Saint Andrew, pray for us.

Saint John, pray for us.

Saint Mary Magdalene, pray for us.

Saint Stephen, pray for us.

Saint Ignatius, pray for us.

Saint Lawrence, pray for us.

Saint Perpetua and Saint Felicity, pray for us.

Saint Agnes, pray for us.

Saint Gregory, pray for us.

Saint Augustine, pray for us.

Saint Athanasius, pray for us.

Saint Basil, pray for us.

Saint Martin, pray for us.

Saint Benedict, pray for us.

Saint Francis and Saint Dominic, pray for us.

Saint Francis Xavier, pray for us.

Saint John Vianney, pray for us.

Saint Catherine, pray for us.

Saint Teresa, pray for us.

All holy men and women, pray for us.

(Add students' names.)

Lord, be merciful. Lord, save your people.

From all evil, Lord, save your people.

From every sin, Lord, save your people.

From everlasting death, Lord, save your people.

By your coming as man, Lord, save your people.

By your death and rising to new life, Lord, save your people.

By your gift of the Holy Spirit, Lord, save your people.

Be merciful to us sinners. Lord, hear our prayer.

Give new life by baptism. Lord, hear our prayer.

Jesus, Son of the living God, save us. Lord, hear our prayer.

Christ, hear us. Lord, hear our prayer.

Lord Jesus, hear our prayer. Lord, hear our prayer.

The students respond loudly: **Amen!**

Song   "Center of My Life" by Paul Inwood from *Today's Missal* (OCP), *Gather (Comprehensive)* (GIA), *Journeysongs* (OCP), *Glory & Praise 2* (OCP [NALR]).

"Gather Us In" by Marty Haugen from *Gather (Comprehensive)* (GIA), *Glory & Praise* (OCP [NALR]), *Today's Missal* (OCP), *We Celebrate* (J.S. Paluch Co., Inc.).

"Take, Lord, Receive" by John Foley from *Glory & Praise* (OCP [NALR]).

Announcements
- parish news
- birthdays
- other

PART II: Remembering *God's Word*

Review last week's session.

1. What happened in last week's gospel?
   - Jesus told us a story about two people praying in the temple. One was a Pharisee and the other was a tax collector.
2. What was the moral of the story?
   - God hears the prayers of those who are in need, who are poor, and who are humble. We shouldn't judge others.
3. What did Jesus say about those who exalt themselves and those who humble themselves?
   - The exalted will be humbled, and the humbled will be exalted.
4. How did you define the word *humble* last week? How did you live out the definition? What did you experience? How did Jesus help you?
   - Let the students respond openly and honestly.

PART III: Understanding *God's Word*

Begin by sharing what makes a saint a saint. Say: **A saint is a person whose life and actions reflected Jesus' life and actions. No saint was perfect, and they were 100 percent human—just like you and me. What makes them special is that they opened their hearts and allowed Jesus to help them live so that everyone could see Jesus through their words and actions. Others recognized Jesus working in and through them. Saints can help us because they can show us the way to be more like Jesus. Each saint was different, and each found his or her own special way to be more like Jesus. We can learn from their examples, and they can pray for us. This is what we mean by the communion of saints.**

This activity will show you how the saints can still help us today, even if the people around us sometimes don't reflect Jesus as they should.

Ask two students to leave the room while you and a few older students create a maze by moving around furniture and other objects. Outside the room, blindfold one of the student volunteers, and tell the other student volunteer that he or she will be the voice of a saint. The blindfolded student should listen only to the saint's voice. That voice will guide the blindfolded student through the maze. (The voice of the saint should be steady, calm, and loud enough for the student who is blindfolded to hear.)

Direct the blindfolded student to the beginning of the maze. Tell him or her to walk through the maze. Ask the other students to give false directions. The voice of the saint should calmly and quietly tell the blindfolded student how to proceed safely through the maze. The blindfolded student will need to decipher carefully the directions.

As time allows have other students to take turns being the saint and the blindfolded student. Change the maze for each new student. The students will quickly learn to tune out the shouting and listen to the voice of the saint. This activity is a lot of fun.

Proclaim Matthew 5:1–12a. Tell the students that we all have the potential to be saints. We just need to put Jesus' teachings into practice. Jesus will help us if we ask.

Materials Needed

All Students
- Bible
- blindfold
- four volunteers
- a simple maze (created with chairs, cones, wastebaskets, tables, boxes—be creative, but keep it simple)

Younger Students
- paper
- crayons

Older Students
- journals
- pens

Reflection

Use the following questions and activities to help students further understand the gospel reading.

Younger Students

1. Distribute to the students paper and crayons. Direct them to draw a picture of themselves with their favorite saint.

2. Whom do you know who truly reflects Jesus and his teachings by the way they live?

3. What changes do you need to make to become a saint?

Older Students

Allow time for the students to respond in their journals to the first question.

1. Reread the gospel. Which beatitude is the easiest for you to live? Which is the most difficult?

2. What do the Beatitudes tell us about God's kingdom?

3. What eight qualities characterize kingdom people? Are these qualities admired by everyone? Why or why not?

Closing Prayer

Gather the students in a circle. Say: **Quietly reflect on people in your life who have touched you in a deep, spiritual way. Who has brought Jesus' love and teachings to you? Say a quiet prayer in your heart for these people.** Go around the circle. Invite the students to share the name of a person who has reflected Jesus for them. Hold hands as you conclude the session with the Lord's Prayer.

Making God's Word Our Own

This week put the Beatitudes into practice. Choose a new one each day, and invite Jesus to help you live it out. Try it! You just might be surprised at what happens when you put Jesus' words into action.

If you are choosing a student for next Sunday's opening prayer, do so now.

Thirty-First Sunday *in* Ordinary Time

Readings

Wisdom 11:22–12:2
2 Thessalonians
    1:11–2:2
Luke 19:1–10

Theme

Jesus' love transforms all people and all things!

Scripture *Background*

The reading from the Book of Wisdom is part of a song celebrating the wonderful mercy of God.

All creation is nothing compared to the greatness of God. Part of God's greatness is a tender concern for everything created, no matter how small. God's love creates everything that exists. Nothing could continue to exist without the continued care of God. All things live by the Spirit of God, the breath of God. God even forgives sinful humans because he created them.

The gospel passage describes Jesus' witness to the inclusive love of God. Zacchaeus was a tax collector and a rich man. Everyone assumed, without proof, that he was a sinner. They presumed that he overcharged and extorted funds from others. When Jesus announced his intentions to stay at Zacchaeus's house, the people criticized Jesus: "He has gone to eat with a sinner." Zacchaeus defended himself against these accusations. He stated that he customarily gave half his income to those who were poor. If in some way he had overcharged anyone, he would repay the error four times over. He was a righteous man.

Jesus defended Zacchaeus. He pointed to him as an example of a true descendant of Abraham. Like Abraham, Zacchaeus was lost because his neighbors ostracized him. These people also were lost because they had failed to understand Zacchaeus's true character. Jesus criticized their intolerance by going to eat with someone who was scorned by his neighbors. The underlying message here, as in the parable of the prodigal son, was that God eats with all people, including those whom society deems undesirable. Christian table fellowship includes those who might be excluded from social situations. The Christian table excludes no one, just as God excludes no one.

In his letters to the Thessalonians, Paul dealt with the problems that arose because the Thessalonians expected the glorious return of Jesus at any moment. Paul reminded them that it was God's work to decide the day of the Lord. Their work was fidelity to their call. They must practice their faith and continue to glorify God without being unduly agitated about the end of the world.

Irene Nowell OSB

PART I: Gathering *for God's Word*

Opening Prayer

Alternative: *Ask one of the students to lead the opening prayer.*

Open the session by saying: **Welcome! May God's peace rest on everyone here. Have you noticed that it's getting darker earlier and the days are much shorter? Remember, we are children of the Light, and as long as we stay close to Jesus— our true Light—everything will be good. I invite the Church to stand for our opening prayer. We begin by recalling that we are sons and daughters of God because we are baptized** (make the sign of the cross) **in the name of the Father, and of the Son, and of the Holy Spirit.**

> *Jesus, may your love transform us just as it did Zacchaeus, the tax collector. Fill our hearts with great anticipation of encountering you daily in our lives. Continue to bless these students, their families, and their teachers. Keep them always warm and safe in your love. We ask all these prayers in your name.*

The students respond loudly: **Amen!**

Song

"Amazing Grace," Traditional from *Gather (Comprehensive)* (GIA), *Glory & Praise* (OCP [NALR]), *Today's Missal* (OCP), *We Celebrate* (J.S. Paluch Co., Inc.), *Lead Me, Guide Me* (GIA).

"God Is Love," several versions by different composers in various hymnals.

"I Have Loved You" by Michael Joncas from *Glory & Praise* (OCP [NALR]), *Today's Missal* (OCP).

"Jesus Said: Zacchaeus Come Down" by Christopher Walker from *Stories and Songs of Jesus* (OCP).

"Open Our Eyes This Day" by Carey Landry and Carol Jean Kinghorn from *A Wonderful Song of Joy* (OCP).

Announcements

- parish news
- birthdays
- other

PART II: Remembering *God's Word*

Use the following questions to review the Thirtieth Sunday in Ordinary Time.

1. What happened in last week's gospel?
   - Jesus told us a story about two people praying in the temple. One was a Pharisee and the other was a tax collector.

2. What was the moral of the story?
   - God hears the prayers of those who are in need, who are poor, and who are humble. We shouldn't judge others.

3. What did Jesus say about those who exalt themselves and those who humble themselves?

   • The exalted will be humbled, and the humbled will be exalted.

4. How did you define the word *humble* last week? How did you live out the definition? What did you experience? How did Jesus help you?

   • Let the students respond openly and honestly.

Use the following questions to review All Saints' Day.

1. What is a saint?

   • A saint is a person whose life and actions reflected Jesus' life and actions.

2. What do the saints do for us today?

   • They show us how we can also become mirrors of Jesus and other saints. They pray for us and help us live as Jesus did.

3. What are the Beatitudes? Why are the Beatitudes important to us?

   • The Beatitudes are road maps that lead us to Jesus and help us build his kingdom. This is what we must follow if we truly want to be Jesus' followers. (If time allows, have the students try to recall all of the Beatitudes.)

4. Which beatitude did you live out last week? How did Jesus help you?

   • Let the students respond openly and honestly.

PART III: Understanding *God's Word*

Scripture

Materials Needed

All Students
 • Bible
 • role-play script (page 230)
 • student volunteers

Younger Students
 • paper
 • crayons

Older Students
 • journals
 • pens

This is a fun and creative activity that the students will love. The goal is to connect the students with the gospel story. When they are finished working and molding the gospel, they will be ready to listen to God's word in a new way.

Ask for volunteers to help you proclaim the gospel. Direct the students to listen carefully to what Jesus did for Zacchaeus and how Zacchaeus responded to Jesus' loving invitation. Using the script on page 230, proclaim the gospel slowly and reflectively.

After the reading, ask the students if they have any questions about the story. Once all the questions have been answered, ask them what Jesus meant when he said, "Today you and your family have been saved."

Use the following questions and activities to help students process the readings.

Younger Students

Reflection

1. Distribute to the students paper and crayons. Direct them to draw a picture of Zacchaeus and Jesus meeting and talking to each other.

2. It sounds as if Zacchaeus was very excited to see Jesus. When do you get excited to see Jesus?

3. How did Jesus' love change Zacchaeus? How can Jesus' love change you?

Older Students

Allow ample time for the students to respond in their journals to the first question.

1. Zacchaeus was a small man. What do you do that makes you feel small?

2. Why do you think Jesus invited himself to Zacchaeus's house for dinner? What would you do if Jesus invited himself over to your house?

3. What do you think Jesus and Zacchaeus talked about over dinner? What would you and Jesus talk about if you had dinner together?

Closing Prayer

Gather the students in a circle. Invite them to close their eyes and picture themselves standing in front of Jesus. Say: **Jesus is looking at you, and you are looking at him. Jesus has a peaceful smile on his face and a twinkle in his eye. You can tell he wants to say something to you. You both sit down and start a conversation. Jesus starts by saying, "I love you." Continue the conversation with Jesus. Let him say what he wants to say; listen to him, and say whatever you want to say to him.**

After about five minutes of quiet time, conclude the session with the Lord's Prayer.

Making God's Word Our Own

Spend time this week finishing your conversation with Jesus. Sit with Jesus for fifteen minutes each day. Repeat the closing prayer experience, or come up with one that fits you better. Ask Jesus to help you if you have difficulty sitting and talking with him. You will be amazed and blessed by being open to Jesus in this way.

> *If you are choosing a student for next Sunday's opening prayer, do so now.*

Role-Play Script—
Jesus and Zacchaeus

*Remind the students that tax collectors were hated. They were considered sinners and traitors of the Jewish faith. Zacchaeus was a **chief** tax collector.*

Narrator: Jesus was going through Jericho, where a man named Zacchaeus lived. Zacchaeus was in charge of collecting taxes and was very rich. Jesus was headed his way, and Zacchaeus wanted to see what Jesus was like. But Zacchaeus was a short man and could not see over the crowd. So he ran ahead and climbed up into a sycamore tree. When Jesus got there, he looked up and said . . .

Jesus: Zacchaeus, hurry down! I want to stay with you today.

Narrator: Zacchaeus hurried down and gladly welcomed Jesus. Many who saw this started grumbling.

All: This man Zacchaeus is a sinner! And Jesus is going home to eat with him.

Narrator: Later that day Zacchaeus stood up and said to the Lord . . .

Zacchaeus: I will give half of my property to the poor. And I will now pay back four times as much to everyone I have ever cheated.

Narrator: Jesus said to Zacchaeus . . .

Jesus: Today you and your family have been saved, because you are a son of Abraham.

Narrator: The Son of Man came to look for and to save people who were lost.

Thirty-Second Sunday *in* Ordinary Time

Readings

2 Maccabees 7:1–2,
9–14
2 Thessalonians
2:16–3:5
Luke 20:27–38

Theme

We are resurrection people.

Scripture *Background*

The Books of Maccabees were written to tell the story of the second-century B.C. revolt and of those who gave their lives for the freedom to worship. One of the legendary heroes of this revolt was the mother of seven sons whose story is told in the first reading. She encouraged her sons to accept martyrdom bravely rather than abandon their faith. When the youngest was the only one left, the mother spoke to him in their native language, unknown to the executioner. She begged her son to accept death rather than sin so that she, who gave birth to him, might have him back in the resurrection. She told him that God would restore his life if he remained faithful. The mother was last to die, after all her sons.

In the gospel story, the issue of resurrection was raised by the Sadducees, who did not believe in resurrection. They posed to Jesus a problem from the Mosaic law. The law stated that if a man died without children, his brother must marry the widow to raise the children of the dead man. The necessity for children in this case was so the dead man would live on in his children and in memory. That was essentially his only hope of "eternal life." The problem became exaggerated. Seven brothers married the same woman. Whose wife would she be in the resurrection?

Jesus stated a belief in life after death and also corrected the Sadducees' presumption that life after death must be just like this life. Marriage, Jesus said, belonged to the life we know now, in which people die. Life after death would go on forever. Thus there would be no need for marriage and the bearing of children. The Sadducees were asking the wrong question.

In 2 Thessalonians, Paul continued to admonish the people who were expecting an immediate end of the world. He encouraged them to stand firm and persevere in the tradition. He also asked them to pray for him and his ministry. His final encouragement was to remain tenacious.

Irene Nowell OSB

PART I: Gathering *for God's Word*

Opening Prayer

Alternative: *Ask one of the students to lead the opening prayer.*

Open the session by saying: **Welcome. May God's peace fill you with laughter and joy. Let's do something different today. I invite the Church to stand and echo a spirit-filled chant with me. Let's see how loud you can be. Are you ready? Give me an R. Give me an E. Give me an S. Give me a U. Give me an R. Give me another R. Give me an E. Give me a C. Give me a T. Give me an I. Give me an O. Give me an N. What's that spell? Resurrection!**

We are a resurrection people. Without the death and resurrection of Jesus, we wouldn't have been given the gift of the Holy Spirit. Without the Holy Spirit, we wouldn't have the bonding force or glue that makes us a Church—the Body of Christ. Because Jesus rose from the dead, we are baptized into his life, death, and resurrection. So let's begin our prayer (make the sign of the cross) **in the name of the Father, and of the Son, and of the Holy Spirit.**

> *Lord Jesus, you have called us to be a resurrection people, living in joyful hope for the day when we will live with you forever. Open the minds and hearts of your children; help us understand the true gift that you offer us—the gift of life without fear of death. Grant us the strength to live as resurrection people. We ask all this in Jesus' name.*

The students respond enthusiastically: **Amen!**

Song

"I Am the Bread of Life" by Suzanne Toolan from *Glory & Praise* (OCP [NALR]), *Gather (Comprehensive)* (GIA), *Today's Missal* (OCP), *We Celebrate* (J.S. Paluch Co., Inc.), *Lead Me, Guide Me* (GIA), *Celebrating Our Faith* (Harcourt Religion Publishers, GIA).

"I Am the Resurrection" by Jim Anderson from *Today's Missal* (OCP), *Journeysongs* (OCP).

"You'll Be in My Heart" by Phil Collins from *The Tarzan Soundtrack* (Disney Records).

"Your Words Are Spirit and Life" by Bernadette Farrell from *Spirit & Song* (OCP), *Today's Missal* (OCP), *Journeysongs* (OCP).

Announcements

- parish news
- birthdays
- other

PART II: Remembering *God's Word*

Review last week's session.

1. To whom did Jesus reach out last week?

   • Zacchaeus

2. Who was Zacchaeus? What did Jesus do for him?

   • Zacchaeus was a tax collector. Jesus offered him salvation.

3. What does this message of Jesus found in the gospel have to do with us today?

   • Let the students respond open and honestly. (Jesus continues to offer **all** people salvation, forgiveness, and love.)

4. What did you and Jesus talk about last week?

   • Let the students respond openly and honestly.

PART III: Understanding *God's Word*

Scripture

There are many ways to do this activity. Be creative and mold the activity to the shape and needs of the students. The goal is to have them realize what life would be like if there was no resurrection and how believing in the resurrection actually frees us to truly live.

Before the session, print the following words on sturdy strips of paper: "Sons and daughters of the resurrection are sons and daughters of God."

Divide your large group of students into smaller groups (four students per group). Ask half of the small groups to represent the people who believe in the resurrection (they share eternal life with Christ) and the other half to represent those who do not believe in the resurrection.

Pass out blue sheets of paper to the small groups who represent those who *believe* in the resurrection and red sheets of paper to those groups who are designated as those who *do not believe* in the resurrection. Have each blue group list five ways their lives and actions are changed because they believe they will be raised to new life after death. Have each red group list five ways their lives and actions would change if there were no resurrection and no life after death. After ample work time, invite the small groups to share their lists.

Proclaim Luke 20:27–38 to see what Jesus says about the resurrection. Pass out the 1 1/2" X 5" strips of paper on which the quote "Sons and daughters of the resurrection are sons and daughters of God" has been printed. Invite the students to decorate the strips of paper and take them home to use as bookmarks.

Reflection

Discuss the readings further using the following questions and activities.

Younger Students

1. Jesus says that those who are raised from the dead will be God's children forever. Distribute to the students paper and crayons. Direct them to draw a picture of a deceased friend or family member as a child of God in heaven.

Materials Needed

All Students
• Bible
• pre-printed 1 1/2" X 5" strips of sturdy paper (one per student)
• colored makers
• ribbon
• blue and red sheets of paper (one piece of paper for each group)
• pencils (one for each group)

Younger Students
• paper
• crayons

Older Students
• journals
• pens

---

2. Jesus tells us that the sons and daughters of the resurrection will live forever with God. How do you feel when you think about that?

3. Sometimes we feel sad when someone we love dies because we miss him or her. Have you ever experienced the loss of a loved one? What do you think Jesus meant when he said, "God is the God of the living"?

Older Students

Allow students time to respond in their journals to the last question.

1. Do you feel freer or more fearful about death after hearing Jesus' words about life and death? Why?

2. What is your idea of heaven? What does this passage say about what it will be like? Does it reinforce or change your idea of what heaven will be like?

3. How does believing in the resurrection change your life?

Closing Prayer

Gather the students in a circle. Jesus calls us to believe that death is a doorway to life. We are called to live in joy, laughter, and love and to put aside all fear. We are called to live as sons and daughters of the living God. Go around the circle, and have the students share how they could be a living reminder of the resurrection.

Making God's Word Our Own

This week's prayer challenge is to live your gift of life to the fullest. Do something new each day for one week. Ask Jesus to show you if you are not sure what to do each day. God is not the God of the dead but of the living. So live!

If you are choosing a student for next Sunday's opening prayer, do so now.

Thirty-Third Sunday *in* Ordinary Time

Readings

Malachi 3:19–20a
2 Thessalonians 3:7–12
Luke 21:5–19

Theme

The day of the Lord is a day of hope and joy.

Scripture *Background*

The first reading is from the Book of the prophet Malachi, written during the fifth century B.C. The people had again sunk into complacency. The prophet reminded them that the day of the Lord was coming, a day on which the righteous would be vindicated and the wicked would be punished.

God's day was coming like a fire. The wicked would be consumed by the fire. But, for the righteous, the fire would be like the sun. It would provide warmth and light, the symbols for life. The righteous would frolic like calves, and the wicked would be the burned ashes under their feet. The prophet was warning them that the time to choose was now. When the day came, it would be too late.

The Thessalonians expected the day of the Lord—the second coming of Christ—to arrive immediately. Some had stopped working and were simply waiting. Paul urged them to live in the present and to continue their work. They should stop working only if they were also willing to stop eating! Paul offered himself as an example. He had worked tirelessly and at great cost to spread the gospel of Christ. They should imitate him and continue to do what was right.

The gospel passage is Luke's version of Jesus' apocalyptic discourse concerning the end of the world. Two sets of images are interwoven. They include the destruction of Jerusalem in A.D. 70 by the Romans and the coming of the Son of Man at the end of time. At the time the Gospel of Luke was written, it had become evident that the return of the Son of Man was not going to happen immediately. Christians needed to live in the present. They also needed to remain vigilant and ready for Christ's coming. The fall of Jerusalem should provide an example. People pointed to the glory of the Herodian temple, but Jesus warned that the day would come when all would be destroyed. Luke's contemporaries noted the gospel warnings that the day of the Lord would come suddenly, like a trap. Christians should not worry about the time. Christians should persevere in faithfulness. Then they will always be ready.

Irene Nowell OSB

PART I: Gathering for God's Word

Opening Prayer

Alternative: *Ask one of the students to lead the opening prayer.*

Open the session by saying: **Welcome! God's peace be with all of you. Raise your hands if you know how to hope or if you have hope in something. Great!** (Take a minute or two to ask the students for what they hope.)

We are getting ready to end one liturgical season and begin another. We are ending Ordinary Time and moving toward Advent, which will begin in two weeks. But before we move into the Season of Advent, our Scripture readings invite us to think about something very special—the day of the Lord. All creation waits in joyful hope for Jesus' coming at the end of time.

Please stand for our opening prayer. We begin by recalling who we are—sons and daughters of God in God's kingdom; (make the sign of the cross) **in the name of the Father, and of the Son, and of the Holy Spirit.**

Come, Lord Jesus, come! May we not be afraid, but rather may we be filled with hope, love, and excitement as we await your return. May the day of the Lord come quickly so that peace will reign, your healing presence will fill the land, and your justice and mercy will rule the earth. Bless these students; fill them and all present with hopeful anticipation of your return. We ask all this in your name.

The students respond loudly: **Amen!**

Song

"Amazing Grace," Traditional from *Gather (Comprehensive)* (GIA), *Glory & Praise* (OCP [NALR]), *Today's Missal* (OCP), *We Celebrate* (J.S. Paluch Co., Inc.), *Lead Me, Guide Me* (GIA).

"In the Day of the Lord" by M.D. Ridge from *Spirit & Song* (OCP), *Journeysongs* (OCP), *Glory & Praise 2* (OCP [NALR]).

"Patience, People" by John Foley from *Journeysongs* (OCP), *Glory & Praise* (OCP [NALR]).

"This Is the Day" by Bobby Fisher from *Today's Missal* (OCP), *Spirit & Song* (OCP), *Journeysongs* (OCP).

"This Is the Day" by Marty Haugen from *Gather (Comprehensive)* (GIA).

"This Is the Day (Psalm 118)" by David Haas from *Walking by Faith* (Harcourt Religion Publishers, GIA).

Announcements

• parish news
• birthdays
• other

PART II: Remembering *God's Word*

Review last week's session.

1. What was the main theme of last week's gospel?

- God is the God of the living. There is life after death.

2. What was the question that the Sadducees asked Jesus?

- The question, intended to trap Jesus, was in regards to a woman who was married seven times and wanted to know whose wife she will be in heaven.

3. What did Jesus say about those who rise from the dead? What will they be like?

- They will be like angels—free from death.

4. Jesus said the following about God: God is not the God of the dead, but _____.

- God is not the God of the dead but of the living! All are alive in him.

5. How did you enjoy and celebrate the gift of your life last week? What did you learn about God? What did you experience about yourself and others?

- Let the students respond openly and honestly.

PART III: Understanding *God's Word*

Scripture

Materials Needed

All Students
- Bible

Younger Students
- paper
- crayons

Older Students
- journals
- pens

Read Luke 21:5–19. Answer any questions the students have. Then read the following story of a father and three sons from *Storytelling, Imagination, and Faith* by William J. Bausch (Mystic, CT: Twenty-Third Publications, 1984). Again, answer the students' questions.

There was once a village chief with three sons. Each of them had a special talent. The oldest had the talent of raising olive trees and would trade the oil for tools and cloth. The second was a shepherd and when the sheep were ill he had a great talent for making them well again. The third was a dancer and when there was a streak of bad luck in the family or when everyone was bored during hard winters and tired of work, this was the son who would cheer them up and dance.

One day the Father had to go away on a long journey and so he called his sons together and said, "My sons, the villagers are depending on you. Each of you has a special talent for helping people and so, while I am gone, see to it that you use your talents as wisely and well as possible so that, when I return, I will find our village even more happy and prosperous than it is now." He embraced his sons and departed.

For a while things went well. Then the cold winter winds began to blow and the blizzards and snows came. First, the buds on the olive trees shrank and cracked, and it was a long time before the trees could recover. Then the village, because of the especially long winter, ran out of firewood. So the people began to cut down the trees but in the process they were denuding and destroying the village.

Then, too, the snow and ice made it impossible for the traders to come up the river or over the mountain pass. The result was that the villagers said, "So, let us kill the sheep and eat them so we do not starve to death." The second son refused for a time, but finally had to give to the hungry villagers. His remark was, "What good would it be to spare the sheep only to have the villagers perish?"

In this way, the villagers got just enough wood for their fires and food for their tables but the bitter winter had broken their spirits and they began to think that things were really worse than they were and they even began to lose all hope. So much so, that family by family, they deserted the village in search of a more hospitable environment.

As spring began to loosen the icy grip of winter, the village chief, the father of the three sons, returned only to find smoke rising from his own chimney. "What have you done?" he asked when he reached his house and spoke to his sons. "What has happened to the villagers?"

"Oh, father, forgive me," said the oldest son. "The people were freezing and begged me to cut down the olive trees and so I did. I gave away my talent. I am no longer fit to be an orchard keeper." "Don't be angry Father," said the second son. "The sheep would have frozen to death anyway and the people were starving and I had to send my flock to the slaughter."

But the father understood and said, "Don't be ashamed, my sons, you did the best you could and you acted rightly and humanely. You used your talents wisely in trying to save the people. But, tell me, what has become of them? Where are they?"

The two brothers looked with fixed eyes on the third son who said, "Welcome home, father. Yes, it has been a hard time. There was so little to eat and so little firewood. I thought that it would be insensitive and improper to dance during such suffering and, besides, I needed to conserve my strength so that I could dance for you when you came home."

"Then, dance, my son," said the father, "for my village is empty and so is my heart. Fill it with joy and courage once again. Yes, please dance!" But as the third son went to get up, he made a face of pain and fell down. His legs were so stiff and sore from sitting that they were no longer fit for dancing. The Father was so sad that he could not even be angry. He simply said to the third son: "Ours was a strong village. It could have survived the want of fuel and food but it could never survive without hope. And because you failed to use your talent wisely and well, our people gave up what little hope they had left. So now? Now the village is deserted and you are crippled. Your punishment has already fallen upon you."

And with these words he embraced his two sons and wept.

Compare both stories. Bring out the elements of hope, joy, and sharing what God has given us as we await his return. Use the following questions to guide your discussion.

- Do you know and love the "father" enough to trust and believe that he will return?
- Do you use your energy following things or following what other people say is important? Are you using your energy to develop the talents that God has given you?
- Do you freely use your talents to share with others as you wait for Jesus' return at the end of time?
- Do you share with others your hope and joy of Jesus' returning?

Reflection

Use the following questions and activities to help students get to the heart of the gospel.

Younger Students

1. Distribute to the students paper and crayons. Direct them to draw a picture of what they would want to be doing if Jesus returned soon.
2. Would Jesus be happy or sad if he returned today? Why?
3. What can you and your family do to live in joyful hope for Jesus' return?

Older Students

Allow time for the students to respond in their journals to the last question.

1. Would most people be happy or sad if Jesus returned today?
2. How would your actions change if you began to live as though Jesus were returning at any moment? Explain.
3. Do you believe that Jesus is going to return at the end of time? Why or why not?

Closing Prayer

Gather the students together. Invite them to close their eyes, sit quietly, and picture in their minds and hearts Jesus' return. Say: **What does Jesus look like? What does he say? Picture him embracing you and holding you gently in his arms. Feel how everything is made right, everything is made anew. Rest in your thoughts, in your images, in your feelings.** Let the students rest in their thoughts for a few minutes. Then hold hands as you conclude the session with the Lord's Prayer.

Making God's Word Our Own

If you are choosing a student for next Sunday's opening prayer, do so now.

This week's prayer challenge is very special. Meditate for fifteen minutes each day. You can do it if you try. It can be an easy and very powerful experience. Find a quiet place, close your eyes, and think about Jesus' return. Imagine Jesus holding you, speaking to you, and listening to you. Or use a chant, silently repeating in your mind and heart the following phrase: "Come, Lord Jesus, come." Repeat that phrase over and over. Let your mind and heart be filled with thoughts of Jesus. Perhaps try this before you go to sleep at night. Fall asleep with Jesus on your mind and in your heart.

Christ *the* King

Theme

Jesus is our Lord, King, and friend. We share in his reign.

Scripture *Background*

David was a powerful and successful king. He defeated enemies and established prosperity in the land. David was dear to God. God promised him that his throne would last forever, that a son of his would always sit on the throne. Because of this promise and because of David's success, he became an idealized figure. People longed for an age like the time of David, an age of peace and prosperity. After the kingship ceased, the hope became more idealized. Some people hoped for a renewal of the kingdom. Others were looking for a specific person, a messiah of either kingly or priestly rank. Some people simply longed for peace.

Jesus did not fit the common image of the anointed king or messiah. The suffering Jesus endured was especially problematic for the Jewish people of that time. In the Gospels, Jesus seemed to accept the title of Messiah or Christ only in contradictory situations. In the stories of Jesus' infancy, the angel in the Gospel of Luke and the wise men in the Gospel of Matthew both identified Jesus as king and as son of David. In the trial scene, Jesus was asked by the high priest if he was the messiah. He seemed to answer affirmatively, but added an interpretation about the Son of Man coming on the clouds to judge and about his kingdom not being of this world. At the crucifixion he died with the charge nailed over his head, "The King of the Jews." The whole concept of messiah and king had been radically reinterpreted.

In the Gospel of Luke, Jesus promised a place in his kingdom to one of the criminals who was executed with him. The image of the kingdom was no longer an image of peace and prosperity in Jerusalem. The image of the citizens of the kingdom had also shifted radically.

The reading from the Letter to the Colossians elaborates on the new image. Kingship now involved preeminence over all creation. The one through whom and for whom all things live has reconciled all creation to God. This reconciliation occurred at the price of his life. The kingdom has moved into eternity, and he is the first within it. He is truly Christ the King.

Irene Nowell OSB

PART I: Gathering *for God's Word*

Opening Prayer

Alternative: *Ask one of the students to lead the opening prayer.*

Open the session by saying: **Welcome. May the reign of God fill your lives and hearts with security and joy. Today we celebrate Jesus as the king, the power, and source of our lives. This Sunday is the last Sunday of our liturgical year. Next week we will celebrate our "new year" in Christ Jesus with the Season of Advent. I invite the Church to stand for our opening prayer. Remember we were baptized into Jesus' priesthood, prophetic life, and kingship. Therefore we are honored to stand in God's presence and bless ourselves** (make the sign of the cross) **in the name of the Father, and of the Son, and of the Holy Spirit.**

Jesus, you are our Lord and King. Thank you for calling us to be children of the kingdom. Continue to bless all of us; help us realize the great privilege, honor, and responsibility of being children of the kingdom. Open all our hearts, and pour out upon us your Holy Spirit so that we may claim the fullness of your reign in our lives. Jesus, you freely offered up your life on the cross. You showed us how much you love us and that you have power over life and death. May we in turn live our lives showing you that we accept and acknowledge your reign and law of love in our lives. We pray all this in your name.

The students respond: **Amen!**

Song

"At the Name of Jesus" by Christopher Walker from *Today's Missal* (OCP), *Spirit & Song* (OCP), *Glory & Praise 2* (OCP [NALR]), *Journeysongs* (OCP).

"I Have Loved You" by Michael Joncas from *Glory & Praise* (OCP [NALR]), *Today's Missal* (OCP), *Journeysongs* (OCP).

"The King of Glory" by Willard Jabusch from *Today's Missal* (OCP), *Gather (Comprehensive)* (GIA).

"We Have Been Told" by David Haas from *Glory & Praise* (OCP [NALR]), *Gather (Comprehensive)* (GIA), *Today's Missal* (OCP), *We Celebrate* (J.S. Paluch Co., Inc.).

Announcements

- parish news
- birthdays
- other

PART II: Remembering *God's Word*

Use the following questions to review last week's session.

1. What is the "day of the Lord"?

   • The "day of the Lord" is the day when Jesus returns and the fullness of God's kingdom will be established.

2. If this were to happen soon, should we be excited and happy or sad and scared?

   • Let the students respond openly and honestly.

3. What should we do as we await Jesus' coming at the end of time?

   • We should live according to Jesus' law of love, develop the gifts and talents that God has given us, and share our gifts with others until Jesus returns.

4. What did you learn about Jesus when you meditated and chanted last week? What did Jesus share with you? Was this prayer hard for you to do? Why or why not?

   • Allow the students to respond openly and honestly.

PART III: Understanding *God's Word*

Scripture

Materials Needed

All Students
• Bible
• mosaic marbles or flat stones of various shapes and colors
• basket
• small table
• processional cross with stand (the one your parish uses on Sunday for liturgical processions)

Younger Students
• crayons
• paper

Older Students
• journals
• pens

The goal of this activity is to allow the students to examine what it means to be part of God's kingdom and live under Jesus' reign. It will help them discover that they are precious and valuable jewels that make up Jesus' crown of glory.

Divide the room in half, and have all the students stand at one end of the room. Explain to them that the whole room represents God's kingdom, but the empty end of the room represents God's castle. All who live in the castle freely choose to follow Jesus' laws of love. This is called living under God's reign.

Place the processional cross in the middle of the room to mark the boundary of God's castle. Proclaim Luke 23:35–43. Explain to the students that Jesus, out of love for us, embraced the cross to show us that he is king of life and death; he truly loves and forgives us. He is God, and he wants to walk with us and be our king every day. Jesus gave up his life so that we may live with him in his castle; he rose from the dead to show us that eternal life is true. He is the way (the door) into the castle.

Invite each student to consider what he or she is willing to do or willing to give up in order to live in God's castle and live in the reign of God. Have each of the students share what he or she needs to do to allow God to reign more fully in his or her life. As the students share, invite them to walk across the room, touch the cross, and move to the other side of the room.

Use the following questions and activities to help students get to the heart of the gospel.

Reflection

Younger Students

1. Distribute to the students paper and crayons. Direct them to draw a picture of Jesus as king, wearing his crown of glory.

2. Having Jesus as your king means you must follow the king's rules and laws. By which laws do you find it easy to live? Which ones are difficult to live by?

3. You're a living and precious jewel that belongs to God. What can you do to help polish your precious stone to keep it bright, shiny, and beautiful for God?

Older Students

Allow ample time for the students to respond in their journals to the last question.

1. What are the benefits of "truly" allowing Jesus to be Lord and King of your life? What are the drawbacks?

2. There were two people suffering and dying with Jesus. One told Jesus to save himself and them. The other man believed Jesus is King and asked Jesus to remember him in paradise. Which of these two men are you most like right now in your spiritual life. Why?

3. All precious jewels and stones must be cut, polished, and buffed so that their beauty and true value can shine forth. You are one of God's precious jewels. What areas of your life need to polished, buffed, cut, and shined? Why?

Closing Prayer

Place a small table in the middle of the room, and gather the students in a circle around the table. Place mosaic marbles or flat stones of various shapes and colors in a basket on the table. The processional cross should be next to the table. Invite the students to pick a stone from the basket. Have them choose a stone that they feel represents the unique gift of who they are. Then say: **God offered Jesus a crown of glory because Jesus proclaimed God's reign, died for us, and rose from the dead to offer us a way to live in God's reign. We become precious jewels placed on Jesus' crown of glory when we accept Jesus as our Lord and Savior, welcome him into our lives, and try to follow his law of love. Carry your precious stone with you as a reminder of how precious you are to Jesus. Welcome him into your life as Lord and King. Remember that you are part of his living crown of glory and are called to live with him forever in paradise.**

Have the students hold their stones and reflect quietly on how precious they are to God. Then hold hands as you conclude the session with the Lord's Prayer. Place emphasis on the words "your kingdom come, your will be done on earth as it is in heaven."

Making God's Word Our Own

If you are choosing a student for next Sunday's opening prayer, do so now.

Carry your stone everywhere this week. Use your stone as a reminder of how precious you are to Jesus; you are called to live in his kingdom. Say a quiet prayer inviting Jesus into your heart as your Lord and King every time you see, feel, or remember the stone you are carrying. Ask Jesus to show you how to be more open to God's reign in your life. Thank him for calling you to be part of his kingdom.